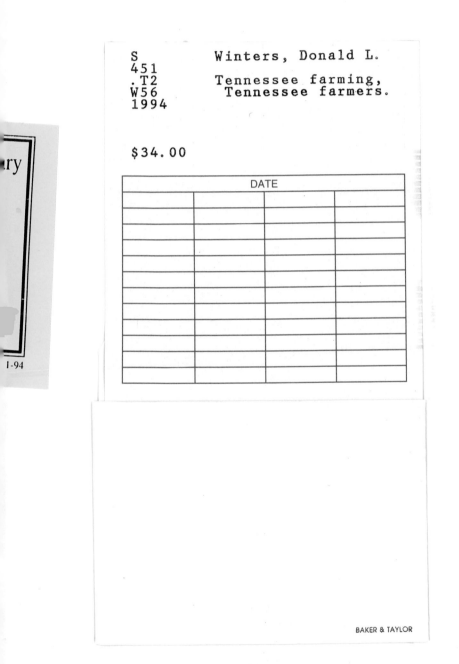

Tennessee Farming, Tennessee Farmers

Tennessee Farming, Tennessee Farmers

ANTEBELLUM AGRICULTURE IN THE UPPER SOUTH

Donald L. Winters

The University of Tennessee Press
Knoxville

Chapters 3 and 4 draw upon material from "Farm Size and Production Choices:
Tennessee, 1850–1860," which appeared in the *Tennessee Historical Quarterly*
52 (1993): 212–24.

Chapters 7 and 9 draw upon material from "'Plain Folk' of the Old South
Reexamined: Economic Democracy in Tennessee," which appeared in the
Journal of Southern History 53 (1987): 565–86.

Chapter 9 also draws upon material from "The Agricultural Ladder in Southern Agriculture: Tennessee, 1850–1870," which appeared in *Agricultural History* 61 (1987): 36–82.

Library of Congress Cataloging-in-Publication Data

Winters, Donald L.
    Tennessee farming, Tennessee farmers: antebellum agriculture in the
upper South / Donald L. Winters.
          p.   cm.
    Includes bibliographical references and index.
    ISBN 0–87049–860–6 (cloth: alk. paper)
    1. Agriculture—Tennessee—History—19th century. 2. Farmers—
Tennessee—History—19th century. 3. Agriculture—Economic aspects—
Tennessee—History—19th century. 4. Farm life—Tennessee—History—
19th century.   I. Title.
S451.T2W56   1994
338.1'09768'09034—dc20   94-20835
                                                                    CIP

For my mother
and the memory of my father

Contents

Maps

Tables

Preface

Agriculture has been a central part of Tennessee's rich history. More than any other factor, the opportunity to farm drew people to the Tennessee territory in the late eighteenth and early nineteenth centuries. Agriculture was the dominant sector of the state's economy during the nineteenth century and remained an important one well into the twentieth century. Over the years farming has provided a livelihood for millions of Tennessee families. As late as 1950, more than a quarter of the state's labor force worked in agricultural occupations, a greater proportion than in any other area of employment. The commercial farmers' need for services such as marketing, transportation, and finance created economic opportunities for thousands more Tennesseans. So, too, did their need for agricultural supplies and equipment and for household goods. Today farming accounts for barely 1 percent of the personal income and 2 percent of the employment in the state, but throughout most of Tennessee's long history, agriculture played a critical role in the state's economy and in the well-being of its citizens.

The importance of agriculture reached beyond its economic role. Tilling the soil has been the preferred way of life for many generations of rural families. Farming became a social organization for cultivating and preserving values, and for passing them on to succeeding generations. It bestowed worth and self-esteem on the individual, it sustained the family and strengthened the community, and it enabled rural residents to live satisfying and rewarding lives. Farmers and their families have found in rural life an independence, a sense of dignity, and a feeling of achievement that no other setting could provide them.

The purpose of this book is to explore the development of Tennessee's agriculture in the years before the Civil War. During that period, farmers transformed the state from an undeveloped wilderness into a cluster of mature agricultural regions producing a wide variety of commodities. They created a complex agricultural system that provided goods for household consumption and for sale in markets off the farm.

Many of them improved the efficiency of their farms and the quality of their products by participating in a widespread agricultural reform movement that included the adoption of animal-drawn equipment, better cultivation techniques, new crop strains, and improved livestock. Producing for outside markets made it necessary for Tennessee farmers to become more knowledgeable about business matters and more skillful at operating within the extensive commercial network created to carry their goods to those markets. Although much of their effort and attention centered on commercial activities, farmers also sought to enhance the quality of rural life for themselves and their families. They cultivated friendships, cooperated with neighbors, engaged in community endeavors, and took part in a variety of leisure activities. They established religious, educational, and social institutions to meet the diverse cultural needs of their households. They strove to acquire land, not only as a way to increase their own wealth and sense of independence but also as an inheritance to pass on to their children so that future generations might continue to enjoy the benefits of an agricultural life. As farmers pursued their objectives, they set priorities and selected from competing options. Their decisions, the contexts in which they made them, and the ways in which they implemented them form the agricultural history of the state and the content of this book.

Tennessee farming and Tennessee farmers have left an indelible heritage. The history of agriculture in the state embodies tradition and change, success and failure, pride and stigma, joy and pathos. It encompasses developments that were peculiar to Tennessee and developments that extended well beyond the state's boundaries. Farmers created an agricultural system adapted to the particular geographic, climatic, and locational conditions in their state. Tennessee, as a consequence, came to occupy a transitional position between the semitropical staple agriculture of the South and the grain-livestock agriculture of the North. The state's farmers also participated in activities that were part of a wide spectrum of change occurring across the South and across the nation. They were Tennessee farmers, but they were also southern farmers and American farmers. Their story is sometimes ambiguous, often complex, and always fascinating. This book contains part of that story.

Acknowledgments

Many people assisted me in the preparation of this book. I was fortunate that much of my research drew on sources at the Tennessee State Library and Archives in Nashville. The staff there could not have been more helpful or more cordial. They quickly brought the material I requested and, after becoming familiar with my project, made useful suggestions. Wayne Moore, in particular, not only provided excellent archival service but also permitted me to tap his considerable knowledge of Tennessee agriculture. Librarians at Vanderbilt University's Jean and Alexander Heard Library also assisted in finding and obtaining research material. Carroll Van West and Caneta Skelley Hankins at the Center for Historic Preservation of Middle Tennessee State University in Murfreesboro advised me on a number of subjects and allowed me to use valuable material from their Century Farms Program. Dorothy Curtis, formerly director of the Oscar Farris Agricultural Museum in Nashville, shared her knowledge and time, instructing me on some of the more arcane aspects of nineteenth-century farm technology. Blanche Henry Clark Weaver and Harriet C. Owsley consented to my use of information they had gathered from the manuscript censuses of 1850 and 1860. My wife, Raena F. Winters, helped with the research, constructed the maps, and gave encouragement from the beginning of the project to the end. I am grateful both for her spousal assistance and for her willingness to be acknowledged for providing such assistance. Vanderbilt University granted academic leaves on two occasions to allow me free time to work on the project.

Paul K. Conkin and V. Jacque Voegeli, two of my colleagues at Vanderbilt University, drew on their vast knowledge and powerful editorial eyes to critique an early version of the manuscript. They made many valuable suggestions for revision, which have saved me from factual errors, faulty logic, and fuzzy exposition. Jeremy Atack and R. Douglas Hurt, both excellent agricultural historians, read the completed manuscript for the University of Tennessee Press and offered their own suggestions for improvement, many of which I incorporated in the book. Any weaknesses that remain are, of course, my responsibility. The staff at the University of Tennessee Press has provided expert assistance in moving the project from manuscript to published book. Karin Kaufman's expert copyediting and Stan Ivester's skillful management have greatly improved the final project.

Portions of this book have previously appeared in three scholarly journals. I wish to thank the editors of *Agricultural History, Journal of Southern History,* and *Tennessee Historical Quarterly* for permission to use material from articles they have published.

I dedicate this book to my mother and to the memory of my father, for reasons she will understand.

1

The Setting

The land that received Tennessee's first aspiring white farmers in the last years of the eighteenth century varied broadly in topography, soil type, vegetation, and climate. Some areas were ideally suited for a wide assortment of agricultural activities, some only for a narrow range of production. Other areas were incapable of sustaining any form of farming enterprise. The Indian population in the eastern portion of the land that eventually became the state of Tennessee had learned much earlier how to exploit at least some of the territory's rich agricultural potential. They grew a variety of crops to supplement a diet comprised largely of meat from hunting and fishing, and fruits and nuts from gathering. Their farming practices were neither highly developed nor extensive. Yet within a few decades after the arrival of white immigrants, the Tennessee wilderness had given way to a broad and diverse array of agricultural activities.

Those early settlers must have been disappointed at their first view of the new land.[1] As they crossed the boundary of North Carolina into the territory to the west, they encountered the rugged Unaka Mountain chain (see map 1.1). The region embraced a number of individual ranges, some with elevations exceeding six thousand feet. Its tall peaks, jagged ridges, and deep gorges created a formidable barrier that threatened to deny settlers access to the lands beyond. Had it not been for an occasional river valley and a few low passes through which travelers moved on the risky trek, it might well have succeeded. Dense forests and thick ground vegetation covered the lower elevations. On crossing the area in 1784, John Liscomb noted "the buckeye four feet through and Populars nine feet through, and Cain grew on the Mountain side very thick."[2] Perhaps a few of the more optimistic among the early migrants recognized the possibility of grazing livestock on the grassy upper slopes of the mountains or of cultivating the isolated riverine coves, which had received alluvial deposits from periodic flooding. But the steep, irregular, inaccessible terrain and the thin, leached, unproductive soils that covered most of the region quickly discouraged any who had come with the intention of creating a new life based on agriculture.

The hardy migrants who traveled beyond the lofty mountain barrier that separated North Carolina from the Tennessee territory found more promising circumstances. As the Holston River and its tributaries cut northeastward and the Tennessee River and its tributaries cut southwestward through a series of narrow forested ridges to the west of the Unaka Mountain chain, they formed the broad, level, and readily accessible eastern valleys. A mixture of limestone, shale, and sandstone, the soils of these valleys would in time sustain an assortment of grains and specialty crops and support a variety of farm animals. Early farmers soon discovered what Gilbert Imlay noted in his journal when he visited the area in the late eighteenth century: "This country has mountains on every side but the southwest, and is interspersed with high hills in most parts of it. The vallies are extremely fertile, and everywhere finely watered."[3] Francis Asbury, a Methodist minister traveling across the northern section of the eastern valleys, declared that "the low lands are very rich, the uplands barren."[4] French botanist François André Michaux echoed this assessment a few years later when he reported that the region was well "watered by the small rivers issuing from the adjacent mountains, which cross it in every part. The best land is upon their borders." He noted that "the nature of the soil, somewhat gravely, appears more adapted for the culture of wheat, rye, and oats." He was less enthusiastic about the elevated woodlands that separated the river valleys, commenting that the "remainder of the territory, almost everywhere interspersed with hills, is of a middling quality, and produces nothing but white, red, black chincapin."[5] The Holston and Tennessee river systems not only drained this part of the territory, as the region's first white visitors had observed; in time the Tennessee River would also provide the eastern valleys with a vital transportation route to the outside, despite troublesome navigational obstacles downstream.

While many settlers remained and took up farming in the fertile eastern valleys, others moved across the hill country, the Cumberland tableland or plateau, and the eastern edge of the highland rim into the central basin of Middle Tennessee. A series of low-lying ridges, some reaching elevations of thirty-five hundred feet, and narrow valleys formed the hill country, at the northeastern edge of the Cumberland tableland. Few of the valleys were broad enough to accommodate ag-

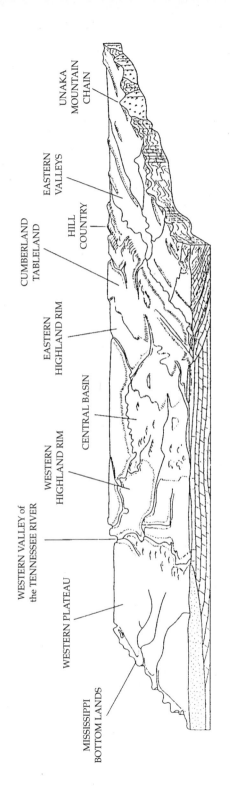

Map 1.1. Major physiographic regions. Source: Tennessee State Division of Geology.

MISSISSIPPI BOTTOM LANDS

WESTERN PLATEAU

WESTERN VALLEY of the TENNESSEE RIVER

WESTERN HIGHLAND RIM

CENTRAL BASIN

EASTERN HIGHLAND RIM

CUMBERLAND TABLELAND

HILL COUNTRY

EASTERN VALLEYS

UNAKA MOUNTAIN CHAIN

riculture, and those that were contained poor quality land. In 1785 a German traveler, Lewis Brantz, commented that in this part of the territory "nothing grows but grass. . . . the land in these barrens is uncommonly poor in comparison with that on the Cumberland [River]; however, it is believed that it may produce grain."[6] On to the west, the tableland and, at a slightly lower elevation, the rim were level and, for the most part, free of natural impediments to farming. Except for the long, narrow lowland cove located in the Sequatchie River Valley, however, the area possessed deficient soils, generally thin, porous, and of low fertility. A short distance west of the eastern valleys, Michaux reported, "the soil is uneven, stony and very indifferent, of which it is an easy thing to judge by the quantity of pines . . . that are in the forests."[7] The Reverend Asbury noted that on the tableland "the soil is generally barren and broken."[8] The area appeared much the same to J. M. Brewer a decade later: "The glades renders the country entire sterile. . . . [The land] is very poor, and much of it is barren & covered with shrubby oak and blackjack."[9]

It is small wonder that a region of such limited agricultural potential saw virtually no white settlement as more favorable areas to either side steadily gained in population. Francis Baily remarked as he crossed the area in the late 1790s that "this state may be divided into two parts, the eastern and western, which are separated from each other by a wilderness which is possessed by the Indians." On leaving the central basin in route to the eastern valleys, he penned a stark depiction of the Cumberland tableland: "I took my farewell of all kind of society till I arrived at the opposite end of the wilderness."[10] General farming, limited tobacco cultivation, and livestock grazing would eventually reach this elevated and infertile plain, but only after settlers had pursued more inviting agricultural opportunities in the eastern valleys and central basin.

The central basin is a cluster of lowlands bounded on the east, south, and west by the highland rim. Often called the "garden" of Tennessee, prospective farmers quickly recognized its potential. Much like the rich Kentucky Bluegrass region to the north, it possessed clayey, calcareous soils with generous amounts of phosphate and humus, which supported dense woodlands interspersed with open ranges of lush natural grasses. When he crossed the basin in the 1790s, Francis Baily recorded that the "country all round consists of a layer of fine black mould on a bed of limestone." His overnight camp on one occasion was "surrounded on each side with a deep wall of woods. I enjoyed the serenity of the evening in silent mediation."[11] Michaux was likewise impressed with the fertile soil and fulsome vegetation: "It is usually, in point of colour, of a dark brown, without the least texture of stony substances. The forests that cover the country clearly indicate how favourable the soil is for vegetation, as most of the trees acquire a very large diameter." He was struck by the thick stands of cane, or native bamboo, "which grow so close to each other, that at the distance of ten or twelve feet a man could not be perceived was he concealed there."[12] The region's natural endowments in time enabled its farmers to produce an abundance of cereal, cotton, and tobacco crops, and to feed an assortment of livestock. The region also enjoyed a rich riverine legacy. The Cumberland River and several smaller rivers provided both drainage and transportation outlets for the saucer-shaped basin. Those streams would play a crucial role in the settlement and growth of the region.

Indian occupation and prior land claims stalled settlement for a time at the far edge of the central basin. Once westward movement resumed, arriving farmers discovered yet more diversity in Tennessee's natural endowments. Beyond the western edge of the highland rim they came again upon the Tennessee River, now as it made its way northward to the Ohio River after reaching its southern extension in Alabama. The narrow, irregular valley that contained the river on its northerly course enclosed some tracts of excellent alluvial bottom land, others of anemic or marshy soils. The western valley of the Tennessee River could not offer the advantages of the eastern valleys or the central basin, but the region's settlers eventually developed grain and livestock farming, and, to the north, lucrative tobacco production. By the time the Tennessee River reached the point where it headed northward, it had passed the navigational obstructions that impeded its course in the eastern valleys. Its way was now clear to provide the region with a convenient and unhampered connection to the Ohio and Mississippi River routes.

As settlers moved farther west, they entered a region that rivaled the central basin in its capacity to support agricultural production. The plateau of West Tennessee—also called the coastal plain—began as a high shelf at the edge of the western valley of the Tennessee River and sloped gently downward to a steep escarpment overlooking the Mississippi River Valley. Its deep, brown loam soils, relatively free of rocks and forests, ranked among the most fertile in the territory. The loess soils, which covered much of the northern half of the region, were especially rich, but were at the same time loose and subject to wind and water erosion. Although this part of the Tennessee territory sustained the production of a broad range of crops, farmers who migrated to the region soon found it ideally suited to the cultivation of two commercial crops. Well before white settlement reached the western plateau, Gilbert Imlay recorded in his travel account that "the high grounds near that river [Mississippi] are particularly favourable to the culture of indigo and cotton. The article last mentioned must be a constant source of wealth to the planter, because its value is considerable when compared to its weight, and it must be in constant demand in foreign markets."[13]

Imlay's enthusiasm for indigo production would prove to be misplaced, but he accurately foresaw that cotton would become a mainstay of the economy of this rich agricultural region. If cultivated less extensively than cotton, tobacco nonetheless held a similar position in farming to the north. Imlay again revealed his prescience in noting the potential of this crop: "The soil is not only fertile, but easily cultivated. Six hogsheads of tobacco for one man does not require more labour than three hogsheads in the atlantic states."[14] Traveling across the same area half a century later, agriculturist Solon Robinson commented similarly on the quality of the soil. It was, he reported, "requiring of a great deal of hard toil to prepare it for culture, but affording an assurance to the husband-man that when once cleared, he will have a soil that no judicious system of culture can ever wear out."[15]

The western plateau possessed no direct transportation outlet of its own, but it commanded access through a number of tributaries to either the Tennessee River to the east or the Mississippi River to the west. In time these waterways became important outlets for the commercial products of the region.

The Mississippi River Valley, or bottom lands, formed the extreme western region of Tennessee. About ten miles wide at its northernmost point, this thin strip of land nearly disappeared to the south as the Mississippi River encountered the high bluffs that formed the boundary of the western plateau. The region, primarily alluvial flood plain, contained some of the state's richest and poorest soils. An English visitor in 1761 remarked, with some exaggeration, that the "land is so rich and the soil so deep that in many places one may run a soldier's pike up to the head without meeting a rock or a stone and capable of producing everything." A few years later, another English observer portrayed the area, also with a measure of embellishment, as "luxuriantly rich and fertile, even beyond a possibility of description."[16] Christian Schultz, on a trip down the Mississippi River in 1808, noted that the country around Chickasaw Bluffs, near the future site of Memphis, was "apparently of an excellent soil, but extremely uninhabited."[17] At the time of settlement, dense vegetation, lakes, and marshes covered most of the northern section of this region, and much of the terrain was subject to periodic flooding. Still, in those areas where farmers could drain the land and secure it from yearly flooding, cotton cultivation eventually flourished. Moreover, with the Mississippi River forming its western boundary, this part of the territory possessed the best water link to the outside of any of Tennessee's regions.

Tennessee's climate, like its topography and soils, varies from region to region.[18] Just as the farmers who established the agricultural foundations of Tennessee had to adjust to differences in natural physical conditions, so too they had to accommodate variation in climate. Rainfall is generally uniform across the state, averaging between forty-five and fifty inches annually with fairly balanced distribution throughout the year. Rainfall, therefore, placed few constraints on the production choices open to early Tennessee farmers. The length of the growing season is far less uniform, and it became a key factor in at least some of those choices. The farming areas of East Tennessee have from 150 to 170 frost-free days per year, which limited settlers there to relatively fast maturing summer crops, such as oats and corn, and to livestock farming. The long, mild winters usually provided ample snow cover, which made this area especially favorable for winter wheat. Conditions were less suitable for other crops. Michaux noted that although the eastern valleys supported the cultivation of small grains, "that of cotton is little noticed, on account of the cold weather, which sets in very early."[19] Moving from northeast to southwest, the growing season lengthens, exceeding 250 days per year in the extreme southwestern corner of the state. The factors affecting crop options open to farmers changed accordingly. Because the variable winters brought alternating freezing and thawing, and produced little protective snow cover, winter wheat was a less attractive choice than it was in the east. On the other hand, the longer growing season made the southwestern quadrant more conducive to cotton, which for varieties available in the antebellum period required a minimum of 210 frost-free days to ripen.

Tennessee's diverse geographical and climatic regions combine to form the three grand divisions of the state. The Unaka Mountain chain, the eastern valleys, and the hill country comprise the division of East Tennessee. The area between the eastern and western valleys of the Tennessee River—the Cumberland tableland, the highland rim, and the central basin—constitutes Middle Tennessee. The western valley of the Tennessee River, the western plateau, and the Mississippi bottom lands join to form West Tennessee.

Prospective farmers not only discovered unfamiliar terrain, soil, and climate conditions when they arrived in the Tennessee territory, they also encountered an indigenous population. The Indian presence affected white occupation of the territory in different ways. Indian resistance to encroachment on their lands periodically delayed settlement and impeded agricultural development. At the same time, white farmers sometimes benefited from observing and emulating indigenous agriculture. The newcomers were, of course, already familiar with Indian methods; white farmers had long since assimilated many native practices. Still, the agriculture developed by the Indians in the Tennessee territory was the result of many years of trial and error and adaptation to local conditions, and the settlers found an advantage in incorporating at least a few of the native practices into their own farming systems.

Among the Indian tribes residing in the future state of Tennessee, only the Cherokees, who occupied the eastern valleys, had moved beyond hunting and gathering by the time white settlers appeared.[20] They had selected the most favorable locations along the rivers, usually sites rich in loamy alluvial soils. They often chose canebreaks because they had learned from years of experience that land supporting this kind of vegetation was also good for farm crops. They cleared the land of trees by girdling with stone axes and of brush with fire and hand tools. The Indians divided their improved fields into individual household allotments, but they worked them communally.

The Cherokee's principal crop was corn, but they also grew a number of other crops, including beans, squash, pumpkins, potatoes, sunflowers, gourds, and tobacco. They produced several strains of corn, varying in color, shape, size, hardness of kernel, and time required for maturation. Each type had a special use. One type was harvested early, roasted, and eaten from the cob. Another, which was allowed to reach maturity, provided ground meal for cornbread. Still others became ornamentation for their dwellings. The Cherokees employed intercropping, a method that mixed several different crops in the same field. In this way they made efficient use of their cleared land and enabled the crops to reinforce one another's growth. For example, cornstalks provided poles on which beans planted between the corn rows could grow. The beans, in turn, replaced the small amount of nitrogen drawn from the soil by the corn, although the Indians were unaware of this benefit. Squash vines planted in the same field inhibited the growth of weeds. The Cherokees also practiced multiple cropping, under which they sowed two corn crops a season on the same field. They planted an early variety, which they picked green and roasted, as soon as the threat of frost had passed, followed by a late variety after the first crop had been picked and the field cleared. The Indians also kept domesticated dogs, which provided a source of meat.

The Cherokees followed a customary division of labor. The men usually cleared the land and perhaps assisted in the planting. The women and children performed most of the farming tasks. They sowed the crops, weeded them during the growing season, harvested them at maturity, and prepared them for consumption or storage. For the most part, they used simple hand tools crafted from sticks, stones, shells, and animal bones, though some had adopted more advanced hand tools introduced by early white travelers to the region. In return for these responsibilities, women were apparently vested with the ownership of the products. For it was from them, not the men of the tribe, that early travelers and settlers in the eastern valleys purchased foodstuffs. This activity, ironically, made the Cherokee women the first commercial farmers of Tennessee.

The first settlers in the new land brought with them considerable knowledge about agriculture, but they also learned from observing Indian methods. The Indians had already identified crops and techniques appropriate for the particular conditions in the territory. Imitating Indian practices, such as intercropping and cultivating canebreaks, allowed white farmers to avoid at least some of the uncertainty and difficulties that normally accompanied the establishment of farming in a strange environment. The Indians had also located and cleared areas that were favorable for agriculture. Sometimes white settlers followed Indian examples in selecting their own farm sites; sometimes they merely took over Indian lands after the indigenous population had left voluntarily or been forcibly removed.

Topography, soil type, and climate set the parameters of Tennessee's agriculture. They determined the areas suitable for farming and established the crop and livestock choices available to farmers. Tennessee settlers in the late eighteenth and early nineteenth centuries had to discover for themselves the state's natural parameters. Through experimentation and observation they gradually learned the full spectrum of agricultural possibilities and the relative merits and drawbacks of each. This information defined the range of possibilities from which they chose in establishing and developing their farming activities.

The physical environment represented only one set of considerations influencing their decisions. There were others—family needs, desires, and aspirations; an appropriate mix between production for the household and production for the market; and circumstances affecting the management and conduct of commercial relationships. The kind of life farmers sought, the size of inheritance they wished to pass on, the degree of financial risk they were willing to assume, the ways they chose to carry out market transactions, the activities they elected to fill their leisure time—those factors and many others figured in their decisions and influenced their farming practices. The manner in which each household dealt with such questions and adapted to its particular situation constituted the substance of the agricultural history—indeed, of the rural way of life—of Tennessee during the antebellum period.

2

Settlement and Farm Making

The first permanent white settlers began to filter into the Tennessee territory in the late 1760s. Preceded by an assortment of hunters, trappers, and traders, they set up residence in the wilderness and undertook the arduous task of creating a routine of subsistence agriculture. Those early settlers congregated along the Watauga and Holston rivers just across the Unaka Mountain chain in the northeast corner of what later became the state of Tennessee. In the years following the end of the American Revolution, immigration accelerated and extended well into the interior of the state. By the turn of the century, the population exceeded 100,000 and was concentrated in two locations, one in the eastern valleys and the other along the Cumberland River in the central basin. Migrants continued to arrive in growing numbers and to push westward during the first decades of the nineteenth century. By 1830, when the state's population had reached almost 700,000, all regions of the state had passed beyond the pioneer stage of settlement, contained a sizable number of permanent residents, and established a strong agricultural base.

Settlement would have moved more rapidly had it not been for conflicting claims to ownership of the Tennessee territory.[1] North Carolina had earlier contended that, under conditions originally set out in its colonial charter, it held title to the lands beyond its western border. During the revolutionary war, the state granted millions of acres in land warrants as bounties to members of the military. To redeem these warrants it set aside a large, ill-defined military reserve in the western area to which it laid claim. The state also sold enormous tracts of land in the same area to speculators. The legislature sought to reinforce its land and jurisdictional claims by establishing Washington County in 1777 to govern the Watauga-Holston community, and Cumberland County in 1783 to govern the central basin community. That the state's authority in the territory was tenuous became clear in 1784, when the citizens of Washington County and the surrounding area declared themselves the independent state of Franklin. Still, notwithstanding the dubious grounds for its actions, North Carolina had already transferred massive amounts of land in the future state of Tennessee to private hands by the time the flow of settlers to the territory quickened after the revolutionary war.

The jurisdictional question was at least partially resolved in 1789, when North Carolina renounced its western claims, ceding the territory to the federal government. Congress organized the area into the Southwest Territory the following year and officially opened it for settlement. But North Carolina had attached conditions to its cession. The federal government agreed to honor titles to western land sold by North Carolina and to recognize the validity of its military warrants. The second condition proved particularly troublesome, because the military reserve established earlier to satisfy the warrants failed to cover the large number of outstanding claims, and eventually the federal government had to set aside additional land. Adding to the confusion and discord, Tennessee sought control over the federal lands within its borders after it became a state in 1796. Through a series of piecemeal agreements and concessions, culminating in 1846 with an outright grant of what remained of the public domain in the state, the federal government gradually relinquished its authority. Although North Carolina's cession in 1789 had resolved the narrow question of jurisdiction over the Tennessee territory, the problems precipitated by the accompanying agreement and the conflict between the federal government and Tennessee over control of the public domain affected settlement and land distribution for some time afterward.

North Carolinians were not the only claimants to lands west of the Unaka Mountain chain; the Indians also asserted title to the territory. In fact, the Cherokees and the Chickasaws, who had lived in the territory long before the intrusion of white immigrants, flatly rejected the notion that the new arrivals held any rights to the land. English traveler Francis Baily recognized the adamancy of the Indians on this matter in 1797: "Though the [white] inhabitants claim the whole of the [Tennessee] territory, . . . they do not possess more than a quarter of that tract in *full right and sovereignty.* . . . The Indians dispute every inch of ground with the Americans, and will not let them encroach upon their territory."[2] Early settlers in the Watauga-Holston community had to obtain permission from the Indians to reside in the area. Others who came later leased and then purchased land from the Cherokees.[3] Similarly, the small group that located along the Cumberland River had to lease the Indian lands they occupied.[4] But these were clearly temporary expediencies; permanent and large-scale settlement of the territory depended on eradicating Indian claims.

The first step toward accomplishing that end came in 1777. The Cherokee nation had unwisely allied with the British in the American Revolution and suffered a humiliating defeat at the hands of the North Carolina militia early in the war. Under the terms of surrender, the Indians ceded a large tract of land in the eastern valleys. The cession was ratified after the Revolution in a treaty between the Cherokees and the central government under the Articles of Confederation. As the white population increased, conflicts between settlers and Indians inevitably multiplied. Resolution of these differences, just as inevitably, brought further concessions from the Indians. By the second decade of the nineteenth century, the Cherokees and the Chickasaws had, through a succession of informal agreements, sales, and treaties, surrendered all of their claims to land in East and Middle Tennessee. The Chickasaws managed to retain control of West Tennessee until 1818, when they finally surrendered the last of the Indian claims within the state. In a little more than forty years, between 1777 and 1818, undisputed title to the Tennessee territory had gradually passed from the Indians to the white settlers.

While the issue of control and ownership of Tennessee lands moved toward resolution, settlers streamed in from the east. The newcomers were a homogeneous lot. Most came from the Piedmont of Virginia and North Carolina and had descended from English and Scots-Irish ancestors. As settlement continued, some immigrants began arriving from more distant states, such as South Carolina, Georgia, and Pennsylvania, and with more diverse backgrounds, such as German, Irish, Welsh, and French. The early introduction of black slaves added yet another component to the population mix. Still, Anglo-Saxon ethnic groups continued to represent the dominant element among Tennessee's settlers. The immigrants were similar in another respect. They came almost exclusively from rural settings; they and their families before them had long been engaged in agriculture and been members of farming households.

Several factors account for the homogeneity of the settlers. The geographical proximity of the principal states of origin—Virginia and North Carolina—and of other south-Atlantic states that sent people was, of course, a major factor. Migration to a pioneer territory was never easy, but normally the shorter the distance settlers had to travel, the fewer problems they encountered. North Carolinians who held claims to land in Tennessee had an additional reason to come to the territory. Moreover, most settlers understandably preferred an area similar in climate, soils, and vegetation to the one from which they had come.[5] Such a preference helps to explain the preponderance of immigrants from states immediately to the east and the dearth of immigrants from the North and from foreign countries. The existence of slavery doubtlessly also discouraged some northerners and foreign immigrants from coming as well. Because the primary states sending people to the new territory were themselves preponderantly Anglo-Saxon, the large majority of Tennessee's settlers naturally came from the same ethnic roots.

The motivations of the immigrants varied, yet they shared a common belief that western lands offered the opportunity to live satisfying and reasonably comfortable lives. Many were encouraged in this belief by hunters and trappers who related stories of rich land and friendly Indians beyond the mountains. Some of them even prepared crude maps to guide the first settlers. Travelers to the area brought back similar information. James Robertson, who later participated in the establishment of the Cumberland settlement in the central basin, returned to North Carolina from a visit to the Tennessee wilderness in 1770 to report on the natural beauty and the economic opportunities of the area.[6] Gilbert Imlay was likewise impressed when he crossed East Tennessee two decades later. "Few places are more healthy, there is none more fertile," he wrote in his journal; "and there is hardly any other place in which the farmer can support his family in such a degree of affluence." He concluded that "there are few places that present fairer prospects to the man who is looking for a settlement."[7] Equally encouraging were the remarks of people who had already taken up residence in the territory. "So great is the fertility of the soil," reported one settler to the *Philadelphia Gazette* in 1795, "that the inhabitants with little labour raise thrice as much grain as supplies their families, and the balance is hospitably given up to the emigrant, or those who from accident have been deprived of sustenance."[8] The reports coming out of the West, notwithstanding an understandable amount of exaggeration, doubtlessly convinced many who were already predisposed to migrate, and perhaps some who were not.

The reasons settlers gave for migrating to Tennessee were consistent with the promise of those accounts. Joseph White, who acquired a farm in Jefferson County in 1808, came for the rich land, the soil in his native Virginia having been depleted by repeated cropping.[9] If the judgment of Charles Augustus Starr was sound, prospects in Virginia had not improved over the three decades that followed. He left "impoverished Virginia" in 1836 to take up farming in Shelby County, a "veritable land of milk and honey."[10] After investigating prospects in Kentucky and Tennessee, Matthias Boon moved his family to Madison County in 1824, where he purchased 150 acres of unimproved land.[11] The decision to migrate to Tennessee was easier, as noted, for those who held military warrants that they could exchange for land. On settling in Blount County in 1808, Samuel Henry redeemed a warrant he had received from the North Carolina government in lieu of delinquent pay from the revolutionary war.[12] William Garner claimed land in Blount County in 1839 with a warrant he had inherited from his father, who had also served in the North Carolina militia.[13] Some people came for less tangible, but nonetheless compelling, reasons. Distressed over the death of her husband, Mary Elam Scruggs moved from South Carolina with her children and a few slaves to make a new life in Bedford County in 1830.[14] William Jeffries's explanation for moving to Blount County in 1816 was even more cryptic; he was simply responding to the "restless spirit of the times."[15]

The immediate concern of the new settlers was to secure the essentials for survival. Their first activities involved selecting a satisfactory site, constructing a simple dwelling, and planting food crops. Normally the entire family took part in these activities, but sometimes the men of the household came first, usually arriving in late winter or early spring to set up the farmstead and returning for the rest of the family after sowing the first crop. If the area already contained a number of established households, settlers customarily received assistance from their neighbors; if not, they were on their own. In localities where Indians were a threat, groups of settlers constructed a primitive fort called a "station," in which they lived while erecting their household dwellings and preparing their land.[16] By the time the first crop came in, members of the family had either succeeded in providing for their basic needs or they had returned to their former home.

Successful settlers understood the criteria for selecting a viable farm site. They sought a location with good soil, reasonably level and well-drained terrain, a supply of timber, and a source of fresh water.

Beyond these essential requirements, they looked for outcroppings of limestone for fertilizer lime, stones for chimneys and fences, a stand of oak or red cedar for furniture and utensils, and, perhaps, falling water for a future gristmill.[17] Those anticipating the possibility of commercial ventures at a later time—by all indications, the vast majority of them—often chose sites with transportation links to potential markets. Gilbert Imlay acknowledged the importance of such considerations in noting that the Watauga-Holston community "is not above 340 miles from Richmond in Virginia, along a good wagon road; whence we may conclude that the settlers on the Holston [River] will preserve a considerable intercourse with the atlantic states."[18] A resident writing to an eastern newspaper in the 1790s thought it worthwhile to make a similar point: "So great are the natural advantages of water in this country, that it is asserted with truth, there is not a spot in it 20 miles distant from a boatable navigation, from whence the farmer . . . may with cheapness, safety, and ease, convey his articles for foreign markets, down the great Tennessee, or Cumberland, into the Ohio and Mississippi, and thence to New Orleans."[19]

Gaining title to a farm site was relatively easy, even for those of limited means. Settlers carrying certificates of purchase or military warrants issued by the government of North Carolina needed only to lay claim to eligible land. Under the terms of North Carolina's 1789 cession, the federal government had to honor those obligations, a responsibility that shifted to the state of Tennessee as it gained control over the public domain. Settlers simply converted their claims into titles at the nearest land office on choosing a farm site. The military warrants were negotiable—that is, they could be bought and sold—and many immigrants acquired them after they arrived at their destinations. The market in warrants was well developed, and purchasers usually had little difficulty securing them. A Clarksville agent, for instance, offered in the local newspaper to "procure land warrants . . . on reasonable terms."[20]

Other settlers purchased land from individuals. Speculators, such as William Blount in the eastern valleys and James Robertson in the central basin, had amassed enormous tracts either by purchasing land directly from North Carolina or by buying up military warrants, usually at bargain prices, from veterans not interested in exercising them. The speculators were, of course, eager to sell farm sites from their holdings to incoming settlers. Newspapers across the state carried abundant advertisements offering land for sale. Beginning in the early 1790s, the *Knoxville Gazette* regularly listed raw land, not only in the nearby eastern valleys but also in the central basin.[21] A single entry in an 1811 issue of the *Tennessee Gazette*, published in Nashville, listed for sale six parcels ranging in size from 197 to 1,503 acres. Later in the month, the same newspaper advertised the sale of individual units from a fifteen-thousand-acre tract.[22] The *Memphis Appeal* informed its readers in 1843 of a "regular auction" of farm real estate in Shelby County.[23] Much of the land offered for sale was unimproved. But some parcels were partially cleared and broken, and some included crude structures; others appeared to be fully established units. Previously developed sites offered both advantages and disadvantages to potential buyers. The greater the improvement, the sooner the purchaser could bring the land into production, but the higher the price he had to pay. Christopher Houston, who came to Maury County in 1816, doubtlessly echoed the opinion of many settlers when he recommended that "for the man who can buy improved land, even if rated high, it is far better than to begin in the woods."[24]

The large supply of land on the market during the settlement stage apparently kept prices low. Francis Baily remarked in the summer of 1797 that the "price of land about the vicinity of this place [Nashville], unimproved, is from one to four and five dollars [per acre], according to its situation and neighbourhood."[25] Little had changed by 1802, when François André Michaux reported that the "price of the best land does not exceed five dollars per acre in the environs of Nasheville, and thirty or forty miles from town they are not even worth three dollars. They [settlers] can at that price purchase a plantation completely formed, composed of two to three hundred acres, of which fifteen to twenty are cleared and a log-house."[26] In 1824, Matthias Boon purchased 150 acres of raw land in Madison County at four dollars an acre.[27] Advertisements for the sale of land rarely included prices, but those that did were consistent with these observations.

The flexibility of owners in negotiating sales also testified to the abundance of land on the market. They understandably preferred full cash payment, but they frequently indicated a willingness to accept more lenient terms. Half the price as a down payment, the balance in six to twelve months was a typical arrangement. The *Tennessee Gazette* listed several tracts for sale on even more generous terms; one seller wanted a third down in cash and the balance in "approved negotiable paper" in twelve months.[28] Another advertisement merely offered land for sale on "accommodating terms."[29] Sometimes the seller would accept payment in slaves or marketable goods. "Negroes and cash will be taken," read the notice of one dealer selling plots from an extensive tract in the central basin.[30] It is possible to detect a sense of desperation in the owner of a seven-hundred-acre parcel who declared that "I will sell part or all; negroes will be received in part payment."[31] Sellers frequently accepted cotton in partial payment, and one agreed to take "horses if they are under 8 years old."[32] Another was willing to trade his Tennessee property in "exchange for lands in some one of the Southern Territories or Atlantic States."[33] Prospective buyers occasionally used the newspapers to announce their interest in purchasing land, as with the person in the central basin who wanted to "purchase 80–120 acres at a fair price."[34] One wonders whether another had any response to his offer: "I have long laboured under a complaint—for ready money only. This is to give notice—that my wife jane—will be exchanged for good arable land."[35]

Despite low prices and the owners' willingness to negotiate attractive terms, some newcomers were still unable, or perhaps unwilling, to purchase land. They had two alternatives open to them. They could, as Michaux observed, easily find land to rent: "Among the emigrants that arrive annually from the eastern country at Tennessea there are always some who have not the means of purchasing estates; still there is no difficulty in procuring them at a certain rent; for the speculators who possess many thousand acres are very happy to get tenants for their land, as it induces others to come and settle in the environs. . . . [and] speedily enhances the value of their possessions."[36] A nonresident landowner in West Tennessee appeared to bear out Michaux's contention: "I have about 25,000 acres on the Hatchie River and on the Mississippi below the mouth of the Hatchie, for most of which I should be glad to get good tenants."[37]

Prospective tenants, as with prospective buyers, had only to consult the local newspapers, which frequently contained offers to rent property. "I have 150 a. of good open land to rent," read an 1802 advertisement in the *Tennessee Gazette*. Another in the same newspaper was directed specifically at recent arrivals: "To new commers, this place ought to be an object, & to any persons with a few hands who will engage to make improvements to a certain extent, he [owner] will give a long lease & and make the terms accommodating."[38] Sellers of land sometimes indicated their intention to rent out their property, normally for a single season only, if they failed to find buyers. Owners with land to rent, like those with land to sell, appeared to be flexible in negotiating arrangements. They frequently used adjectives such as "liberal," "accommodating," and "reasonable" in describing rental terms, which typically called for improvements—erecting buildings and clearing land, for instance—in exchange for the use of property. Two travelers in the territory in the early nineteenth century found that one-year leases on unimproved land commonly required tenants "to clear and enclose eight or more acres, to build a log-house, and to pay the proprietor eight or ten bushels of maize for each acre cleared."[39]

The other alternative open to settlers without the means or the inclination to purchase land was to become a squatter. Many availed themselves of the opportunity to move onto unoccupied land, private or public, and take up farming. The owners rarely complained about such intrusions; many private owners, in fact, encouraged the practice because it brought improvements, and thereby enhanced value, to their property. If the owner put up his land for sale later, as was usually the case, he customarily offered the squatter the privilege of first refusal. In the case of public land, the squatter normally held preemption rights entitling him to purchase his improved parcel at the government's minimum price. Squatters hoped that when the property on which they settled was eventually placed on the market, they would be in a strong enough financial position to purchase it.

After obtaining a farm site, settlers had to turn quickly to the tasks of constructing the family dwelling and putting in the first crop. A crude log cabin, erected in a week to ten days—less with help from the neighbors—usually provided their first house. Typically, a single, square room, measuring fifteen to twenty feet on a side, it was made from round logs, notched at both ends and with the bark removed. If the family was fortunate enough to have help from neighbors, the builders sometimes hewed two sides of the timbers flat and squared the logs to achieve a better fit. They then filled the gaps between the logs with small pieces of wood, broken rocks, and moss, binding the assortment of fillers with clay or mud. The roof consisted of poles running the length of the cabin and covered with clapboards fastened with wooden pegs. Once the shell of the structure was in place, workers cut holes in the sides, which served as doors and, perhaps, as windows. The interior walls remained unfinished. Dirt floors were the norm, though some settlers installed puncheon floors formed from split logs with the flat sides up. A fireplace with a chimney of sticks and mud usually completed the first year's construction.[40]

This was an ideal design for a first dwelling. The occupants could build the cabin quickly from materials close at hand. Although the average family found the accommodations cramped, the single room provided protection from the weather and wild animals. Moreover, when time permitted, they could easily double the living quarters by adding a companion cabin facing the original cabin, with the two units joined under a single roof and sharing a connecting porch. They might also cover and enclose the porch to gain even more living space. In fact, this type of structure was so common on the Tennessee frontier that it was eventually identified as an architectural type: the dog-trot design. In time, many settlers constructed larger and more elaborate houses, but the log cabin served them well in their first few years in the territory.

After completing their dwelling, settlers faced the task of sowing their first crop of foodstuffs. They rarely had time to break land. Some settlers cultivated fields that previous occupants—farmers who had moved on or, more likely, Indians who had abandoned the land—had already broken. Most planted among the stumps of trees felled for the construction of their cabins. The forest soils were easy to work and, having been shaded from the sun, were relatively free of undergrowth. Using a stick or a hoe, settlers dug an irregular line of holes among the stumps and dropped in the seed. They usually brought seed with them, though they sometimes obtained it from nearby farmers who had a crop from the previous year.[41] Until the first crop ripened, settlers subsisted on food carried from their previous homes, supplies provided by neighbors, wild fruits, fish, and game, such as deer, buffalo, turkey, and squirrel. A small number had driven livestock to their new locations, which enabled them to supplement the limited household diet with meat and dairy products.

The most important crop for the new farmer was corn. Virtually every settler planted more than enough to ensure a supply to meet family needs. It was a staple in the diet of every household. *De Bow's Review,* a popular journal in the antebellum South, aptly described the importance of corn to early Tennesseans. Of all crops, corn is best adapted to the condition of a pioneer people; and if idolatry is at all justified, Ceres, or certainly the goddess of Indian corn, should have had a temple and a worshipper among the pioneers of Tennessee. Without the grain the pioneer settlements could not have been formed or maintained. It is the most certain crop—requires the least preparation of ground—is most congenial to virgin soil—needs not only the least amount of labor in its culture, but comes to maturity in the shortest time.

The grain requires also the least care and trouble in preparing it. It may safely stand all winter upon the stalk, without injury from weather, or apprehension of damage by disease, or the accidents to which other grains are subject.[42]

It would be difficult to exaggerate the centrality of corn to the Tennessee farm family's way of life, especially during the settlement stage.[43]

Settlers also put in an array of vegetables and occasionally small grains. They adopted the Indian practice of planting beans, pumpkins, and squash between the irregular corn rows. They grew sweet and Irish potatoes, carrots, onions, peas, tomatoes, and beets in small garden patches. On previously cleared fields or on grassy plots requiring little preparation, they sowed oats, barley, and buckwheat. Because stumps and roots on newly cleared land obstructed the growth of broadcast crops in particular, farmers cultivated very little small grain during the first few years at a new site.[44]

The work routine did not slacken once the crops were in; it only changed. The settlers next turned to the laborious task of clearing and breaking more land. This required the felling of more trees, which the household used for firewood the following winter and, perhaps, for additional construction. The farmer normally cut all of the trees on a planned field. But if the growth were particularly dense, he might cut only some of the trees with the intention of returning later to clear the rest. This strategy involved a tradeoff: it saved time in preparing new fields for cultivation, but it reduced the yields of the first year's crops. The trees that remained blocked the sun and thereby slowed plant growth. Christopher Houston learned this principle when he opened virgin land in Maury County. He chose to leave some of the trees standing on his new fields; "hence it is much shaded," he discovered; "but I expect a half crop. . . . This is the first time I have begun in the woods, and were it not for its being so heavily timbered, I might soon have a plantation."[45]

The presence of tree stumps required another decision. The settler might remove the stumps by excavating or burning them, or he might work around them until they rotted out. The former option had the obvious disadvantage of requiring considerably more time and labor. The second option took less effort, but it also had disadvantages. The field would contain less precious planting space, and the stumps would inhibit cultivation.

Once a field or two had been cleared, another cluster of activities took place. Members of the farm family might safely leave mature corn in the field until it was needed, as *De Bow's Review* pointed out, but they had to bring in vegetables from the garden and preserve them to last through the approaching winter. The women of the household gathered the vegetables and processed them by drying, pickling, or storing in a cool place. They also made warm clothing, usually from cloth brought with them, in anticipation of the approaching seasonal change. The men broke the recently cleared fields and planted them in winter wheat or, if they had cattle or draft animals, grasses which could be used as feed. They cut and split logs for firewood and prepared the cabin for cold weather.

It was only at this point in the year that the pace of work slowed, if only moderately. As the weather permitted, family members continued to clear land. Winter was a good time to construct the second half of the dog-trot cabin. It also was a good time to build furniture, such as tables, benches, and beds, or tools and kitchen utensils. And the slower work pace allowed more time for hunting and trapping.

Much of the routine of the first year persisted for several years. The job of clearing and breaking land went on for some time; it normally required a minimum of five or six years to reach the optimum number of improved acres. John J. Boon reported that his father, who purchased raw land in Madison County in 1824, "year after year . . . cleared new land until he had a considerable farm."[46] Because Tennessee, along with other southern states, followed the traditional colonial practice of allowing livestock to graze freely on open range, farmers had to protect their cultivated fields with fences.[47] They normally constructed the fences from chestnut rails or stones, both of which were close at hand if they had been careful in selecting their farm site.

The task of constructing buildings likewise remained. Some families, to be sure, continued to live in crude log cabins many years after arriving at their new locations. While crossing the central basin in 1797, Francis Baily stopped at a farmstead established almost a decade earlier. "His [owner's] house was formed of logs," Baily reported, "and consisted of only two rooms; one of which served for all the purposes of life, and the other to hold lumber, &c." Another farmer, Baily wrote, "had got a good deal of land about him, a great part of which was in a rude state of cultivation. His house, remained the same as when it was first built—and of course cut no very striking figure."[48] In fact, it was not uncommon to find people living in similar dwellings on the eve of the Civil War. J. R. Miles recalled that in the 1850s his family in Weakley County occupied "a log shack two rooms with flore made of split slabs cracks you could run your hand in."[49]

Many farmers, however, improved their original dwellings as soon as they had the opportunity, not only by expanding with a dog-trot design structure, but by finishing off the interior and adding amenities. Others in time erected larger and more elaborate log structures. "The inhabitants live in comfortable log houses," observed François André Michaux, as he traveled from Nashville to Knoxville in 1802.[50] John B. Masterson described his Wilson County home, built later in the century, as "a hewed popular log house with 4 rooms and a 16 foot hall. It had a fireplace to each room. The house was weatherboarded, lathed and plastered and had cedar shingles."[51] M. L. Morrison remembered that his family lived in a log house in Roane County until his father "built a frame house of three rooms and a 'hall-way.'"[52] Michaux also saw stone houses that "consisted of four large rooms on the ground floor, one story, and a garret." Because such houses usually required hiring a mason to assist in the construction, they were not the typical farm residence.[53] Some plantation houses were even more elegant. William Hunter, a slave owner in Putnam County, eventually built a large brick dwelling on his five-thousand-acre tract.[54] The erection of buildings with special functions—smokehouses, springhouses, barns, tool sheds—also occupied much of the farmers' time in the early years.

After five to seven years, the diligent family had carved a farm out of a piece of the Tennessee wilderness. The farm provided their basic needs and a few modest luxuries that made frontier existence a bit more tolerable. Their food was plentiful and wholesome, if not par-

ticularly varied or succulent. Their house was functional and reasonably comfortable, if not spacious or elegant. Their furnishings were ser-
viceable, if not well finished or fashionable. All members of the family
had toiled long and resolutely to realize their goal; all would have to
continue to work to sustain it. Although some settlers were doubtlessly
unhappy with their situation, many more were satisfied with their new
life. Their daily routine was arduous, and they experienced unanticipated hardships and disappointments. But many who moved to the
Tennessee territory eventually realized their aspirations for a better
life. More importantly, perhaps, their new home held the promise of
an even better standard of living for their children and grandchildren.

The process described above recurred in Tennessee thousands of
times beginning in the late eighteenth century and stretching well into
the nineteenth century. As the members of each family brought their
own farm into existence, the state gradually changed in almost imper-
ceptible steps from an undeveloped wilderness into an extensive and
productive agricultural area. The conversion occurred at an irregular
pace, hurried on at times by conditions that quickened settlement,
slowed at other times by conditions that inhibited it. Still, the pace was
relentless, as one by one the regions of the state were settled and brought
into production.

East Tennessee was the first of the state's three grand divisions to
move beyond the frontier stage of settlement.[55] William Bean, thought
to be the first permanent settler in Tennessee, and a group of his relatives from Virginia took up farming along the Watauga River in 1769.[56]
Within a few years, a number of small settlements extended from the
Watauga-Holston area south to the Nolichucky River. The Cherokee
cession in 1777 accelerated the movement of settlers into East Tennessee. They flowed primarily into the valleys of the Holston and Tennessee river systems, locating farms on the fertile soils of the region. The
rise of several commercial centers to service the growing farm population, estimated at thirty-six thousand in 1790, was another measure of
the stage of settlement.[57] Knoxville, which had about two hundred dwellings in 1802, had become the area's leading service center as early as the
1780s. Several other smaller communities scattered throughout the northeast corner of the state emerged as the rural population expanded.[58]

By the time Tennessee came into the union in 1796, East Tennessee's
agriculture was already well established. Gilbert Imlay was impressed
with the variety and quality of its farm products. "The soil," he re-

ported, "produces wheat, barley, indian corn, hemp, and flax, in great
perfection." "In this country," he continued, a settler "would live with
great affluence, or become rich, by that measure of industry which, in
the other situation [a colder climate], would hardly be sufficient to support a miserable life."[59] J. M. Brewer, who drove a herd of horses from
Nashville into Virginia in 1814, was also struck by the prosperity and
the productivity of the eastern valleys. "In this part of the state live some
very wealthy farmers," he inscribed in his log as he passed through the
Knoxville neighborhood. "There is much small grain maid in this part
of Tennessee." Of the area to the northeast near Rogersville, he wrote:
"This country is thickly settled. . . . The land in this end of the state is
much richer and consequently more productive than the land on [the]
Emory river & the land before we come to it."[60]

Soon after the opening of the Watauga-Holston settlements, another group established an outpost along the Cumberland River in the
central basin of Middle Tennessee. Two parties set out from the northeastern communities for the Cumberland country in the fall of 1779.
One party led by James Robertson followed an overland route across
the Cumberland tableland and arrived at its destination in late December. Another party led by John Donelson followed a more circuitous route
along the Tennessee and Cumberland rivers and joined the Robertson
contingent in the spring of 1780. Together they built several stations and
began the tedious job of clearing land near the future site of Nashville.
Although individual settlers had preceded them in the Cumberland vicinity, this group established the first permanent community in Middle
Tennessee.

The population of Middle Tennessee, about eight thousand in 1790,
grew more slowly than that of East Tennessee, partly because
the Cumberland settlers encountered considerable resistance from Indians.[61] "They had to support, for several years, a bloody war against
the Indian Cherokees," explained Michaux, "and till 1795 the settlements at Holston and Kentucky communicated with those in Cumberland
by caravans, for the sake of traveling in safety."[62] The conflict not only
discouraged settlement, it also hindered farm making and cultivation.
Most of the early settlers lived in the stations along the Cumberland
River, leaving during the day to work on their own sites. Even then,
the Indian threat forced them to divide their attention and time. "Father and the older men made corn and I chased Indians," recalled the
son of one settler.[63] When John Donelson attempted to harvest the first

crop from his new farmstead in the fall of 1780, Indians denied him access to his land and killed two members of his party.[64]

Once the white immigrants had subdued the Cherokees in the Nickajack Expedition in 1794, the flow of people into the central basin quickened.[65] Imlay noted the results of improved relations: "Several thousand crossed the Cumberland mountains in September, October, and November last [1795], in detached families, without guard, and without danger. The Indians treated them with kindness, visited their camps at night, and supplied them plentifully with venison."[66] Michaux offered a similar assessment a few years later: "Since peace has been made with the natives, . . . they travel there [central basin] with as much safety as in any other part of the Atlantic states."[67] Treaties signed with the Indians in 1805 and 1806 further encouraged settlement. A wagon road built across the Cumberland tableland connecting East and Middle Tennessee facilitated movement into the region. From the mid-1790s, immigrants poured into the Cumberland community and fanned out along the tributaries of the Cumberland and lower Tennessee rivers.[68]

With amicable Indian relations and better access from the east, settlers in Middle Tennessee rapidly developed the region's agriculture. As early as 1792, Imlay praised the farm production of the Cumberland community: "Wheat, barley, oats, rye, buckwheat, indian corn, pease, beans, potatoes of both sorts, flax, hemp, tobacco, indigo, rice, and cotton, have already been planted in that settlement, and they all thrive in great perfection."[69] In some respects, Imlay's enthusiasm was excessive. Indigo and rice may have been cultivated in the central basin, but they hardly "thrived in great perfection."[70] His report is entirely plausible on other counts. A decade later Michaux was likewise impressed with the region's crops, especially the corn: "The harvests of this grain are as plentiful as in Kentucky; the blades run up ten or twelve feet high; and the ears, which grow six or seven feet from the earth, are from nine to ten inches in length, and proportionate in size."[71] Indian problems and a remote location may have delayed the central basin's agricultural development, but it lagged behind East Tennessee's by no more than a decade or two.

Like East Tennessee, the central basin saw the rise of agricultural service centers. "Nashville is a recently founded place, and contains only two houses which, in true, merit that name," was Lewis Brantz's observation five years after the first permanent settlers had arrived.[72] By 1796 the community had grown to about one hundred dwellings and had become the region's leading center.[73] At the same time a number of other communities appeared nearby. "There are several other little towns in the neighbourhood," Baily reported in 1797; "in fact, the banks of the Cumberland river, on both sides, are well cultivated for a considerable distance." The "civilized appearance" of the Nashville area clearly surprised Baily: "We even met, within three or four miles of the town, two *coaches*, fitted up in all the style of Philadelphia or New York, besides other carriages, which plainly indicated that [the] spirit of refinement and luxury had made its way into the settlement."[74] Even if the farmers of the central basin agreed with Baily's assessment, they probably did not share his delight with Nashville's "spirit of refinement and luxury." Yet the agricultural economy they had created in Middle Tennessee by the end of the eighteenth century in large measure sustained the affluence implied in that description.

Other areas of the state trailed behind the eastern valleys and the central basin in settlement and agricultural development. The Cumberland tableland and the eastern extension of the highland rim situated between the white occupied regions to either side remained an agricultural wasteland until well into the nineteenth century. Their soils and terrain simply lacked the quality to attract a large-scale immigration of prospective farmers. Baily wrote in 1797 that "this state may be divided into two parts, the eastern and western, which are separated from each other by a wilderness which is possessed by the Indians." He estimated that the unoccupied territory began some sixty miles east of Nashville, "though the whole of that distance is scarcely better than a wilderness after you proceed about a half-a-dozen miles from the town; the houses are so far apart from each other, that you seldom see more than two or three a day." He stopped at several farms between Nashville and the eastern edge of the highland rim to obtain supplies for a journey across the Cumberland tableland. But he found the settlers "so poor, or so distressed for provisions themselves, that I could get nothing."[75]

Brewer's impressions of the Cumberland tableland in 1814 revealed a significant change. Inhabitants now occupied several small pockets in the region. Their circumstances, though, seemed little better than those Baily had encountered two decades earlier among the farmers on the western perimeter of the tableland. Brewer recorded in his journal that the land around the Caney Fork River had been "settled by some families of poor appearance." Farther on near the Obed River, he came

upon an area that was "thickly settled; but the land is [so] poor that
they [inhabitants] make but little produce and rely on what they can
pick up from passengers."[76] At a time when farming was flourishing
in the eastern valleys and the central basin, settlers of the area in between were barely eking out an existence. Their situation would improve as the Cumberland tableland and the highland rim became better
integrated into the state's economy, but the poor natural endowments of
the two regions placed narrow limits on their agricultural potential.

The reasons for the delay in the settlement of West Tennessee were
quite different. Unlike the tableland and rim, much of this region was
ideally suited to agriculture, and settlers were eager to move in and
develop its resources. They paused at the western valley of the Tennessee River only to await eradication of the remaining Indian claims
in the state. Under the Jackson Purchase of 1818, the Chickasaws surrendered title to all land in West Tennessee. With the last impediment
to white occupation removed, the settlement of West Tennessee pro-
ceeded rapidly. A steady stream of immigrants in the 1820s swelled to a
torrent the following decade. The transition from frontier stage to established stage of settlement that had required twenty to thirty years in East
Tennessee and the central basin took half that time in West Tennessee.

The rise in traffic on the Mississippi River and its tributaries provided one measure of the pace of growth and agricultural development. Herndon Haraldson saw considerable activity on one tributary
as early as 1821: "When I left the Forked Deer [River] there were three
keel-boats at Alexander's landing one and one-half miles below Doak's,
freighted with corn, bacon, and whiskey, etc. Many boats had stopped at
Key Corner and cribbed their corn."[77] By the early 1830s, steamboats
regularly plied the Forked Deer and Hatchie rivers, and Memphis had
established its first steamboat line to New Orleans.[78] The cotton receipts at Memphis, the region's principal commercial center, tell a similar story. They rose from three hundred bales in 1826 to one thousand
bales in 1830, and then to thirty-five thousand bales in 1840.[79] Within
two decades after the removal of the Indians from West Tennessee, the
region had reached a level of agricultural development equivalent to
that of the eastern valleys and the central basin.

By the time the last settlers reached the Mississippi River, more
than half a century after the first settlers had entered the territory from
the east, Tennessee was enjoying one of the most productive agricultural economies in the country. Those settlers had brought the state

from a wilderness with rich potential to a cluster of mature farming regions. Agricultural production had moved well beyond the objectives of the early immigrants, who initially strove primarily to realize a reasonable level of self-sufficiency. Tennessee's agriculture was now comprised of several farming regions that not only provided food and fiber for the farmers of the state but also served local and distant markets and rested on an extensive commercial network.

3

Providing for the Household

The Tennessee farm household during the antebellum period was a largely self-reliant unit. Members of the household produced much of what they consumed and wore and some of what they used in the home and on the farm. Settlers on the frontier were, of course, self-sufficient out of necessity, as their isolated location denied them access to commercial sources of household goods and farm supplies. Farmers in established areas, on the other hand, had the option of purchasing supplies and services in nearby towns or, perhaps, from neighbors, but they often elected to pursue a self-sufficient course. Although rural families rarely achieved total self-sufficiency, many strove to come as close as their limited resources permitted. Their objectives sometimes reflected individual circumstances, sometimes economic conditions, and sometimes broadly held values. In any case, providing for the household was a traditional element of Tennessee farm life.

Farmers chose a self-sufficient strategy for several reasons. A chronic shortage of cash, especially in the early antebellum period, restricted the purchase of household goods. In his travels through Tennessee in the first decade of the nineteenth century, François André Michaux identified the problem and the solution: "I am persuaded that not one in ten of them [farmers] are in possession of a single dollar; still each enjoys himself at home with the produce of his estate."[1] Even after the supply of circulating currency increased with the appearance of commercial banks, farmers often found the money of uncertain value and negotiability, and they hesitated to use it. Moreover, many farmers were short of cash at certain times of the year. Whatever the reason, the scarcity of money encouraged families to provide as much as possible for their household needs from the farm.

Their determination to meet family subsistence requirements was also part of a rural way of life that placed value on independence from the outside world. For some who pursued the elusive goal of self-sufficiency, the primary motivation was the personal satisfaction of supporting one's family without resorting to sources off the farm. For others, it was the desire to avoid the risks inherent in the commercial activities necessary to procure goods and services from the outside. Alexander Cartwright, who grew up on a Davidson County farm in the 1830s, succinctly stated the principle followed by many families: "Everything was made at home that could be."[2]

Providing food for the family received high priority. Corn was the mainstay of the household diet, just as it had been during the frontier period. Although some regions offered conditions more favorable to corn cultivation than others, the plant was hardy enough to do well across the entire state. Moreover, it produced more nourishment per acre than any other crop Tennessee farmers might grow. It was a versatile food. Harvested early and roasted while still young and tender, it supplied a nourishing fresh food. Allowed to ripen and dry, it provided ground meal for bread and mush. Farmers with access to a still might distill surplus corn into whiskey. No other crop could be grown with so little trouble and put to so many uses. It was the ideal foodstuff for the farm household that strove to achieve self-sufficiency.

Small grains also contributed to the family's diet. Most farmers planted wheat for household consumption. Because wheat cultivation was both riskier and a less efficient use of the soil than corn cultivation, wheat flour became something of a luxury. Households often reserved it for breads, biscuits, or pastries to be consumed on special occasions.[3] Many farmers grew barley, rye, oats, and buckwheat, but these small grains were even less common in the rural diet than wheat. Households ground the four grains into flour for breads, muffins, and pancakes, and they added barley kernels to soups and stews as a meat extender. Although farmers normally preferred corn whiskey, they also used small grains for the distillation of alcoholic beverages.

Farmers usually departed from a self-sufficient strategy when it came to grinding grain. Some families, particularly during the pioneer period, undertook this arduous, time-consuming task themselves over the slack winter months. It required a large mortar and pestle or some other pulverizing device, like a corn crusher, and an enormous amount of effort. But households generally hired someone else to convert their grains to flour and meal. Most localities contained a farmstead or two equipped to grind grain and willing to sell or trade the services to neighbors. The mill was sometimes a primitive contraption consisting of two millstones, the bottom one stationary and the top one driven by livestock circling on an earthen floor. Farmers located near enough to a swiftly running stream constructed water-powered mills, which were far more common, as well as vastly more efficient. John Burtis's mill in Fayette County, for instance, provided "a place for the community to grind their own corn and wheat."[4] As the population increased, commercial gristmills appeared. These establishments ground grain for payment in cash or kind, customarily an eighth or a fourth of the load. Diaries and account books indicated that farmers regularly hauled grain to nearby mills for processing. Typical entries included John Barker's: "98 bushels of wheat to Warden's mill, made 3650 pounds of flour"; and Herndon Haraldson's: "2 waggons to mill below Jackson, 15 bushell wheat & 12 of corn."[5]

The garden and orchard were major sources of food. Every household set aside a large plot near the house on which the family grew a wide variety of vegetables. The typical garden contained most of the following crops: several kinds of beans, Irish and sweet potatoes, peas, carrots, onions, beets, cabbage, squash, pumpkins, tomatoes, celery, turnips, parsnips, cucumbers, asparagus, melons, peppers, and radishes. Many farmers put in orchards that, after several years, provided apples, peaches, cherries, and plums; they sometimes planted strawberries and peanuts on the floor of the orchards and grapes along the edge of the orchards or gardens.

When the produce of the gardens and orchards was in season, family members ate fresh vegetables and fruits. But they always harvested ample amounts of preservable varieties to see them through the winter and early spring. They placed apples and root crops—potatoes, carrots, and turnips—in underground bins, cellars, or springhouses, where cool temperatures slowed their deterioration. They dried some fruits, such as peaches, apples, and plums, and kept them in closed containers. In the 1840s glass jars with sealable lids became available for the first time, and some farm families canned cooked vegetables and fruits. Because the jars were expensive and undependable—the loss from spoilage was high—canning was not widely practiced. They pickled cucumbers, beets, and cabbage with homemade apple vinegar. They sweetened peaches, strawberries, cherries, and grapes with maple sugar or honey and stored them as jams and jellies. Apple cider and grape juice were popular beverages; blackberry wine and peach brandy provided stronger alternatives.

The family's food supply included ample amounts of meat. Pork was the most common type of meat. Farmers butchered hogs only during the coldest part of the year to reduce the risks of spoilage, but the winter's slaughter had to supply pork for the entire year. Wiley Bagwell, who farmed near Clarksville, butchered twenty-three hogs in December 1844 and "laid in for my family 4075 lbs."[6] John Bills, a large slave owner in Hardeman County, during the same winter "put up pork. . . . Enough for my fifty constant eaters and visitors."[7] Household members consumed fresh pork during the cold months, but they salted and smoked most of the meat to preserve it through the warm weather. They usually prepared the pork in their own smokehouses, though wealthier farmers sometimes sent theirs to a commercial pork house for processing. An establishment in Clarksville, for example, promised farmers to "pack Pork on the same terms that it is done in Louisville, and in a manner not surpassed anywhere."[8] In this way, rural households assured themselves an adequate supply of hams, sausage, and bacon throughout the year. Moreover, lard was their only cooking grease.

Beef also contributed meat to the diet, but much less so than pork. Farmers raised fewer cattle than hogs because they took longer to reach slaughter weight and were more costly to maintain, and because their meat was more difficult to preserve. Some farmers butchered for beef only cattle with a poor ability to produce milk. Madison County farmer Robert Cartmell, for example, complained about several cows he had purchased on a neighbor's advice: "Bought them without seeing them on his sayso. Not worth anything for milk—do for beef."[9] Cattle, like hogs, were usually slaughtered in the winter to slow the deterioration of the meat, but family or social gatherings large enough to require a sizable quantity of food might serve as an excuse for killing a beef cow in warm weather. Rural households normally ate beef fresh, though they occasionally dried and stored beef jerky for consumption later. Families almost always kept a few cows to supply dairy products. They drank some of the milk and cream, and made butter and cheese from the rest, which they kept along with the root crops in cool storage.

Farmers hardly ever raised sheep primarily for their meat. They kept the animals for their wool, butchering those that no longer produced fiber in adequate amounts or of acceptable quality. Cartmell acknowledged the double purpose of sheep when he commented on his purchase of "a pair of sheep being a good mixture of South Downs & Cotswold; fine for wool and mutton."[10] While farm diaries routinely recorded the slaughter of hogs and cattle in the antebellum period, entries like the following from James Matthews's daily log were rare: "Butchered a mutton."[11] Most families kept chickens, turkeys, ducks, and geese, which they killed as needed. One spring Betty Gleaves, the wife of a farmer in Cheatam County, obtained some "young chickens; look very nice."[12] The family used them for eggs and meat.

Domesticated plants and animals were the family's primary source of nourishment. But the forests and streams supplemented the food produced on the farm and added variety to the household fare. Most of the buffalo had either migrated west or been killed by Indians before the arrival of the first immigrants. Early settlers hunted the few that remained in the western half of the state.[13] Deer, rabbits, squirrels, ducks, turkeys, and boars were a more abundant source of wild meat. Farmers' diaries included references to hunting throughout the year, but especially in the winter months. The take of game was often quite large. Herndon Haraldson killed three deer on one day, forty-four ducks on another, and twenty-two squirrels on yet another.[14] John Barker bagged ten rabbits and twenty-four squirrels in a single outing.[15] Although fishing was a minor source of food, George Washington, a wealthy planter in Robertson County, considered his catch of two large trout noteworthy enough to record in his daily journal.[16] One senses that the opportunity to leave the farmstead chores for awhile was as important as the day's catch for Betty Gleaves of Cheatam County: "I take the boys & go fishing, catch enough for us to eat."[17]

The forests and natural grasslands also provided fruits, nuts, and sweeteners. Family members gathered strawberries, grapes, blueberries, blackberries, huckleberries, walnuts, hickory nuts, chestnuts, and chinquapins from the wilds. They tapped maple trees for syrup. William Hunter of Putnam County encouraged the growth of maple trees in a grove near his house expressly for this purpose.[18] Others enticed honey bees to take up residence in their hives.[19] John Barker was understandably disappointed when his "wife's bees swarmed 1st time and left her." Robert Cartmell was more optimistic about his prospects the day he jotted in his log: "Got a good chance of honey"; so, too, was Herndon Haraldson when he "took in Wild Beehive."[20]

With such a plentiful and varied supply available on or near the farmstead, antebellum households approached self-sufficiency in foodstuffs. Still, most farmers found it necessary or chose to purchase some food from the local store. What they did purchase were often non-essential items that added a small measure of pleasure to a life of numbing regularity. James Harrison's family always looked forward to their infrequent trips into Shelbyville to pick up supplies, especially those that were not absolutely necessary.[21] Annually, almost to the day every January, Wiley Bagwell drove his wagon to Clarksville and brought back a year's supply of coffee—sometimes Javanese, sometimes Brazilian—and refined cane sugar.[22] The taste of others ran to tea, spices, and chocolate or hard candy; that of still others to whiskey and, rarely, European wines and brandies and West Indian rum.[23] Even though households produced their own soft cheese, it was always a treat to purchase a block of well-aged New England cheddar or English stilton to serve during the holidays. When supplies of basic goods ran out, as they did on occasion, farmers had to purchase such items as flour, lard, and bacon to tide them over until the next harvest or the next slaughter.[24]

Farm families also made most of their own clothes. Tom Bryan remembered from his childhood days on a farm in Montgomery County that his "mother spun and wove all of our clothes from the skin out. She made the buttons that went on our shorts. We raised the cotton, the flax, and the wool, and it was all worked at home."[25] Betty Gleaves and Jane Margaret Jones must have been typical farm women; their diaries reveal that they devoted much of their time to making clothes for members of the household.[26] The *Southern Agriculturist,* a widely read farm journal, advised slaveholding families to use pregnant slave women to spin thread and sew clothing as a way to reduce expenses.[27] Making clothes was as important as producing food for those farm families that strove to attain self-sufficiency.

Households, such as the Bryan's, that owned the necessary equipment, performed all of the clothes-making tasks, from carding the fiber, through spinning and dyeing the thread, to weaving the cloth and sewing the garments. William Mantlo, who spent his childhood in such a family on a Robertson County farm, recalled that his mother "would cord & spin & weave cloth & make clothing for the family."[28] Betty Gleaves, who also performed all of the work from raw fiber to finished product, proudly declared in her diary one day that "I'm up & at the loom early & by dint of hard work get my cloth out."[29] John Barker seemed equally pleased with his wife's efforts: "Wife got out 57 yds double cloth."[30]

Households without textile equipment frequently paid a neighbor or local establishment, often in kind, to convert their wool, cotton, and flax into thread or cloth. One year Wiley Bagwell "sent 191 lbs wool to

Gains factory to be carded."[31] John Motheral set up a "machine house" on his Williamson County farm for spinning and weaving, and offered his services to neighbors.[32] An advertisement for a Nashville firm read: "Those who have wool to card are informed that the Carding Engines are in operation, & ready to receive their wool."[33] Some families simply purchased finished cloth from the general stores, which offered a variety of fabrics for sale. For example, rural residents commonly purchased calico, which could not be produced on the farm, from the local merchant.

From the cloth farm families made pants, shirts, and coats for the men of the household, and dresses, blouses, and aprons for the women. From the yarn they knitted sweaters, shawls, and socks. They crafted buttons from lead obtained at the local store or mussel shells recovered from a nearby stream. In addition to clothing, they made blankets, sheets, pillow cases, tablecloths, and corn sacks. Jane Margaret Jones, who lived on a Hardeman County farm, seemed both relieved and satisfied when she "finished the first pair of pant I ever made for my old man; very nice."[34] One day Betty Gleaves was "busy sewing on shirt for Mr. Gleaves"; two days later she "finish[ed] the shirt, commence[d] on other."[35] Some projects took longer. On 16 March 1858, Gleaves "cut some squares for Lizzy May's hexigon quilt"; one day short of a year later, she "finish[ed] Lizzy May's hexigon quilt."[36]

Despite the importance they placed on self-sufficiency, rural households had to rely on sources off the farm for goods they could not produce for themselves. Because few households contained anyone with cobbler skills, they usually had to obtain shoes from the outside. Still, farmers normally supplied the raw materials and paid only for the skill necessary to convert them into finished products. They took their cowhides to a shop that would, according to the announcement of one Nashville firm, "tan on shares."[37] Tom Bryan recalled that his father had leather tanned on a "50/50 basis."[38] Those farmers who possessed no cowhides purchased leather from the general store. One Nashville merchant advertised "a large quantity of upper and soal leather tanned at Frankfort, Ky which we will sell very low for cash."[39] Farmers then took the leather to a local craftsman to be made into shoes for members of the household. Wiley Bagwell, for example, often purchased leather and "paid for shoemaking."[40] Other farmers chose to sell their cowhides, if they had any, and buy their shoes directly from the general store. One day Montgomery County farmer John Barker splurged and "bought 2 pair of shoes."[41]

Households lacking even rudimentary sewing skills had to make similar arrangements.[42] Sometimes they hired a local seamstress to convert cloth purchased in town into clothes. One December Bagwell "paid for cloth for an overcoat"; two months later he "paid Mrs. Adams $3.50 for making overcoat."[43] The other option was to buy ready-made clothes from the local merchant, who usually kept a stock of articles in greatest demand. Even when the members of the family possessed the necessary skills, they occasionally purchased finished products. Gleaves, who made practically all of her household's clothes, one day allowed herself the pleasure of a modest shopping spree: "I go down to Ashland [City]—get me a calico dress . . . [and] silk hankerchief."[44]

Antebellum rural households were self-sufficient in other ways. They built and maintained their dwellings. They raised kitchens, smokehouses, henhouses, barns, and sheds. They cut firewood and put up fences. Less often they made and repaired their household furnishings and farm tools. Flavius S. Landers's father, who farmed in Bedford County, "was a man of all work[;] done his own carpenter work, staked his own plowes, made all of the family shoes. Made the first pair of boots he ever owned, made his own grain cradles and made the first buggy he ever owned."[45] Allowing for a bit of exaggeration, perhaps, Landers described a set of chores performed by the head of a typical rural household. When a task required extra hands or a special skill, as was often the case, farmers turned to help from the local community. Neighbors frequently exchanged assistance and shared expertise. Farmers employed outside labor when necessary, but only as a last resort. On one occasion, Wiley Bagwell, who normally used the labor on his farm for building and maintenance, found it necessary to bring in two hands to roof his house.[46]

Farmers of all sizes supplied household needs from the farm. In the crucial choice between producing for household consumption or for the market, however, smaller farmers seemed to have placed a higher priority on approaching self-sufficiency than larger farmers. At least this was the case with food production. In general, smaller farmers devoted relatively more of their land and labor to subsistence production and relatively less to commercial production. They elected to produce primarily for the household rather than for the market. Although the larger farmers also produced a good deal of foodstuffs, they tended to place relatively greater emphasis on marketable goods.[47]

Examination of data from several sample counties in 1850 and 1860 reveals a systematic relationship between the size of a farm and the

Table 3.1

Corn Output/Improved Acres by Improved-Acre Category, 1850 and 1860

Acre Category	1850	1860
1–49	13.71	12.80
50–99	9.61	7.94
100–199	8.04	6.64
200–299	6.83	5.76
300–499	5.68	4.81
500–999	5.48	4.91
>999	4.21	3.43
All categories	8.37	6.57

Source: Eight sample counties (see appendix).
Note: Corn output measured in bushels.

portion of land used for corn production.[48] Cultivation of this grain, the primary staple in rural diets, occupied a greater percentage of improved acreage on small farms than it did on large farms and plantations. Table 3.1 shows that an index of emphasis on corn production was inversely associated with farm size.[49] The corn index declined as farm size, measured by the amount of improved acreage, increased in both 1850 and 1860; with one exception (500 to 999 acres in 1860), the smaller the farm size, the larger the index. When the scale of operations is measured by the number of slaves (table 3.2), the pattern is the same. As slaveholdings increased, the corn index declined.

Breakdowns of per capita corn production by slaveholding categories in table 3.3 also reveal a close relationship between scale of operations and emphasis on self-sufficiency. Farms with fewer than three slaves in 1850 and fewer than six slaves in 1860 had above average per capita output; those with three or more slaves in 1850 and six or more slaves in 1860 had below average per capita output. Table 3.4, which arranges per capita corn production by improved acre categories, shows a mixed pattern. The smallest farms in both years and the largest farms in 1850 had below-average production; all other categories had above-average production. The reasons for the discrepancies between ordering by slaveholding and by improved acreage are not clear.

Table 3.2

Corn Output/Improved Acres by Slave Category, 1850 and 1860

Slave Category	1850	1860
0	10.14	8.23
1–2	9.41	7.27
3–5	8.99	6.93
6–10	8.48	6.35
11–20	7.98	5.74
>20	5.94	5.05
All categories	8.37	6.57

Source: Eight sample counties (see appendix).
Note: Corn output measured in bushels.

Regression analysis provides a more powerful test of the relationship between farm size and corn production because it uses farm-level information, rather than county-level averages, for farm sizes. If smaller farmers placed greater emphasis on meeting subsistence requirements than larger farmers, regression analysis should show that the corn index was associated with the amount of improved acreage and the ratio of household size to improved acreage (i.e., the ratio of food needs to cultivable land). Put more simply, the relative importance of corn production on an individual farm should have depended on the number of improved acres and the number of mouths to feed per improved acre. The fewer the acres and the larger the household size, the greater should have been the emphasis on corn production. This is precisely what the test revealed: emphasis on corn production showed a negative relationship with improved acreage and a positive relationship with household self-sufficiency requirements.[50] Smaller farmers, especially those with heavy food requirements relative to their cultivable land, clearly placed greater importance on meeting household needs than larger farmers and planters. They were less likely to adopt the alternative strategy of producing commercial goods and buying food.

Impressionistic evidence is consistent with these findings. Entries in the diaries and account books of medium or large slave-owning

Table 3.3

Per Capita Corn Production by Slave Category, 1850 and 1860

Slave Category	1850	1860
0	94	86
1–2	95	95
3–5	80	83
6–10	68	68
11–20	65	59
>20	54	58
All categories	86	82

SOURCE: Eight sample counties (see appendix).
NOTE: Corn production measured in bushels per household member.

planters, such as Wiley Bagwell, John Bills, and George Washington, reveal that they almost always obtained some part of their basic food needs from commercial suppliers. Even though they produced a large portion of what their households consumed, they still regularly bought items such as lard, bacon, and flour from the local store. By contrast, smaller farmers, such as Herndon Haraldson and James Matthews, must have produced and processed most of the food their families needed, for they rarely purchased basic foodstuffs.

The daily journals also implied that these differences extended to other items of necessity. Betty Gleaves and Jane Margaret Jones lived on moderate-sized units, and their logs indicated that they made virtually all of the family's clothes. Betty Gleaves's delight with the calico dress she bought from the general store suggested that the purchase of ready-made clothing was a rare occurrence in her household. Recall also that Tom Bryan's family, which lived on a small Montgomery County farm, produced everything they wore "from the skin out." It was far more common, on the other hand, for the diaries of larger farmers to record the purchase of clothing or the hiring of someone to make clothing. George Washington, for example, regularly paid a woman in the community to sew his shirts. Wiley Bagwell likewise hired people off the farm to make his clothing.

Table 3.4

Per Capita Corn Production by Improved-Acre Category, 1850 and 1860

Acre Category	1850	1860
1–49	70	63
50–99	97	87
100–199	105	100
200–299	98	108
300–499	80	95
500–999	90	95
>999	69	92
All categories	86	82

SOURCE: Eight sample counties (see appendix).
NOTE: Corn production measured in bushels per household member.

Two possible explanations account for the apparent difference in behavior between small and large operators. Small farmers, perhaps, placed less importance on material possessions than the more commercially minded large farmers and planters. Naturally less acquisitive, they were satisfied with a simple life of subsistence provided by the produce of their farms. They chose to use their land and labor to insure that the basic needs of their families would be met, even though greater involvement in the market held the promise of a higher standard of living.[51] The second explanation posits that small farmers adopted a "safety-first" approach because they were at relatively greater risk than wealthier farmers. Their limited equity and restricted access to credit made them more vulnerable to financial adversity than larger operators.[52] If they elected to participate heavily in the market, a year or two of poor weather or low prices threatened the few assets they had acquired. They therefore sought to achieve self-sufficiency first, participating in the market only if they produced a surplus of foodstuffs or possessed the land and labor to cultivate a commercial crop like cotton or tobacco in addition to meeting their basic household needs. Under the circumstances, they were more interested in preserving their limited wealth than in accumulating additional wealth and improving their standard of living.

It is impossible to determine with certainty whether the smaller farmers' behavior resulted from a less-acquisitive mentality that discouraged involvement in the market or from a realistic assessment of their financial circumstances that led them to minimize risk. Both factors were probably at work. It is suggestive, however, that relative emphasis on food production formed, in most cases, a linear relationship with farm size, whether size was defined by improved acreage or slaveholding; that is, emphasis on food production steadily declined as farm size grew. This is precisely the pattern one would expect if land-use decisions reflected financial circumstances rather than personal aversion to participation in the market. As farm size expanded, operators could gradually abandon their safety-first strategy and take on greater risk. If land-use decisions were determined by personal preference, one would not find such a linear relationship between relative emphasis on corn production and farm size. Instead, at some point on the scale running from small farms to great plantations, an abrupt change in production choices would occur, clearly dividing less-acquisitive from more-acquisitive farmers. The gradual shift away from a concern for self-sufficiency and toward a willingness to enter the market that did occur supports the safety-first explanation.

Large farmers, as noted, also produced a substantial share of the foodstuffs consumed by members of their households. From one perspective, this made economic sense because it permitted full use of their labor and equipment throughout much of the year. Labor demands for corn, for instance, came when labor demands for Tennessee's major commercial crops were light. Moreover, livestock were often turned loose to forage on unimproved land and required little care. Labor used to produce foodstuffs, therefore, did not significantly reduce the amount available to cultivate commercial commodities on large farms and plantations.

Food production on larger commercial units perhaps served another purpose. Larger farmers, like their smaller counterparts, may have followed a safety-first strategy and differed only in the margin of safety they required. Because smaller farmers were more vulnerable to risk than larger farmers, they required a wider margin of safety even if it often resulted in food production exceeding family needs. The larger farmers' stronger financial position allowed them to accept a narrower margin of safety, even if it sometimes resulted in a deficiency of foodstuffs. Viewed in this way, large and small farmers differed not

Table 3.5

Percentage of Farm Households Deficient in Food Production, by Improved-Acre Category, 1860

	County			
Acre Category	Greene	Haywood	Johnson	Wilson
		Grain		
1–49	36	29	38	8
50–99	12	19	18	4
100–199	6	13	14	3
200–499	4	21	—	9
>499	—	4	—	—
		Meat		
1–49	54	32	33	44
50–99	21	27	20	22
100–199	16	14	11	12
200–499	4	16	—	15
>499	—	19	—	—
		Total Foodstuffs		
1–49	29	17	30	11
50–99	10	16	12	4
100–199	7	6	7	2
200–499	0	12	—	2
>499	—	4	—	—

SOURCE: Adapted from Robert Tracy McKenzie, "From Old South to New South in the Volunteer State: The Economy and Society of Rural Tennessee, 1850–1880," Ph.D. diss., Vanderbilt Univ., 1988, table 15, p. 55.

in their objectives—both sought self-sufficiency—but in the degree of certainty they demanded in pursuing those objectives.[53]

Whatever their objectives and management strategies, larger farmers were, ironically, often more successful in achieving self-sufficiency than smaller farmers. A study of Tennessee agriculture in the nineteenth century reports mixed findings.[54] In 1859, as table 3.5 shows, nearly 40 percent of farms with fewer than fifty improved acres in two sample counties—Greene and Johnson—were deficient in grain production; approximately 30 percent were deficient in total food production, that is, grain and meat combined. At the same time, larger farms in the same counties were far more likely to meet household needs for both grain and total foodstuffs. By contrast, the range of differences among size categories in the other two sample counties—Haywood and Wilson—was significantly narrower, though a larger proportion of smaller farms still fell short of household requirements. Meat deficiency alone, which was higher across all size categories, likewise revealed significant differences in favor of large farms in achieving self-sufficiency. Despite their strong commitment to self-sufficiency, therefore, smaller farmers were sometimes less successful in realizing their goals than larger farmers.

If some operators fell short of achieving self-sufficiency, farmers as a group produced a surplus of foodstuffs.[55] In the four sample counties from the study noted above, as revealed in table 3.6, total grain output exceeded total farm household needs by anywhere from 50 to 120 percent in 1859; the figures for total foodstuffs output were comparable. In fact, production exceeded the food requirements not only of the farm population but also of the entire county population by 10 to 70 percent. Much of the surplus was sold outside of the state, but some of it was available on the local market.

Farm households that failed to produce enough to feed themselves, therefore, doubtlessly obtained additional food from the surplus of their neighbors. Edward Anderson, who acquired a Sullivan County farm in 1825, usually produced foodstuffs in considerable excess of his family's needs, which he sold to his neighbors.[56] Entries in farm journals indicated that such transactions occurred regularly. John Barker mentioned going to "W. Neblett's sale; bot his corn for 1.02 cts."[57] He also "sold to John Bradley the oats I have to spare."[58] George Washington, on one occasion, sold a side of bacon to a neighbor who had run short.[59] Farmers paid for the extra food in cash or labor. Or they borrowed the produce and re-

Table 3.6

Percentage of Farm and County Household Food Requirements Produced, 1860

	County							
	Greene		Haywood		Johnson		Wilson	
	Farm	County	Farm	County	Farm	County	Farm	County
Grain	220	190	150	140	150	120	210	190
Meat	170	120	170	150	180	100	170	130
Total	210	160	160	140	170	110	200	170

SOURCE: Adapted from Robert Tracy McKenzie, "From Old South to New South in the Volunteer State: The Economy and Society of Rural Tennessee: 1850–1880," Ph.D. diss., Vanderbilt Univ., 1988, table 8, p. 40.

placed it from their own surpluses the following season. One year, for example, James Matthews "loaned 10 bu of wheat to A. H. Davis."[60]

The desire to provide for household needs was not the only factor motivating small farmers to follow a safety-first strategy. They were also determined to hold down their indebtedness. Large farmers and plantation owners routinely used credit as a business necessity; they were rarely free of debt. But many small- and medium-sized farmers had an aversion to owing money to someone else.[61] Unless they were fortunate enough to inherit property, they almost always had to borrow for the purchase of land. Yet they strove to pay off their farm mortgages as rapidly as possible. Madison County farmer Robert Cartmell seemed obsessed with lifting himself out of debt. "I wish to get in that condition," he confided in his diary "which will render it unnecessary for liabilities to rest on my cotton crop." He returned to the subject later: "I *want* to get in that situation which will enable me to say I *owe* no man." He eventually realized his objective: "Paid Pa note $550.00 amt & int being the last cent due and the whole amt I was to pay ($4000.00) on my land. I am out of debt . . . for the first time."[62] Constance Perkins Nance, who grew up on a farm in Davidson County, remembered a similar preoccupation of her father, "who reared a family of 12 children according to the injunction, 'Owe no man anything.'"[63]

Despite their aversion to debt, smaller farmers could not avoid running up bills with local merchants and artisans. Circulating currency, as noted, was scarce in antebellum Tennessee, and farmers rarely had cash throughout the year to pay for the supplies they needed. But most of them settled their accounts promptly after they obtained money from the sale of crops or livestock. Cartmell regularly paid bills he ran up during the year for slave clothing and shoes, bagging, and groceries when he sold his cotton crop.[64] Herndon Haraldson faithfully settled his accounts before each spring. One can sense the relief he must have felt as he inscribed in his diary "paid off several merchants" or "paid off most of my creditors in town."[65] About the same time each year, Wiley Bagwell, using proceeds from his tobacco sales, "settled my account with Moore and Broaddus [merchants]" or "settled my Blacksmith's account."[66] Alexander Cartwright remembered from his childhood on a farm in Davidson County that "long store accounts were avoided, and debt was shunned as a calamity."[67] The diary records of Tennessee farmers clearly bear out his recollections and point up another reason for their interest in being as self-sufficient as possible.

Tennessee farmers sought to provide for much of their families' subsistence requirements directly from their own farms. In the very early stages of settlement, they had no choice; outside sources of household products had not yet appeared. Later, after merchants and artisans located in nearby towns and commercial supplies and services became available, many households continued to meet a large share of their needs. They produced and processed most of the food, much of the clothing, and many of the other items they needed in the home and on the farm.

Households never achieved complete self-sufficiency. Unexpected circumstances, such as poor weather conditions or crop damage from insects, sometimes reduced yields to levels below household requirements, making it necessary for even cautious families to obtain food from elsewhere. This occurred most often on farms that employed a margin of safety too narrow to accommodate a poor crop year. Some farmers deliberately planned to produce below household requirements, intending to use the income from commercial activities to secure extra food. Furthermore, most families did not possess the full range of expertise necessary to meet all of their processing and maintenance needs, and they had to purchase the skills they lacked in the local community. Occasionally, too, they merely indulged themselves and bought non-essential items from local merchants and craftsmen. For a variety of reasons, then, households turned to sources off the farm for supplies.

Farmers differed in the extent of their commitment to self-sufficiency. Some strove to come as close as possible to satisfying household needs because they desired to reduce risk, to escape debt, or simply to avoid dependency on the outside world. Others placed a lower priority on production for family consumption because they were willing to accept greater risk, to employ credit, and to draw on commercial sources of household goods. Despite those differences in attitudes and strategies, antebellum Tennessee farmers varied largely in the degree and intensity of their pursuit of self-sufficiency, not in their objectives. All of them engaged in farming that included some measure of production for household subsistence.

4

Producing for the Market

Tennessee farmers placed a great deal of importance on producing for household consumption, but many of them also vigorously pursued commercial opportunities. Almost from the beginning of settlement, they searched for some product or service that would generate a money income. All farmers needed at least a small amount of cash to cover incidental expenses and to purchase goods they could not provide for themselves. But most of them desired a money income above that necessary to cover basic expenditures, which they could use to expand their assets and to raise their families' standard of living above the subsistence level. They understood that pursuing that goal required involvement in markets off the farm.

François André Michaux perceived such an acquisitive personality not only among Tennessee's farmers but also among Americans in general. As he traveled through the state in the early nineteenth century, he encountered "the desire of growing rich in a short time, a general desire in the United States, where every man who exercises a profession or art wishes to get a great deal by it, and does not content himself with a moderate profit, as they do in Europe."[1] Michaux perhaps exaggerated the intensity of the acquisitive mentality among Tennesseans, although Englishman Francis Baily had detected evidence of a similar—and, to his thinking, deleterious—attitude a few years earlier. He complained that farmers in the state were always willing to pasture a traveler's horse, "if you pay them well for it; the idea of their being hospitable and doing a kindness to strangers for nothing, is false."[2]

Whether one views Tennessee farmers as motivated by unbridled greed, clearly the implication of Michaux's and Baily's remarks, or by a healthy ambition to improve their lot in life, they unquestionably participated in a wide range of commercial activities in the antebellum period. Opportunities to engage in such enterprises emerged soon after white settlers arrived in the Tennessee territory, and they steadily expanded over time. Even on the frontier, farmers found occasion to sell or trade surplus commodities to their neighbors or to travelers. As settlements advanced beyond the pioneer stage, local markets for agricultural products appeared. As commercial networks matured and business activity widened, more extensive markets became available.

Tennessee farmers' initial forays into the commercial world were modest. General stores provided their first markets off the farm. Although most store owners preferred payment in scarce hard currency, out of necessity they accepted farm products in exchange for merchandise. Sommerville & Ore, a Knoxville establishment in the early 1790s, advertised "a large and general assortment of WELL chosen GOODS. From the markets of Philadelphia and Baltimore, which they are determined to sell on the most reasonable terms . . . for CASH." Sommerville & Ore would, however reluctantly, take payment in rye, corn, and oats, as well as animal furs and skins.[3] Another Knoxville store indicated that it would accept corn, bacon, and beef cattle for its pots, pans, kettles, and castings.[4] Nashville store owner Tait Stothart announced in 1801 that he "will sell low for cash or cotton." Yet another Nashville establishment approved a wider assortment of produce, including cotton, hemp, pork, flour, hogs, lard, and butter, in exchange for its retail goods.[5] A merchant in Blountville, J. J. James, advertised that he would accept wool, bacon, butter, flax linen, and cotton in payment for general merchandise.[6] As late as 1844, a Memphis firm continued to take cotton in payment for its supplies.[7]

Michaux speculated that this practice of exchanging supplies for agricultural produce instead of cash worked to the advantage of merchants. "These tradesmen . . . do not always pay in cash for the cotton they purchase," he noted, "but make the cultivators take goods in exchange, which adds considerably to their profit."[8] This may have been true of some merchants. One Nashville store owner offered to exchange his merchandise for "produce that will answer for exportation."[9] A Knoxville dealer advertised in the spring of 1825 that he wished to purchase 100,000 pounds of baled cotton over the coming season, payment to be in salt, iron castings, and groceries at the market price.[10] Merchants such as these at least seemed as interested in profits from reselling farm goods as from selling retail goods. But the advantage in the barter system that Michaux perceived apparently eluded most merchants. As business activity increased and the volume of circulating currency grew, they became more and more reluctant to accept payment in kind; all save a few eventually insisted on cash or short-term credit. The owners of one Clarksville store felt constrained to explain their change in policy in 1818: "The limited credits upon which their [owners'] purchases were made in Philadelphia imperiously demands cash sales, or to punctual customers upon short credit."[11] In any case, when they could maintain an acceptable volume of business without receiving farm goods in payment for merchandise, most store owners simply abandoned the barter system.

Other suppliers of goods and services also provided barter markets for farm produce. A Nashville spinning mill exchanged its finished cotton yarn for raw wool.[12] A Knoxville firm agreed to card wool for flaxseed and grain, and a Nashville firm to gin cotton for hemp, flour, and tobacco.[13] David Ragon, a Monroe County farmer, "would haul pork to salt lick to trade for salt."[14] One itinerant dealer wanted to trade copper and tin for cotton; someone else offered a "coachee" for cash or country produce.[15] The owner of a race horse received farm goods in payment for stud fees: "I will take 1st proof brandy & wiskey . . . bacon, young heifers, & sheep." Another charged eight dollars in cash or nine dollars in produce for the services of his stud horse.[16] Advertisements for the sale of slaves frequently indicated the owner's willingness to accept farm goods in payment.[17] A medicine shop and surgery agreed to take cotton and tobacco for its services, and a magazine to take cotton, hemp, and wheat in lieu of its yearly subscription of four dollars.[18] Newspapers also received payment-in-kind. The owner of Clarksville's *United States Herald* seemed especially desperate when he appealed to subscribers: "Bacon at the market price will be received in payment for this paper if dilivered imediately."[19] The editor of Nashville's *Tennessee Gazette* apparently liked the tactic of his counterpart on the *Herald.* Three years later his newspaper announced that "a few hundred weight of pork would be taken from those indebted to the editor."[20]

It was not long, however, before a more complex money economy for agricultural goods developed at the local level. In fact, cash markets often emerged simultaneously with barter markets. Many of the same merchants who accepted payment in kind for their merchandise also purchased farm products for cash. On the last day of 1791, Knoxville's Sommerville & Ore "Wanted immediately, A quantity of RYE, CORN, and FODDER, for which a generous price will be given."[21] Two years later, J. Sommerville—the fate of Ore remains a mystery—"Wanted to Purchase Seven hundred linen, Linsey good clean hackled, Flax, and a few Chairs."[22] A Nashville merchant, in 1812, advertised to buy fifty to sixty thousand pounds of bacon.[23] Anderson and Wier, on opening their store in Nashville in 1801, offered to "purchase a quantity of Cotton, if delivered immediately."[24] A merchant in Clarksville regularly advertised his policy of paying the highest cash prices for butter, eggs, onions, and poultry.[25] Another in Memphis on one occasion wanted to purchase five hundred bushels of dried peaches.[26] Maury County farmer James Matthews, according to an entry in his diary, "took apples to Wm Starks [merchant] & sold them for $1.00 pr. bushel = $7.50."[27] Buyers sometimes gave farmers a choice of payment, as with the Nashville dealer who wanted to purchase cotton for cash or merchandise to be delivered several months later.[28]

Farmers also had the option of selling their goods on commission through local merchants. General stores often advertised such services in the newspapers. They preferred to handle relatively expensive products, such as apple cider, distilled whiskey, maple sugar, cotton, and tobacco.[29] A Knoxville store, offering to sell any marketable product on consignment, promised "the most advantageous sale, and speedy remittance of proceeds."[30] Occasionally an outside agent sought business. A merchant in Tiana, Alabama, advertised in the Knoxville newspaper that he "will receive, on consignment, . . . the Products, &c of East Tenness, which he will dispose of agreeable to instructions."[31]

Local processors, as well as store owners, offered to buy the farmers' produce for cash. Small cotton and woolen spinning mills, which sprang up as areas passed from the pioneer stage of settlement, were always in need of raw fiber. A new firm opened in Nashville in 1811 and advertised immediately for "fresh, clean cotton"; a Clarksville establishment, for good quality wool.[32] Another mill opened in Knoxville in 1827 and announced that it was "now ready to receive any quantity of Cotton that may be offered."[33] The firm of Erwin, Patten & Hall revealed its plans to build cordage factories near Columbia and near Newport, as well as its anticipated need for hemp. They were confident about obtaining the necessary supplies: "We have no right to doubt the aid of our fellow citizens in furnishing us with hemp." Just for good measure, they appealed to the farmers' patriotism: "We can each claim an equal part in performing a duty we owe to ourselves and our country."[34] Another firm also saw wisdom in signaling its future needs for raw materials. The owners of a factory under construction for extracting oil from flaxseed advised, "Farmers, save your seed."[35] A tailor of ready-made clothes in Nashville was flexible in his demands:

"I will give cash for all kinds of homespun of a good quality"; a hat maker, a bit more particular, would buy only lamb's wool from the fall shearing.[36] Farmers also took advantage of local markets for raw cowhides. An establishment in Memphis wanted to buy, for reasons that went unexplained, "dry sheep hides."[37]

Grain and livestock processors provided additional cash markets. Local gristmills depended on nearby farmers to supply them with grain. Kennedy's Mill in Knoxville needed up to ten thousand bushels of wheat late in 1843.[38] In the 1850s, Nashville's Rock City Mills and Memphis' Center Mills guaranteed farmers the highest prices for their wheat and corn.[39] When a new mill opened in Clarksville in 1857, it urged producers in the area to bring in their grain.[40] In the summer of 1821, a Nashville brewery offered to buy barley delivered to its doors at fifty cents a bushel.[41] Peter Brickey, on his farm in Blount County, "operated a licensed distillery which made a local market for grain."[42] A traveler in 1817 observed in the vicinity of Nashville "a great many distilleries in operation. In this way they convert their surplus produce into cash."[43] A Clarksville pork-packing house sought to attract the attention and the animals of nearby swine producers with a newspaper advertisement that opened, in bold letters, CASH FOR HOGS, and someone in Knoxville offered to buy "milch cows" from local farmers.[44]

Farmers also took advantage of opportunities to sell produce to people passing through their neighborhoods. As drovers moved their livestock to market, they had to depend on farmers along the way for feed and pasture. Farmers in the Knoxville vicinity were especially well situated, for their area was a concentration point for drovers on their way to urban markets to the south and the east. They looked forward to the business generated by the annual drives.[45] One Knoxville merchant advertised to buy one thousand bushels of corn and, in the same notice, informed drovers that his establishment maintained a good supply of grain.[46] J. M. Brewer, who hired on to drive a herd of horses from Nashville to Virginia in the summer of 1814, complained that his employer had to pay farmers as much as a dollar a bushel for corn as they crossed the sparsely populated Cumberland tableland.[47] During the War of 1812, the Tennessee militia needed foodstuffs for soldiers on their way to New Orleans, for which it promised to pay cash.[48] At one stop on his trip through Tennessee in the 1790s, Francis Baily was indignant about the prices charged by an enterprising farmer from whom he had obtained provisions: "When I came to discharge my reckoning,

I found they had the impudence to charge me a dollar for this rough accommodation; that is, for a little bread and butter, and some corn my horses had eaten."[49]

Farmers quickly recognized the benefits to be gained from participating in these local markets. Trading small amounts of surplus food and fiber enabled them to pay their taxes and to obtain goods and services unavailable on their own farms. Early on, the marketed surpluses were usually unanticipated, arising from coincidental production in excess of household requirements. Over time, they resulted increasingly from deliberate decisions to produce more than family members needed with the intention of exchanging or selling the oversupply. In either case, involvement in this simple and readily accessible market represented the Tennessee farmers' first experience in the commercial economy.

As beneficial for early farmers as the local markets were, they were decidedly limited. The commercial choices open to them, however, grew more numerous and potentially more profitable as settlement matured. To take advantage of these broadening choices, farmers had to concentrate on the production of one or two commodities in high demand in remote markets and to use more elaborate and extensive commercial systems. Although they continued to supply many of their own household needs, farmers responded to these emerging opportunities by adopting production strategies that placed greater emphasis on marketable goods. Their commercial ventures shifted from trading or selling small amounts of surplus food and fiber in their own neighborhoods to selling large quantities of basic staples destined, more often than not, for distant urban centers in the United States and Europe.

Tennessee's first important commercial commodity was cotton. The settlement of the state occurred at a time when the demand for cotton was growing rapidly. Mechanization of cloth making in England in the eighteenth century created a market for enormous amounts of raw cotton, far more than could be supplied by existing sources. The establishment of textile industries elsewhere in Europe and eventually in the United States reinforced and sustained the demand for cotton fiber well into the nineteenth century. Areas in Tennessee with climate and soil conditions suitable for the cultivation of cotton enthusiastically responded to this expanding market and its attractive profits.

John Donelson, one of the founders of the Cumberland settlements, planted the first cotton grown in Middle Tennessee soon after his arrival in the spring of 1780. He located his plot on a small clearing about twelve miles from the future site of Nashville. Indians prevented him from harvesting the crop, but his efforts demonstrated the viability of cotton cultivation in the central basin.[50] Others soon followed his example. By the mid-1780s, the region was selling cotton fiber to buyers as far away as Kentucky.[51] When Gilbert Imlay came through the central basin in 1792, he was impressed with the high yields and the excellent quality of the cotton crop. "The usual crop of cotton," he observed, "is 800 pounds to the acre; the staple is long and fine."[52]

Michaux reported that by the turn of the nineteenth century, cotton had already become a major cash crop in the central basin. "West Tennessea, or Cumberland . . . is particularly favourable to the growth of cotton," he wrote in his journal; "in consequence of which the inhabitants give themselves up almost entirely to it, and cultivate but little more corn, hemp, and tobacco than what is necessary for their own consumption." He found that the production of cotton was so profitable that virtually every new farmer planted the crop within the first three years of his arrival in the area.[53] Cotton production, as Michaux discovered, was not primarily for local consumption. He saw cargoes of the fiber leaving Nashville destined for Pittsburgh by way of the Cumberland and Ohio rivers, from where they were "conveyed to the remote parts of Pennsylvania." He reckoned that this commerce "must give a high degree of prosperity to this part of Tennessea."[54] The twenty-four cotton gins in and around Nashville by 1804 further reflected the commercial importance of the crop to the central basin. "John Harmon acquaints his friends that he will gin & bale & deliver cotton on the bank of the Cumberland on the same terms that cotton is ginned & packed at other gins," read the newspaper advertisement of one of them.[55]

The removal of Chickasaw claims to West Tennessee in 1818 opened a region even more conducive to cotton cultivation. As white settlement reached into the lands west of the central basin, farmers turned to production of the fiber as soon as they carved farmsteads out of the virgin soil. Barely three years after the opening of West Tennessee, the region's first commercial cotton gin began operation in Jackson. The demand for ginning facilities grew so rapidly that Joshua Farrington of Brownsville began manufacturing the machines in the late 1820s.[56] In the first decades of the nineteenth century, Middle Tennessee continued to expand its cotton cultivation, but it was West Tennessee that witnessed an explosion of production. In 1816, Middle Tennessee sent an estimated fifteen hundred bales of cotton to market. By 1840, the receipts at Memphis alone, the major commercial outlet for West Tennessee, had reached thirty-five thousand bales.[57]

Cotton never became a significant commercial crop in East Tennessee, largely because the climate and soil discouraged its production. Still, the fiber contributed modestly to the agricultural economy of the southern extension of the eastern valleys during the antebellum period. Michaux listed cotton among the goods sent from Knoxville for sale in New Orleans in 1802.[58] In 1804 sales were brisk enough to justify the erection of a cotton gin in Knoxville.[59] As late as 1825, at least one Knoxville firm still ginned and baled cotton for sale outside the region.[60] In the same year, a merchant sought to buy 100,000 pounds of the fiber from farmers in the area, a quantity he could have disposed of only through external markets.[61]

The young state government recognized the emerging commercial importance of cotton. In 1801, barely five years after Tennessee became a state, the legislature set up an inspection system designed to denote the quality of cotton sent outside the state. It required ginners to mark as "inferior" all bales that could not qualify as "first quality" and to attach a certificate of value. It further stipulated that exported bales had to carry the label TENNESSEE and the name and location of the gin so that distant buyers would be able to identify their source. The severity of the penalties for violation—one hundred dollars for failure to label inferior cotton, five hundred dollars for failure to identify the inspecting gin—testified to the legislators' resolve to protect the reputation of the state's fiber.[62] However, their efforts met with resistance from cotton producers, who believed that the practice depressed the prices of the lower grades. The legislature repealed the grading and labeling provisions in 1811 and dismantled the entire inspection system in 1838.[63] Notwithstanding its unpopularity among producers, the motivation behind the scheme was clearly to open and preserve external markets for Tennessee's cotton.

Further to encourage the development of commercial cotton production, the legislature, in 1803, attempted to remove legal impediments to the use of the cotton gin in Tennessee. It declared that "the cultivation of cotton is increasing in this state, and from the invention and use of said machine like[ly] to become a valuable staple article of exportation." The legislature arranged to purchase permission to use the cotton gin from the holders of the patent rights, Eli Whitney and Phineas Miller. From 1803 to 1807 the state collected a tax on each machine operating in Tennessee, which it remitted to Whitney and Miller.[64] The rapid proliferation of cotton gins that followed the passage of this legislation would probably have occurred without it. Federal patent protection was practically nonexistent at the time. But the legislature's action reflected the importance of cotton to Tennessee's farmers and to the young state's economy.

Michaux reported that the legislature also tried to encourage household cloth manufacturing as a way to reduce the importation of textiles and to stimulate internal demand for the state's cotton. Each year, he noted, it made a cash award to "the female inhabitant who, in every county, presents the best manufactured piece." Apparently the program proved effective, at least at one level of society, for Michaux found that "the higher circles wear, in summer time, as much from patriotism as from economy, dresses made of cotton manufactured in the country [Tennessee]."[65]

The growing commercial importance of cotton was reflected in other ways. The diaries and accounts of individual farmers often included detailed references to it. Robert Cartmell, who farmed in Madison County, recorded that his 1853 crop amounted to eleven bales after ginning.[66] He was pleased with the progress of the following year's crop until a late freeze dashed his hopes of a good yield: "I had a good deal of cotton up but I guess this morning's frost killed all."[67] Satisfaction with the return on his 1859 crop prompted him to ruminate over why so many farmers failed to cultivate the fiber. "Good cottons are in demand," he observed, "but some almost entirely neglect it."[68] John Houston Bills, a large-scale planter in Hardeman County, sold thirty-three bales of cotton in 1846 for more than one thousand dollars, substantial proceeds for a single crop.[69] He seemed even more hopeful about his 1853 crop: "I think my stand of cotton will do well on the fresh 100 acre field south & 25 acres fresh land near cabbins."[70] Herndon Haraldson operated on a smaller scale in the same county, but he was no less enthusiastic about the five bales he sent to market in 1845.[71] Sometimes Tennessee farmers even received recognition for their efforts from outside the state. *Niles' Weekly Register,* in commenting on the crop produced by R. J. Mays of Madison County, wrote that it was "as fine an article of this description of cotton as we have ever seen."[72] In 1851 a cotton sample from John Pope's Shelby County plantation won first place at the World's Fair in London.

Commercial cotton cultivation occurred on farms of all sizes. But just as smaller units placed greater emphasis on corn in their crop choices, so larger units placed greater emphasis on cotton.[73] The procedures used in the previous chapter to examine patterns of self-sufficiency production also demonstrate that larger farms and plantations were more heavily involved in commercial production.[74] Table 4.1 shows that when farms in the eight sample counties in 1850 and 1860 are broken down by improved-acreage categories, the cotton index usually varies positively with the size of unit. Farms in the smallest category devoted relatively more acreage to cotton than those in the next larger category, and plantations of one thousand acres or more devoted relatively less acreage to cotton than farms in the next smaller category. With these two exceptions, located at the extremes, the cotton index increased as farm size grew. When slaveholding is used to measure the scale of operations (table 4.2), no exceptions appear; the cotton index increased in tandem with slaveholding. If larger farmers and planters devoted a smaller share of their improved acreage to corn production, as noted in chapter 3, they also devoted a larger share to commercial cotton production.

Interfarm regression analysis sheds more light on the behavior of commercial cotton farmers. Because of the heavy labor demands associated with cotton production, a farmer's scale of operations depended as much on labor per improved acre as on total improved acreage. Some measure of relative labor supply must, therefore, be included in the analysis. The household-acreage ratio, used in chapter 3 as a measure of subsistence requirements, provides a rough approximation of the relative labor size; the larger the household, the more farm labor it could supply. If larger farmers placed greater emphasis on cotton production than smaller farmers, the cotton index should show a positive relationship with both improved acreage and the proxy for labor per improved acre. That is to say, farms with more improved acreage and more labor per improved acre should have placed greater emphasis on cotton production. Interfarm regression reveals a positive relationship between the cotton index and the other two factors, but the association is not as strong as that found in the analysis of self-sufficiency.[75] The results indicate that farms of similar size varied widely in their commitment to cotton production. Although larger operations tended to emphasize commercial cotton production, the relationship was weaker than the relationship between farm size and corn production.

Table 4.1

Cotton Output/Improved Acres (x 100) by Improved Acre Category,
1850 and 1860

Acre Category	1850	1860
1–49	5.75	5.49
50–99	5.12	5.26
100–199	7.30	6.48
200–299	10.23	8.41
300–499	12.20	11.78
500–999	15.03	15.01
>999	13.31	12.05
All categories	8.38	8.76

SOURCE: Eight sample counties (see appendix).
NOTE: Corn output measured in bushels.

Tobacco ranked second to cotton as a cash crop in antebellum Tennessee. The eastern valleys were the first region of the state to grow the plant. However, although a few large farmers continued to specialize in tobacco, it never became a major marketable commodity in the region during the antebellum period.[76] The principal commercial production occurred in the northern tiers of counties in Middle and West Tennessee. The soils and climate in the northwestern quadrant of the state were ideally suited to several varieties of tobacco. By the end of the eighteenth century, barely twenty years after the arrival of the first settlers along the Cumberland River, farmers in the central basin north of Nashville were already heavily involved in tobacco cultivation.[77] Two decades later, after the removal of the last Indian claims to Tennessee land, tobacco cultivation had spread west into the valleys of the Obion River and its tributaries.[78] From those early beginnings, production of the plant rapidly expanded as more and more farmers moved into Middle and West Tennessee and turned to commercial agriculture.

Tobacco growers responded to both foreign and domestic demand. The coarse, dark varieties of Middle Tennessee were best suited for snuff and chewing, the major markets for which were in Europe. The

Table 4.2

Cotton Output/Improved Acres (x 100) by Slave Category,
1850 and 1860

Slave Category	1850	1860
0	2.90	3.94
1–2	4.83	4.12
3–5	5.75	5.78
6–10	8.36	6.83
11–20	9.96	10.16
>20	16.25	16.76
All categories	8.38	8.76

Source: Eight sample counties (see appendix).
Note: Cotton output measured in bales.

higher quality burley varieties grown primarily in West Tennessee became wrappers for plug tobacco, sold mainly in the United States.[79] Clarksville served as the principal center for marketing Tennessee tobacco, whatever its ultimate destination. Tobacco dealers, commission merchants, and forwarding agents congregated there, offering their services to farmers selling their crop to distant buyers.[80] By 1860 a number of factories processing the leaf for sale in the United States had located in or near Clarksville, creating a local market for more than two million pounds of tobacco yearly.[81]

The Tennessee legislature established a tobacco inspection system, just as it attempted to do for cotton. In 1797, a year after the state's admission to the union, it authorized Davidson County to erect a public inspection station and warehouse on the Cumberland River.[82] Such facilities, legislators reasoned, "will encourage commerce, promote industry, and be an advantage to those citizens of said county."[83] Two years later, the legislature established a state system, with inspection sites in Davidson, Greene, Montgomery, Smith, and Sumner counties. The legislation required that all tobacco sent out of the state be certified as "sound, well conditioned, merchantable, and clear of trash." It specified weighing and packaging procedures, and required that each container carry a stamp identifying the inspection site.[84] In 1811 the legislature established additional stations in Robertson and Dickson counties.[85]

The legislature subsequently attempted to strengthen the inspection system. In 1817 inspectors began assigning grades to tobacco for export, instead of simply certifying that it met minimum standards.[86] Producers objected to the grading requirement, however, on the same grounds as the cotton producers had objected; they claimed that it weakened the market for lower grades. The legislature vacillated for almost three decades before arriving at a compromise. In 1846 it directed inspectors to draw a sample, which would be available to purchasers, from each hogshead of tobacco, but to assign a grade only if requested by the owner.[87] Apparently even this solution caused problems. Inspectors at the Clarksville station published a gentle warning in the local newspaper in 1858. "There has been too great a disposition on the part of some Planters to mix with their good Tobacco small and inferior Tobacco," they complained. "This is wrong, and must be broken up." They declared their intention henceforth to include inferior tobacco in the samples of hogsheads of uneven quality. They concluded with a justification for their newly adopted resolve and, at least by implication, for the inspection system in general: "It is undoubtedly the interest of the Tobacco growers of this country to establish and keep a home market. This can only be done by submitting to a rigid inspection, thereby giving it character abroad."[88]

The legislature's efforts to promote Tennessee's tobacco economy involved more than its inspection system. In 1842 it called upon Congress to pressure European countries to open their markets to United States tobacco. It suggested that retaliatory tariffs might convince foreign governments to lower their trade barriers.[89] There is no evidence that Congress responded to the petition, but the action revealed the importance legislators placed on commercial tobacco production in the state.

The diaries and account books of Tennessee farmers reflected a similar regard for commercial tobacco production. In fact, farmers who cultivated tobacco—more so than with any other crop—meticulously recorded their production and commercial activities throughout the year. In 1844 Montgomery County farmer John Barker began preparing his tobacco beds on 8 February; he sent his first load to Clarksville on 22 March of the following year. His careful record of each step in the tedious process, from seeding through selling, highlighted the crucial role of tobacco in his farming system.[90] George Washington's accounts likewise convey an intense concern with the growing and marketing of his tobacco. Throughout the latter half of 1851, he wrote with regularity and, it appears, with some impatience to his agent in New Orleans with detailed instructions for the disposal of the year's crop.[91]

Tobacco, unlike cotton, was not primarily associated with large-scale farms. The tobacco indexes for 1850 given in tables 4.3 and 4.4 were, in fact, generally higher for the smaller improved-acreage and slaveholding categories.[92] For 1860, farms organized by improved-acreage categories showed a similar pattern, whereas farms organized by slaveholding categories showed no systematic relationship. In the regression analysis, the tobacco index registered a positive association with labor per improved acre in both years. But the improved-acreage measure showed no significant association with tobacco production in 1850 and a negative association in 1860. Moreover, the strength of the relationship between the tobacco index and the other two factors was very weak.[93]

Given the requirements of tobacco production, these results should not be surprising. Cultivation demanded an enormous amount of physical effort, which probably explains the positive association between emphasis on tobacco production and labor supply per improved acre. At the same time, it required relatively little land, which probably explains the negative association between the tobacco index and improved acreage in 1860. Small farmers with a commercial orientation elected, quite appropriately, to cultivate tobacco, providing they had access to an adequate labor supply. These findings are consistent with the nineteenth-century image of tobacco as the small farmers' commercial crop. Large operators, to be sure, cultivated the plant. George Washington, for instance, produced a quarter of a million pounds in 1859. In the years leading up to the Civil War, he was the largest producer in Tennessee and probably in the United States. According to family legend, Joseph Edwin, George's father and the first operator of the family's Robertson County estate, was the second largest tobacco producer in the world; the largest, an Egyptian khedive.[94] Still, smaller farmers took up cultivation of the plant as a way to generate a little cash income, but of course on decidedly more modest scales.

Although cotton and tobacco were the principal commercial crops of antebellum Tennessee, farmers responded to outside demand for other commodities. The markets for grain, especially wheat, and flour in the food deficient areas along the Atlantic and Gulf Coasts and, to a

Table 4.3

Tobacco Output/Improved Acres by Improved-Acre Category, 1850 and 1860

Acre Category	1850	1860
1–49	3.56	4.80
50–99	3.72	4.76
100–199	3.18	4.06
200–299	2.34	3.12
300–499	1.23	2.27
500–999	.65	2.11
>999	1.04	4.76
All categories	2.71	3.58

SOURCE: Eight sample counties (see appendix).
NOTE: Tobacco output measured in pounds.

smaller extent, in Europe steadily expanded in the period before the Civil War. At the same time, grain price increases and improved transportation widened the geographical limits of profitable production, and by the 1830s all of Tennessee fell well within that orbit. The state's farmers took advantage of the growing opportunities created by those developments.[95]

The eastern valleys engaged in a flourishing trade in wheat and flour soon after the region passed from the settlement stage. Michaux, as early as 1802, saw flour destined for New Orleans loaded onto Tennessee River barges at Knoxville.[96] A decade later, in the vicinity of the Clinch River in northeastern Tennessee, J. M. Brewer judged from "the appearance of the farms . . . that wheat is their staple commodity."[97] Over time the eastern valleys found grain markets in cities along the northern Atlantic, but the expensive land routes used for this trade limited its potential. Railroad links increased the volume of trade in the late 1850s, and high quality Tennessee wheat came to command a premium price as far away as New York City.[98] Nearer and more accessible by land routes, the cotton-growing counties of northern Alabama and the port cities of the southern Atlantic provided more attractive outlets. By the 1850s, rail connections had made those coastal

Table 4.4

Tobacco Output/Improved Acres by Slave Category, 1850 and 1860

Slave Category	1850	1860
0	3.00	3.02
1–2	5.14	5.13
3–5	3.45	4.82
6–10	3.11	3.80
11–20	2.50	4.88
>20	1.23	2.69
All categories	2.71	3.58

SOURCE: Eight sample counties (see appendix).
NOTE: Tobacco output measured in pounds.

markets even more accessible.[99] Competition from cotton and tobacco inhibited commercial grain production in Middle and West Tennessee. Still, farmers in those regions eventually entered heavily into the trade, particularly in the 1850s, when the Crimean War stimulated European demand and railroad construction provided links to more distant domestic markets.[100]

The farmers who planted more grain than their families were likely to need as insurance against crop damage or low yields naturally anticipated a surplus in most years, which they intended to sell in the outside markets. Edward Anderson apparently followed such a strategy on his Sullivan County farm. He produced corn and wheat primarily for household consumption, yet he nearly always had a surfeit of grain to market off the farm.[101] Herndon Haraldson similarly disposed of the oversupply from his Hardeman County farm. "Cotter's keelboat goes down River with corn, meal, and Bacon," read an entry in his diary. Six weeks later, "Cotter settles & pays me for trip."[102] Robert Cartmell, a cotton farmer in Madison County, apparently found himself in a precarious position one year. With only a small excess above household needs, he "sent a load of corn to town. . . . I can spare a few barrels as times are hard and with almost a failure must sell something to make *ends* meet."[103]

Large farmers and planters frequently included grain as part of their commercial production. The diaries John Barker and Wiley Bagwell, both of Montgomery County, clearly indicated that tobacco was their chief source of revenue. But they also produced significant amounts of grain, which they sold to dealers and processors in Clarksville. In 1848 Barker began hauling his wheat to town in early May, soon after completing the harvest, and finished the task two weeks later.[104] Occasionally he sold corn and oats, but those grains were less important generators of income. One day, for example, he inscribed in his log: "Sold to John Bradley the oats I have to spare."[105] Bagwell, who followed a similar scheme, regularly sold wheat and rye.[106] Cotton may have been the major source of income from Robert Cartmell's Madison County farm, but his earnings from the sale of wheat were substantial.[107] George Washington, Tennessee's largest tobacco producer, every year sold huge quantities of wheat as well. In one of his more unusual transactions, he entered into what amounted to a futures contract in the fall of 1854 to sell twenty-five hundred to three thousand bushels at $1.10 per bushel from the coming year's wheat crop.[108]

Livestock provided yet another source of cash income for antebellum farmers. They often sold hogs or pork products in the local market. John Barker's diary contains numerous references to neighborhood trade. Sometimes they recorded small transactions—"sold Wm Edmonson 3 sows, 6 pigs for $10"—sometimes, sizable transactions—"drove 32 hogs to Providence at 5 1/2 cts nett amt $514.76." On other occasions he peddled large stocks of pork products—"sold 1092 lbs of bacon, 300 lbs lard at 5 and 6 cents."[109] George Washington's sales ranged from a side of pork to a neighbor to twelve barrels of lard to a Clarksville dealer.[110] Crockett County farmer David S. Nunn sold as much as ten thousand pounds of pork in a single year in the 1830s, and on William Hunter's farm in Putnam County, "hogs [were] fed on beechnuts on open range & driven to market down Cherry Creek Road to Sparta."[111] Betty Gleaves, the wife of a small farmer in Cheatam County, was obviously pleased to enter in her diary that "Mr. Gleaves gets 8 1/3 cts for his bacon."[112] James Matthews, another small farmer, usually had a few extra swine after providing for his family, which he sold locally.[113] Tom Bryan, who grew up on a Montgomery County farm, recalled that his father sold swine in town: "They had a pork house in Clarksville, Tennessee, that done a flourishing business."[114]

Drovers offered another profitable outlet. They purchased or received on consignment livestock from farmers as they moved through the state, usually late in the year after the swine had been fattened on corn. The size of the drives normally varied from three hundred to more than one thousand animals; in exceptional cases they exceeded two thousand. The drives that crossed East Tennessee moved either east to markets along the mid-Atlantic coast or south to markets in Georgia and Alabama. Those that crossed Middle and West Tennessee in most cases terminated in the Gulf Coast states.[115]

Tennessee farmers were the principal suppliers of the swine that reached those markets. The widely acknowledged preference of Georgia buyers for Tennessee livestock led one newspaper to recommend that drovers coming from the state bring documents certifying the origin of their animals.[116] Bryan noted that hogs from his area of Middle Tennessee were "carried on foot all the way to Alabama, Georgia, Mississippi, and Louisiana."[117] According to Christopher Houston, a Maury County settler in 1816, land speculators frequently engaged in the swine business. "They give $4.50 [per acre for unimproved land] and buy some hogs and fatten them," he wrote to a family member back home. "They mostly intend driving to Georgia or S. Carolina."[118]

Other livestock, although of less importance than swine, also contributed to the farm income. In 1802, Michaux encountered farmers in East Tennessee who were raising meat cattle for sale. "To consume the superfluity of their corn," he reported, "the inhabitants rear a great number of cattle, which they take four or five hundred miles to the seaports belonging to the southern states."[119] Drovers preferred swine because they could better endure the long drives, but they sometimes included cattle in their herds. Local markets supplemented the distant markets. "Joseph Engleman, Butcher, wishes to purchase a number of stall fed cattle," read an advertisement in the Nashville newspaper.[120] Barker, on one occasion, "sold Carney 11 head of cattle"; on another, "sold C. B. Peterson 5 beeves."[121] Herndon Haraldson, who farmed on a much smaller scale in Hardeman County, from time to time marketed a few head of cattle locally.[122] In addition to meat cattle, farmers sold sheep, chickens, and turkeys for slaughter. Turkey producers often combined their flocks and drove them to the nearest market center. Bryan recalled seeing a "quantity of turkeys driven to Clarksville and shipped from there to Neworleans."[123]

By the turn of the eighteenth century, pork and beef sales outside of the state had already reached a level high enough to provoke legislative supervision of the trade. In an effort "to prevent exportation of unmerchantable commodities," the legislature required the inspection and certification of pork, beef, and lard sent across state lines. Each container had to carry the label, in bold letters, TENNESSEE.[124] This effort, like those applied to cotton and tobacco, met with resistance from producers and dealers, and the legislature dismantled the system two years later. The legislators placed an explanation for their action in the repeal: "From experience it hath been discovered that the inspection directed and authorized . . . on the articles of beef and pork, to be exported from this state, has been productive of considerable loss to the good citizens there of."[125]

Tennessee developed a reputation as a source of fine riding and racing horses. In his account of a journey through the central basin in 1806, Thomas Ashe counted saddle horses among its "valuable articles."[126] Though not part of the typical farm operation, horse breeding was the chief enterprise of a few prominent landowners. William Giles Harding of Belle Meade Farm near Nashville became famous as a breeder of superior animals. People came from all over the United States and Europe to purchase from his stock.[127] Hubbard Saunders of neighboring Sumner County owned two highly regarded stallions, Commodore Perry and Partnership, the offspring of which were in considerable demand as racing horses.[128] Owners of thoroughbred horses also sold stud services, which they advertised in newspapers and farm journals. "The Thoroughbred celebrated running horse Grey Medley" earned on a sliding scale: four dollars for a single leap, eight for an entire season with no guarantee of a foal, sixteen for an entire season with guarantee of a foal. Advertisements for his services included letters of reference from satisfied customers.[129] So in demand was W. A. Lenoir's prize-winning stud that he spent the summer of 1853 on White Sulphur Springs Farm in Meriwether County, Georgia, upgrading the equine stock of the surrounding area and enriching his Tennessee owner.[130] The state began to regulate the lucrative stud business in 1835 with a law requiring the licensing of stallions used for commercial breeding.[131]

Other farmers operated on a more modest scale. On the rich pastures of the eastern valleys and the central basin, they raised draft horses and mules. Many sold their animals locally. Columbia, well known as a market for horses and, especially, mules, attracted buyers from across the South to its annual sales. Some farmers sold their draft stock to drovers, who in turn sold them to cotton planters in the Gulf Coast states.[132] Mississippi planters, according to one observer, pre-

ferred to purchase Tennessee animals to breeding their own. Joseph
Lamar supplied mules from his Anderson County farm to cotton ginners in South Carolina. Tennessee mules commanded prices as high as
three hundred dollars a pair in the Georgia market.[133] Mule breeders
also offered stud services. Farmers wishing to breed their mares might
purchase the services of King Cyrus, "Master Jack of America," or
Sancho (whose owner made no claims for him) for an entire season for
eight dollars, ten dollars to ensure a foal. The owners charged double
those rates for the use of the same jacks to breed a jennet, apparently
because impregnation was more difficult. The law requiring the licensing of stallions also applied to jacks.[134]

Some farmers kept sheep and sold the fiber. Wiley Bagwell and John
Barker mentioned in their diaries when they had sheared sheep; on one
occasion, Barker "sent wool to Hobson's mill."[135] Robert Cartmell bought
a pair of blooded sheep, which were crosses between South Downs and
Cotswolds, hoping to sell premium quality wool.[136] Mark R. Cockrill, who
farmed five thousand acres in Davidson County, was one of a few very
large wool producers in the state. The local market for the fiber was limited, but there were some outlets. A Memphis buyer wanted to purchase
fifty thousand pounds of wool, a fairly sizable lot, in the summer of
1859.[137] Farmers like Cockrill, with large flocks of sheep, normally sold
their fiber to dealers or mills in the Northeast.

A few farmers cultivated hemp for the market. Early in the nineteenth
century, a Nashville newspaper recommended the fiber as a profitable
commodity. "The price of hemp and spun yarn in our atlantic ports," it
claimed, "is a[s] good security as we could ask, to insure us a saving price
for all our hemp."[138] A report on the agriculture of East Tennessee in
the 1840s suggested that many farmers were missing a lucrative commercial opportunity: "Hemp grows luxuriantly upon our River Bottom Lands, but has hitherto been neglected; although it is believed to
be more profitable than any other crop that can be raised."[139] On a tour
of farms near Nashville, the editor of the *Agriculturist* found a similar
disregard for the crop. "We have long since believed this crop could be
advantageously grown on the black limestone soil of Middle Tennessee,"
he wrote, "and we wonder why it is not more generally cultivated."[140]
During the Mexican-American War, the state legislature petitioned the
federal government to promote hemp cultivation in Tennessee. It argued
that hemp was "an important element of National defence and commercial prosperity, and . . . essential to our safety and independence in

time of war with all foreign countries." The legislature urged the federal government to send an agent to purchase Tennessee hemp.[141] In 1852 the navy built a rope factory in Memphis with the intention of purchasing hemp from Tennessee and Kentucky growers. Unable to secure the quality of fiber it required, the navy abandoned the project two years later and donated the works to the city.[142] Despite enthusiasm in some quarters, hemp never became more than a minor commercial product in the state.

The discovery that silk worms thrived on the leaves of the native mulberry tree and of the Chinese morus multicaulis plant, which grew well in Tennessee, generated a flurry of excitement in the 1830s and 1840s. Agricultural journals enthusiastically recommended production of the fiber, claiming that it was particularly suitable for small-scale, marginal operators.[143] According to the *Southern Cultivator*, it was "admirably adapted to the small farmer, and persons of limited means." The fiber did not require heavy exertion and, the journal wrote, cultivation could be "pursued with profit in the family, by employing the children and females, without detriment to other branches of the labor of the farm."[144] The 1840s report on East Tennessee agriculture was as enthusiastic about the commercial potential of silk as it was about that of hemp: "As a Silk raising country, the climate and soil render it unrivalled. . . . Silk must shortly become one of the staple productions of East Tennessee."[145]

Farmers responded by investing in silkworms and growing native mulberry trees and morus multicaulis plants to nourish them. In 1838 the West Tennessee Silk Company established a nursery for cultivating morus multicaulis seedlings, which it sold to farmers entering the silk business.[146] The editors of the *Tennessee Farmer* were delighted that farmers of the eastern valleys had heeded their advice: "We are happy to learn that a real zeal for the extension of the silk culture is rapidly diffusing itself throughout East Tennessee." The *Agriculturist* reported considerable interest in Middle Tennessee as well. On a tour of Williamson County, its editors found ventures ranging from A. P. Maury's relatively modest 100,000 worms to W. P. Campbell's substantial 1 million worms.[147] Tennessee silk output exceeded one thousand pounds of cocoons by 1840 and reached nearly two thousand pounds by 1850, making the state the largest producer in the country.

Farmers had reason to believe that silk offered a viable commercial option. The fiber returned a reasonable profit. Several silk manufacturing companies located in the state, providing a local market that supplemented a robust outside market. The Tennessee Silk Manufacturing Company and Agricultural School opened in Portroyal "to teach the art of the culture and manufacture of silk." The enterprise apparently enjoyed wide support. Tobacco planter George Washington invested one hundred dollars in stock of the institute, even though he himself produced no silk.[148] For a time, the legislature gave bounties of ten cents per pound on silk cocoons and fifty cents per pound on reeled silk produced in the state.[149] Governor James C. Jones appeared at his 1843 inauguration wearing a silk suit manufactured by the Portroyal institute and donated to him "in acknowledgement of his efficient services to the cause of [the] American industry."[150] A shipment of Tennessee silk sold the same year in Manchester, England, was "pronounced equal to the best silk obtained from France and Italy."[151]

Euphoria soon turned to disillusionment. In the 1850s an unknown disease began killing silkworms in epidemic proportions. Many farmers saw their promising businesses destroyed; others withdrew from production before disaster hit. By 1860 state output had plummeted to less than one hundred pounds and centered on a handful of counties in East and Middle Tennessee.[152] Thus ended one of the more peculiar episodes in the state's agricultural history.

Producing for the market exposed farmers to greater risk than producing for household consumption. Many conditions, of course, threatened both commercial and subsistence agriculture. The possibility of crop damage from inclement weather plagued all farmers throughout the growing season. Late frosts destroyed young plants and early buds. "Very severe frost this mng," lamented George Washington one day. "Fruit all killed. . . . Tobacco plants much injured."[153] At the end of April 1844, John Barker recorded in his diary that "this month has been extremely cold and dry[;] wheat, corn, all vegitables and trees killed." Early frosts could also be a problem. Barker estimated that freezing weather early one October cost him a third of his tobacco crop.[154] Proper amounts of rain at the right times were a constant source of concern. Robert Cartmell complained at a critical time during one growing season: "My cotton is dieing, without a change soon I cannot have a good stand. We need rain now." A diary entry three weeks later—"dry, dry, dry, dry"—indicated that conditions had not improved. "We had a glorius rain today," he inscribed, obviously with considerable relief, after another worrisome week. An especially hard rain later the same year caused him a different problem:

"A great deal of corn is on the ground which will be greatly damaged."[155] On one occasion, Herndon Haraldson noted that "all my Wheat Oats & Rye lost by the rains." On another occasion, he revealed that high winds could be just as threatening: "Corn blown down. Crops injured."[156] So, too, could hail, as Cartmell complained: "The hail on Saturday riddled the corn"; and as Barker complained: "The Tob destroyed by hail."[157]

Although weather hazards affected all crops, they usually represented a greater threat to commercial than to subsistence production. Cotton and tobacco, the state's principal market crops, were particularly vulnerable. Both germinated early, exposing them to late frosts at the beginning of the growing season. They were especially sensitive to rainfall; it had to come in the right amounts at the right times. Grains, the main subsistence crops, were more flexible in their requirements. Corn was especially hardy. Irregular weather conditions might cause a reduction in yield, but they rarely destroyed the entire crop. The grain required ample rainfall, but was less demanding in its timing than cotton or tobacco. Wheat, although more delicate than corn, could also accommodate abnormal weather better than cotton and tobacco.

A variety of pests and other perils contributed additional risks to cultivation. Nearly every year worms threatened the tobacco crop. Agricultural journalist Solon Robinson commented on the problem while on a trip through Tennessee in 1845: "The greatest pest in the cultivation of this crop, are the worms that prey upon the leaves, and unless destroyed, will destroy the crop."[158] In most years farmers could remove them before they caused excessive damage. Occasionally, though, they came in such great numbers that farmers had difficulty keeping up with them. Other types of worms and insects were less selective. Barker noted that "the army worms are destroying every kind of crop."[159] The *Southern Cultivator* advised farmers in 1839 that the cut worm "is doing immense mischief and damage to our gardens, corn and cotton fields."[160] John Bills complained one year that "bugs [are] sucking it [cotton] to death & destruction," and Cartmell complained the following year that "some lice [are] on cotton in places."[161] Grasshoppers and locusts ravaged a wide variety of vegetation every few years, and the hessian fly and a type of weevil devoured wheat crops on a regular basis. Barker recorded in 1844 that "the wheat crop [is] destroyed by the weavel."[162] Rust, a type of fungus, attacked small grain, particularly after a field had been planted in the same crop for several successive years. In his diary remarks on July 1856, Cartmell noted that he had "made but little wheat on account of rust."[163] Fire was another hazard. One year tobacco harvested from two of George Washington's fields burned: "Total destruction of both crops [of] Tobacco."[164] Barker's neighbor experienced a fairly common misfortune among producers of fire-cured tobacco: "J. L. Clarks barn burned down full of Tob."[165]

Livestock, as well as crops, were at risk. Hog cholera epidemics were rare, but they were devastating when they occurred. The disease visited Tennessee in 1859. Cartmell charted its course as it approached his property. In March he penned in his log that the "*hog cholera* has played sad havoc with hogs throughout the country for months—is nearer me now than I like." It arrived at his farm two months later and continued to infect animals into July: "Still have hog cholera. . . . I have lossed so far I guess 2/3 of mine. . . . Nothing seems to prevent it or stay its progress." At the end of August, he assessed the damage and found that he had "about 45 hogs in all [out of 130] . . . balance died with cholera."[166] Barker also failed to escape the devastation, recording in December 1859 that he had "lost 16 of my pork hogs by cholera."[167]

Other, less serious threats affected livestock production. Because some animals went unpenned and unattended throughout most of the year, predators were always a problem. Dogs and wolves killed sheep, bears killed swine, cougars killed young cattle, and raccoons and foxes killed chickens. There was little farmers could do to prevent attacks by wild animals. But the state legislature enacted a law holding owners liable for the value of sheep killed or injured by their dogs.[168] Farmers had to watch what animals ate. Bloating was a serious problem, as Haraldson found when a "young mare died Eating new corn."[169] Cartmell learned the same lesson when his "cows ate too many apples. . . . I expect all of them but 1 (3 in no.) will die to night. I was not aware that there was enough apples to injure them." All three eventually died.[170] Animals also wondered off or were stolen. The legislature again tried to install remedies. The law required the finder of a stray to notify the county justice of the peace and to present it on prescribed days for display at the courthouse. If no one claimed the animal for a year, the finder could keep it on payment to the county of two-thirds of its estimated value.[171] The legislature instituted an exceedingly harsh penalty for horse stealing: the guilty person was condemned to "suffer death without benefit of clergy."[172] Either the law had a strong deterrent effect or it went unenforced, for there is no record of an execution for horse stealing.

One set of risks uniquely applied to commercial agriculture. When a farmer committed himself to the production of a commodity for the market, he could only guess at the price it would bring. Prices fluctuated widely from year to year and sometimes throughout the year. At a favorable time, a commercial product might bring in enough to provide a comfortable profit. At a poor time, it might only return costs of production. At a disastrous time, revenue might fall below expenses, leaving the farmer with a loss for his year's efforts. Successful farmers produced as efficiently as possible and hoped for reasonable prices when they brought their produce to market.

The timing of a sale was often a crucial factor. In 1856, with the Crimean War raging in Europe, Cartmell agonized over when to put his cotton on the market. He finally decided to sell in early February, even though the price was at a relatively low seven cents a pound. He reasoned that "in [the] present condition of things cotton is uncertain[;] it may go up or down," and he was unwilling to risk the latter. By late April prospects for an end to the European war had improved and so had the price of cotton. "Peace now certain, cotton averaging 10 cts or more," Cartmell ruefully recorded in his diary. "If I had held on to mine, [I] would have gotten a good price. Hereafter will try and do better." The following year, in the midst of the Panic of 1857, he applied his newly adopted strategy, but with confusing logic: "I have sold no cotton, preferring to wait until things get worse or better."[173]

The assumption of risk was an integral part of agriculture. Weather, crop pests, animal diseases, and a multitude of other conditions produced uncertainties that farmers, whatever their degree of commercial orientation, had to accept. Producing for the market usually entailed the greater risk, however, because the commodities were often more vulnerable and the operating expenses were always greater. Added to that were the price fluctuations that affected only commercial operations.

Enterprising Tennessee farmers not only pursued the most promising agricultural opportunities, they also took advantage of special circumstances to add to their incomes. Those situated near running water sometimes built mills, which they operated as commercial ventures. On his Blount County farm, Richard Burns ran a mill for grinding grain and cutting lumber. John Burtis's mill in Fayette County provided "a place for community to grind their own corn & wheat"—for a price, it should be added.[174] Madison County planter Daniel Hopper owned the first cotton gin in his community, a mule-powered contraption, the use of which he sold to his neighbors. David Coleman operated a commercial steam-powered cotton gin on his property in Carroll County.[175] Robert Cartmell's principal source of income was cotton, but he made extra money by ginning and baling cotton for his neighbors.[176]

Farmers located along heavily traversed routes earned income by providing services to travelers. Francis Baily found, as he crossed the state in 1796, that "almost all the farmers who live near the road will take in strangers and travellers, giving them what is called 'dry entertainment.' For this entertainment they generally take care to charge enough."[177] William Carter's farm bordered a stage coach route from Nashville to Washington, D.C. Among the guests he lodged over the years was Andrew Jackson, who stayed there while on the way to his presidential inauguration in 1829.[178] The White County farm that Calvin Crook grew up on must have been conveniently located. He recalled that in addition to performing much of the farm work, his father "also kept tavn and took care of traveling public."[179] River locations sometimes provided possibilities to make extra money, as Baily learned on his arrival at one point along the Cumberland River. Forced to hire the intractable farmer whose property stood on the banks to carry him across, he complained that "to the advantage of cultivating his own plantation, he unites the profits of the ferry."[180] Benjamin Prater, whose farm was similarly situated on the Tennessee River, made the best of his location. He put up travelers in his house and transported them across the river on "Prater's Ferry."[181]

Farmers capitalized on special skills to turn a profit. Isreal Woolsey of Greene County and John Bond of Williamson County operated blacksmith shops in addition to running their farms.[182] In their spare time, Robertson County farmer Benjamin Elliot built cabinets and caskets, and Union County farmer William Kelly built furniture.[183] William Aydelott, whose family operated a small farm in Maury County, noted that his "father worked on farm and did carpentering at times for neighbors."[184] Edward Anderson's family made woolen and beaverskin hats on their Sullivan County farm, and an anonymous Knox County resident advertised that he would tan and curry leather on his farm.[185] Even though cities and smaller commercial centers provided many of these services, sparsely settled rural neighborhoods always seemed to have a need for them.

Tennesseans' fondness for alcoholic beverages created yet another avenue to extra cash. François André Michaux spent the night with a General Smith, who lodged travelers in his house just east of Nashville. "The General," he wrote in his journal, "has a beautiful planta-

Table 4.5

Commercial Production, 1840–60

	1840	1850	1860
Cotton	27,701	77,813	118,586
Tobacco	29,550	20,149	43,448
Wheat	4,570	1,619	5,459
Swine	2,927	3,105	2,347
Wool	1,060	1,364	1,405
Silk	1,217	1,923	71

SOURCE: Federal Agricultural Censuses, 1840–60.
NOTE: Cotton, tobacco, and wool measured in thousands of pounds, wheat in thousands of bushels, swine in thousands, and silk in pounds of cocoons; crop production from previous year.

tion cultivated in Indian wheat [corn] and cotton; he has also a neat distillery for peach brandy, which he sells at five shillings per gallon."[186] In Meigs County, John Stewart ran a commercial distillery on his farm property. The owner of a plantation must have thought that its distillery was an attractive resource, for he highlighted this feature of the property in the advertisement offering it for sale.[187] Alexander Cartwright purchased a farm in Davidson County as much for its distillery as for its land. "The product of my distillery," he recalled, "was a good article of sour mash copper boiled distilled whiskey which I sold only by the barrel in the Nashville market at 25 cts pr gallon, rarely higher." Perhaps he should have considered raising the price, for his product failed to return a profit. He eventually "sold the still and was glad to get out of the business."[188]

Antebellum Tennessee farmers saw in agriculture enormous commercial potential. For them farming was, at least in part, a business offering a variety of profitable opportunities. Farmers were imaginative and exhaustive in searching out and exploiting those opportunities. Each farmer found a combination of products and services that best suited his particular circumstances and objectives. This required adjusting his production to the topographical and climatic conditions of his area, to the size and nature of his farming operations, and to the goals and aspirations of his family. Table 4.5 reflects a significant and growing involvement in commercial agriculture in the last two decades of the antebellum period. It reveals sharp increases in the production of cotton and tobacco, substantial production of wheat and swine, and steady production of wool. Silk production, had it not encountered the destructive effects of an unknown disease, would undoubtedly have continued to expand in commercial importance. In addition to these major profit makers, farmers also sold on a smaller scale such commodities as beef cattle, dairy products, and hemp, and provided a variety of services.

Virtually all farmers participated at some level in the pursuit of profitable ventures. They understood that to realize their ambition to improve their own material well-being and that of their offspring required involvement in a commercial world beyond the farm. Though their success varied widely, they shared a commitment to the business of farming.

5

The Commercial Network

Participation in the market meant more than merely producing goods and supplying services for sale off the farm. Farmers also had to become involved in an extensive commercial network with a complex assortment of functions and relationships. They depended on the services of a wide array of intermediaries: merchants to sell and dealers to buy their products, agents to transport them to market, bankers and others to provide financing, and media to supply vital information. Such a network would in time be identified as agriculture's "commercial infrastructure"; to the antebellum farmer it was simply a collection of people with whom he had to deal, directly or indirectly, as part of his involvement in the market.

Commodity dealers and merchants provided a crucial link in the commercial chain connecting farmers and the consumers of their products. They were normally the first to handle agricultural goods as they made their way through the market system.[1] Their services were vital to both farmers and those who purchased the farmers' products. Many established their businesses in the state's major marketing centers of Knoxville, Chattanooga, Nashville, Clarksville, and Memphis; others in smaller regional centers, such as Jonesborough, Tullahoma, and Jackson.

Farmers usually had several options when they took their products to market. First of all, they might sell them outright in one of the state's commodity centers. Dealers in the major centers—less often in the smaller regional centers—purchased cotton, tobacco, grain, and other commodities for resale in markets along the Atlantic and Gulf Coasts and in Europe. Montgomery County farmer John Barker apparently elected this option. Each year throughout the 1840s and 1850s he sold his tobacco crop to the same buyer in Clarksville. "Sold my crop Tob to Dunlop for $3.50 per 100," he entered into his diary late in 1845. Three years later he "sold several thousand lbs of tobacco to Dunlop." Toward the end of 1858 he "finished delivering Tob crop 40292 lbs to

Dunlop."[2] Wiley Bagwell, who also farmed in Montgomery County, sold his tobacco over several years to Clarksville agent H. F. Beaumont.[3] One year Madison County farmer Robert Cartmell, who normally shipped his cotton to more distant markets, decided to sell some of the crop to the ginhouse in nearby Jackson.[4] Newspapers regularly carried advertisements to buy produce. A Clarksville dealer offered to purchase tobacco delivered to a landing on the Cumberland River; a Nashville dealer to purchase tobacco and cotton brought to his warehouse.[5] Some buyers came to the farms. "Dunlop came to see my tob," Barker recorded on one occasion.[6] He was still responsible, however, for delivering the produce to Dunlop's warehouse.

The advantage to farmers of selling directly was that they normally received full payment at the time or soon after delivery of the produce. The disadvantage was that the price was lower than the goods would have brought in other markets. The dealer had to discount the prices he paid in order to cover the costs of handling and the risks of reselling in a market whose prices fluctuated weekly. John Park, a merchant in Memphis, tried to allay concerns about the differential between what he offered and what farmers might receive in the coastal markets by assuring customers that he paid the "highest price the New Orleans or European markets will justify."[7] Still, if farmers preferred the convenience and certainty of immediate sale, they had to accept a discounted price in payment for it.

Tobacco growers in Middle Tennessee had another option. Clarksville ran an international tobacco market, drawing buyers from throughout the United States and Europe to its annual sales. Warehouse auctions began in late January and continued for six to eight weeks. One of the locations, S. A. Sawyer's warehouse, announced in 1851 that its sales would commence on 21 January and be held every Tuesday and Friday throughout the season.[8] Bagwell at least tested this venue for disposing of his crop. In early 1846 he recorded in his diary that his tobacco had sold at auction for an "avrage of $3.25/100."[9] Putting tobacco up for auction guaranteed competitive bidding among buyers; one need not accept the local dealer's assurance that the price he offered was fair. But the price the farmer received was probably lower than he could expect in the larger, if less certain, coastal markets.

Another option open to farmers was to hire a local commission merchant to sell their produce in one of the coastal centers. The merchants stored the goods, arranged for shipment, obtained insurance on the cargo, and found buyers. Those in Middle and West Tennessee dealt almost exclusively in the New Orleans market; those in East Tennessee, in the New Orleans and Atlantic coast markets. They received a percentage, usually 8 to 10 percent, of the selling price of the produce. Throughout the year newspapers in the major centers carried advertisements for commission merchants. Often they gave farmers a choice. A Nashville dealer announced that he would either buy cotton and tobacco or ship the goods on commission to New Orleans "for the best price." Another would arrange to sell merchandise at local auction or send it on to New Orleans.[10] H. F. Beaumont, to whom Wiley Bagwell often sold his tobacco, and S. A. Sawyer, at whose warehouse annual tobacco auctions occurred, also acted as commission merchants for farmers in the Clarksville area who elected to sell their tobacco in New Orleans.[11]

The competition among commission merchants for the farmers' business appears to have been brisk. Their advertisements held out inducements to entice producers to deal with them. Agents who represented large houses in the coastal markets often offered cash advances.[12] The Clarksville agent of Wingfield, Trice, & Co. of New Orleans provided "liberal cash advances on produce." Beaumont, who also worked as an agent for a New Orleans firm, advertised "cash advances and other facilities afforded to parties shipping to the above house, by H. F. Beaumont, Agent."[13] N. Anderson & Son in Memphis, a bit more cautious perhaps, gave cash advances only "when amply covered by produce in hand."[14] Facilities for storing produce before shipment provided another inducement. A Nashville merchant assured farmers that he had an "abundance of space," and several others touted their fireproof warehouses.[15] Easy access could also attract business. An agent at Lindwood Landing on the Cumberland River near Clarksville claimed to be located on "one of the best Turnpike Roads in the state."[16]

Quality of service was probably the farmers' chief criterion for selecting a commission merchant, as dealers well understood. When a new agent bought out S. A. Sawyer's business in Clarksville, he reassured potential customers: "Planters who may entrust me with their Tobacco either for sale at auction or for shipment, may rely upon my prompt and strict attention to its disposition."[17] "One of our firm," promised an independent agent, "will go to New Orleans at the opening of the business season there, and will remain for the purpose of superintending the inspection and sales of all produce sent to him by our house in Clarksville."[18] A Memphis commission merchant believed that good service included advising farmers to employ proper ginning and baling procedures for their cotton, for "upon that depends its bringing the best market price."[19] The Nashville representative of a Baltimore firm included a list of references in his advertisement.[20] Sometimes the message was more subtle. Independent agents emphasized their local connections and commitment to the community, implying that area farmers could trust them to represent their interests. Agents of outside firms emphasized their preferential access to a wide array of facilities and services in the coastal markets.[21]

Farmers occasionally arranged on their own to send merchandise to the coastal markets, where they hired an agent to manage the sales. As this practice bypassed the interior commission merchant, it usually enabled them to reduce handling costs by seeking out the least expensive suppliers. But most farmers had neither the time nor the business connections to book the shipping, purchase the river and fire insurance, and arrange for sale of their goods in the coastal markets. Moreover, they were vulnerable to fraud and dishonesty at each stage of the transaction.[22]

A few tobacco or cotton farmers operated on a scale large enough to justify such an approach. For two decades, George Washington shipped his tobacco directly to a New Orleans agent. A shrewd businessman, Washington doubtlessly calculated that the practice benefited him financially. But the cost in time and inconvenience was considerable. Despite regular communication by mail with his New Orleans agent, misunderstandings seemed unavoidable. Moreover, Washington had to settle up for freight, insurance, drayage, inspection, cooperage, and weighing charges in New Orleans from his Robertson County farm. One year, perhaps out of frustration over trading at long distance, he tried dealing with a local commission merchant in Clarksville, but he returned to his New Orleans agent the following year.[23]

Farmers situated near a river landing sometimes found direct shipment to their advantage, particularly if they were some distance from a market center. After sending his cotton by flatboat to Memphis in 1854, Madison County farmer Robert Cartmell decided to "sell 16 bales of it in Memphis; balance 30 bales reship from Memphis to N Orleans."[24] Herndon Haraldson had access to a steamboat landing directly from his Hardeman County farm, which he used to send goods to market. One day in 1845 he "finished ginning 5 bales cotton"; the following day he "haled the 5 bales cotton to the River for the Steamboat."[25]

Whatever selling scheme farmers chose, their products required transportation to market. In an early day when no alternatives existed and hauling distances were relatively short, roads served this purpose. Several years before his better known son, François André Michaux, toured the state in 1802, André Michaux learned on a similar visit that Jonesborough merchants in northeastern Tennessee traded by land route with Philadelphia.[26] Gilbert Imlay reported in 1796 that a road had been cut across the Cumberland plateau connecting the eastern valleys and the central basin, over which "passed . . . 30 or 40 waggons in the fall."[27] A few years later, François André Michaux claimed the same road was "as broad and commodious as those in the environs of Philadelphia."[28]

In 1836 the state government began subsidizing road construction.[29] The program concentrated on local and regional networks, with Middle Tennessee the principal beneficiary, that facilitated the transport of products from the farms to trade centers in the state. In time those trade centers gained road access to markets outside of Tennessee.[30] Reasonably good wagon roads linked Knoxville with Baltimore, Philadelphia, and other Atlantic ports. A report on agriculture in the 1840s noted that "there are also wagons from every part of East Tennessee sent to Augusta [Georgia] with bacon, lard, flour, feathers, &c."[31] The land routes were extensive enough to convince a commission house in Lynchburg, Virginia, to set up agents in several East Tennessee towns in the 1840s to sell the area's farm products on the Atlantic coast.[32] In Middle Tennessee, roads linked Nashville with Louisville and Lexington, Kentucky, to the north, and Natchez, Mississippi, to the south. The latter road was the famous Natchez Trace, which François André Michaux, in 1802, described as "only a path that serpentined through these boundless forests."[33] By the 1830s, state and federal improvements had converted it into a thoroughfare of major commercial importance.

Notwithstanding the expansion and improvement of the road system, the success of Tennessee's commercial agriculture depended on the development of water transportation. The state was well endowed with natural waterways, something on which virtually every early visitor commented. Gilbert Imlay, who crossed the Tennessee territory in 1792, reported that vessels of forty to fifty tons could negotiate the Tennessee River, with the exception of a stretch in the vicinity of Muscle Shoals, from its mouth on the Ohio River to the Virginia state line.[34] François André Michaux concurred in this assessment, commenting that the

"Tennessea [River] . . . has, in the whole, a navigable course for near eight hundred miles: but this navigation is interrupted six months in the year by muscle shoals."[35] Vessels of similar size could navigate the Cumberland River from its outlet into the Ohio River all the way to Nashville. The river above Nashville and most of its tributaries could accommodate boats of smaller size. On a trip through the central basin in 1806, Thomas Ashe observed that the "Cumberland is a very gentle stream, navigable for loaded batteaux about three hundred miles without interruption; then intervene some rapids of fifteen miles in length, after which it is again navigable for seventy miles upwards, which is within two miles of the great Cumberland Mountains."[36] Francis Baily gave a similar account of the Cumberland: "It is navigable upwards of 200 miles from its mouth; that is, in large vessels to Nashville, and thence in boats to the mouth of Obed's river."[37] Imlay noted that five navigable rivers flowed across West Tennessee, emptying eventually into the Mississippi River. He concluded that "the whole country is well intersected by rivers; and most of those rivers are navigable by large boats; some of them by ships."[38]

Tennessee's settlers lost little time in taking advantage of the natural waterways. Nashville resident Martin Martin participated in the first organized effort to use the Cumberland and Mississippi rivers to carry produce to market. "It is not surprising to learn," he recorded in his account of the trip, "that it was 1789 before Middle Tennessee farmers as a group produced enough surplus farm produce to send a small convoy of flatboats down the Mississippi."[39] In 1793 Daniel Smith reported that settlers in the central basin used the river routes to reduce transportation costs: "Pork, flour, or the other produce, may be taken from Nashville to New-Orleans at less than three eighths of a dollar the bushel."[40] A decade later, François André Michaux observed a significant development in the state's riverine commerce. "When I was there [Nashville] in 1802," he wrote, "they made the first attempt to send cotton by the Ohio [River] to Pittsburgh, in order to be thence conveyed to the remote parts of Pennsylvania."[41] He found Knoxville residents similarly exploiting Tennessee's other great river: "They send flour, cotton, and lime to New Orleans by the river Tennessea."[42]

Flatboats, keelboats, and barges provided the water transport in the early days.[43] Michaux had seen this type of craft plying the Cumberland and Tennessee rivers. About the same time, operators began to advertise for freight to carry to New Orleans and other points on the Mississippi River.[44] Propelled downstream by current and upstream by staff, these vessels traveled slowly—twenty to thirty miles a day—but carried a sizable cargo and required only a few hands. Because of the difficulty of upstream navigation, owners of flatboats and barges often dismantled them once they reached their destination and sold the material for lumber. Lighter and better designed, keelboats negotiated the upstream passage with less effort, although they carried smaller payloads.[45]

In time the flatboats and keelboats gave way to more efficient steamboats on the major waterways, but they remained in use on remote or shallow streams throughout the state. A report in the 1840s on East Tennessee agriculture commented that flatboats on the tributaries of the Tennessee River routinely carried farm goods to Knoxville.[46] Tom Bryan remembered seeing them in commercial use as he grew up on a Middle Tennessee farm in the 1830s and 1840s. "They built flat boats at Portroyal and carried the produce to Neworleans," he recorded in his memoir. "The parties who owned the boat sometimes bought the produce and sometimes they taken the goods down and charged freight on them."[47] In the early 1820s, West Tennessean Herndon Haraldson wrote that on the "Forked Deer [River] there were three keel-boats at Alexander's landing . . . freighted with corn, bacon, etc."[48] Twenty years later, Solon Robinson, a northern journalist traveling in West Tennessee, observed traffic on the same river: "Out of this stream, the cotton from this region is sent in flat boats to the Mississippi."[49] Haraldson himself sent his produce to market on "Cotter's keelboat" in the 1830s, and Robert Cartmell still employed flatboats for transporting his cotton in the early 1850s.[50]

The central basin was the first area of the state to acquire regular steamboat service.[51] The *General Jackson*, engaged in trade on the Ohio and Mississippi rivers all the way to New Orleans, was the first steamboat to try to reach Nashville. After at least one aborted attempt in the spring of 1818, it finally succeeded, arriving in March of the following year.[52] Operators of the locally owned *Rifleman* announced in late 1819 that they were available to transport freight and passengers on a regular basis from Nashville to New Orleans. A year later the *General Robertson* joined the competition.[53] By the end of the 1820s several lines provided weekly or semiweekly service between Nashville and New Orleans during the shipping season. One company advertised that its steamboat "will leave for New Orleans on the first rise of the Cumberland river, and will run as a regular packet between Nashville, Clarksville, and

New Orleans, during the season."[54] The majority of the lines operated between Nashville and New Orleans. "THE NEW ORLEANS & NASHVILLE TRADE, . . . and all intermediate landings on the Mississippi, Ohio, Cumberland," read one advertisement.[55] Some lines served ports eastward on the Ohio River, such as Cincinnati and Pittsburgh. Nashville's superior steamboat connections enabled the city to become the principal center for the shipment of Middle Tennessee farm products. "From Nashville and Clarksville," *De Bow's Review* reported in 1846, "there passes on the Cumberland annually . . . 50,000 bags of cotton, and 12,000 hogsheads of tobacco."[56]

The Cumberland River, as early travelers had reported, was navigable throughout most of the year for some distance above Nashville, a natural advantage on which government projects improved in the 1830s.[57] Its tributaries, often shallow and obstructed by shoals, could easily accommodate small vessels like flatboats, but were far less suitable for steamboats. The Stone's and Harpeth rivers were typical of the secondary streams in that steamboat traffic depended on weather conditions that occurred infrequently.[58] A similar situation prevailed on the tributaries of the Tennessee River that reached into Middle Tennessee. Not until the spring of 1839, for instance, did a steamboat reach Columbia, and then only because heavy rains raised the water in the Duck River to unusually high levels.[59] As a result, steamboat service on those streams was at best irregular and always uncertain. Farmers, commodity dealers, and commission merchants in this part of Tennessee without access to the Cumberland River had to depend on flatboats or wagons to deliver their merchandise to Nashville or some other market center.[60]

East Tennessee suffered from navigational problems as well. The obstructions on the Tennessee River at Muscle Shoals severely inhibited steamboat traffic. It was 1828 before a vessel successfully negotiated its treacherous channel all the way upstream to Knoxville. Before then, East Tennessee shippers either sent farm produce destined for New Orleans overland to Nashville, from whence steamboats carried it to market, or floated it downriver on flatboats during periods of high water. In the 1830s regular steamboat service was established between Knoxville and Muscle Shoals, and between Muscle Shoals and New Orleans, with cargoes ferried around the obstructions.[61] Knoxville lines customarily operated only on their side of the shoals; other lines picked up the cargoes beyond the shoals.[62] River improvement projects funded by the federal and state governments eventually cleared away some of the worst obstacles, allowing uninterrupted trips to New Orleans for part of the year. One Knoxville firm advertised in 1841 that its steamboat "is designed expressly for the New Orleans and Tennessee River trade and will run regularly."[63] A report on East Tennessee in the 1840s could state that "steam boats are sent for several months of the year from Knoxville to New Orleans, taking the produce of the country."[64] Still, East Tennessee never achieved the level of service enjoyed by Middle Tennessee.

In West Tennessee, Memphis was ideally situated to provide steamboat service. Steamboats had plied the Mississippi River since 1811, and, by the time this region began to send farm goods to market, the river already supported substantial traffic. Memphis simply tied into that traffic, establishing its first steamboat line in 1834.[65] The number of lines rapidly proliferated. By the 1850s, steamboats provided regular runs year around to New Orleans and, except when prevented by cold weather, to Ohio River ports, making Memphis the principal marketing outlet for West Tennessee's agricultural produce.[66]

Some of the West Tennessee streams flowing into the Mississippi River supported limited steamboat traffic. Vessels reached Bolivar on the Hatchie River and Jackson on the Forked Deer River. On his trip through West Tennessee in 1845, Solon Robinson noted that the Hatchie River was deep enough to accommodate steamboats for some distance upstream.[67] Herndon Haraldson, as mentioned, had access to a steamboat landing on the Forked Deer River by the mid-1840s.[68] Still, the service on these tributaries failed to meet the expanding needs of farmers in the interior. Like their counterparts on the Cumberland River tributaries, they too relied primarily on flatboats and wagons to carry their products to market locations.[69]

Toward the end of the antebellum period, railroads gave shippers in some areas yet another mode of transportation. Chattanooga, in 1850, became the first Tennessee market center to acquire rail connections outside of the state. The Western and Atlantic Railroad linked the city to south Atlantic ports by way of Atlanta. Four years later, Middle Tennessee gained rail access to the Atlantic coast with the completion of the Nashville and Chattanooga Railroad. The Memphis and Chattanooga line tied West Tennessee into the southeastern coastal system in 1857. Knoxville acquired similar connections when the East Tennessee and Georgia Railroad was completed to Chattanooga the following year. The same year, the East Tennessee and Virginia line gave the city a north-

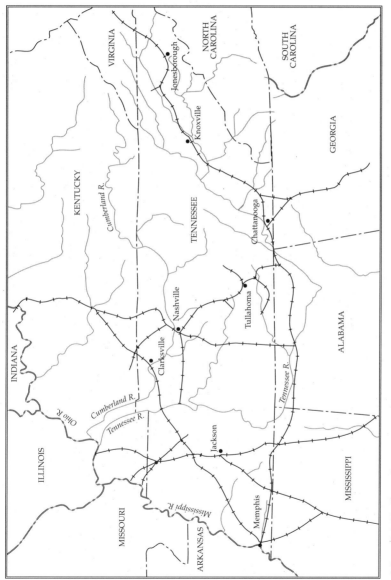

Map 5.1. Railroads, 1861. Source: Corlew, *Tennessee*, 204.

ern route to the Atlantic coast through Richmond, Virginia. Nashville and Memphis also procured rail links to Louisville and to New Orleans and Mobile, respectively.[70] By the outbreak of the Civil War in 1861, Tennessee, as map 5.1 shows, was participating in a fairly extensive railroad network.

The flurry of railroad building in the 1850s had several results. It reduced transportation costs and expanded markets, especially for areas in East Tennessee that had heretofore sent their goods to the Atlantic coast by road. Jonesborough, in extreme northeastern Tennessee, experienced a significant increase in agricultural trade after completion of the East Tennessee and Virginia Railroad.[71] Other communities in the eastern valleys received similar benefits from rail access to the south Atlantic coast. The *Farmer and Mechanic* observed with satisfaction that East Tennessee "now . . . has a railway communication with Charleston and Savannah, and can send its wheat direct to Atlantic ports, from whence it may be shipped direct to Europe."[72]

Railroads also gave Tennesseans broader market options. Farm goods that Nashville and Memphis had routinely sent to New Orleans by river could now be sent to the east coast by rail.[73] In the late 1850s, for instance, rail service diverted much Middle Tennessee grain to more lucrative markets on the Atlantic.[74] Farmers also used railroads for transporting their goods within the state. Joseph White sent produce from Jefferson County, where his farm was located, to Knoxville on the East Tennessee and Georgia Railroad.[75] In West Tennessee, Robert Dew remembered as a boy on a farm in Weakley County "hauling tobacco to Crockett Station on the Mobile and Ohio Railroad, our nearest shipping point."[76] Madison County farmer Robert Cartmell, who earlier had sent his cotton to market by flatboat, now hauled it to a railhead in neighboring Fayette County for shipment to Memphis. Farmers in his area were understandably pleased when they finally received rail connections to the outside. Some four thousand of them attended a ceremony in Sommerville in 1857 "devoted to celebrating the arrival of the cars on the Mississippi central & Tennessee railroad."[77]

Railroads vigorously competed for the agricultural commodities business. They regularly published their rate schedules in the newspapers. The Nashville and Chattanooga Railroad offered rate reductions on flour. The Memphis and Chattanooga Railroad promised "fast freight arrangement" for farm goods sent from Memphis to Charleston and Savannah. Toward the end of the 1850s, railroad advertisements appeared in the Memphis newspaper for shipping cotton to New Orleans and Mobile.[78] Advantages in some markets, coupled with aggressive advertising and promotions, enabled railroads to make inroads into the river-borne trade. But on the eve of the Civil War, steamboats remained the predominant means of transporting Tennessee agricultural products to distant markets.

If the antebellum marketing and transportation systems served Tennessee farmers reasonably well, the same can not be said of financial institutions. Commercial agriculture, except at the barter level, required a dependable medium of exchange. To complete their sales, farmers needed either circulating currency or a system of money accounts among which transfers could be made. Moreover, they depended on access to credit for marketing transactions, living and operating expenses, and the purchase of land and slaves. Mechanisms emerged in response to the farmers' financial needs, but they were not entirely satisfactory.

A shortage of specie plagued Tennessee farmers, as it did most other rural residents in the United States during the antebellum period. Gold and silver coins minted by the federal government were extremely scarce. François André Michaux recognized the situation in 1802: "I am persuaded that not one in ten of them [farmers] are in possession of a single dollar." He approved of the Tennessee legislature's encouragement of domestic cotton cloth manufacturing as "the only means of preserving the little specie that is in the country, and of preventing its going to England."[79] The scarcity created a market in specie, with holders of coin offering to sell to the highest bidders.[80] One farmer was clearly in difficult circumstances when he appealed for specie in the local newspaper: "Money. Wm Reasons wants money to pay his taxes, and he has cotton to give for it."[81]

The legislature sought to increase the amount of circulating currency by authorizing the creation of note-issuing banks. In 1807 it chartered the state's first commercial bank, a privately owned institution located in Nashville. Four years later, it chartered another bank in Knoxville.[82] The economic boom following the end the of War of 1812 persuaded legislators to approve thirteen more privately owned banks scattered throughout the state. With the inability of all save one—the Knoxville bank—to continue redemption of their notes after the Panic of 1819, legislators created the Bank of Tennessee, a state owned institution located in Nashville with a branch in Knoxville. This bank operated throughout the 1820s, but it too encountered problems and ceased operations in 1832. The legislature subsequently chartered several more privately owned banks, including two in Nashville and one in Memphis.[83] By the 1840s, more than forty privately owned charter banks were operating in Tennessee.[84] In 1838, the legislature established the second state owned bank, which remained open up to the Civil War.[85] Until its charter ran out in 1836, the Second Bank of the United States maintained a branch in Nashville.

Because of the inadequate supply of specie, farmers had to resort to bank notes for their commercial transactions. A variety of notes were available to them, including those issued by Tennessee banks, by banks chartered in other states, and by the First and Second United States banks. Dealing in paper money involved varying degrees of risk. As long as a bank redeemed its notes on demand at face value, they circulated at little or no discount. If a bank suspended redemption because of unsound practices or poor economic conditions, a frequent occurrence during the antebellum period, its paper money was severely discounted or even refused in commercial transactions. The notes of failed banks were, of course, worthless.

It was often difficult or even impossible to ascertain the market value of bank notes. Notes issued by the United States banks were always sound. Even during the Panic of 1819, when many state chartered banks were failing or suspending redemption of their notes, the currency of the Second Bank of the United States carried an insignificant discount of .5 percent in the state. Paper money from banks located outside the state was far more precarious. In the midst of the economic instability of 1819, for instance, notes on the Union Bank of Philadelphia circulated at 50 percent below their face value.[86] A short while earlier, the Bank of St. Louis was obviously trying to restore confidence in its notes with a reassuring notice in the Clarksville newspaper: "The public mind having become tranquilized, the bank of St. Louis opened for business on Tuesday last, redeemed its paper in specie; and the public is hereby notified, that it will continue to redeem its paper in specie on presentation."[87] Commercial farmers understood that dealing in notes of out-of-state banks could be risky.

Accepting notes issued by Tennessee banks involved uncertainty as well. Herndon Haraldson heard a report in the midst of the Panic of 1837 that Union Bank of Nashville had suspended payment on its notes, which seemed confirmed when he inscribed in his diary "Union Bank paper refused." A short time later he learned that the report was false, entering for that day: "Alarm for nothing."[88] As it turned out, the report was only premature. Two years later Union Bank and several other Tennessee banks did suspend specie payments, seriously depressing the value of their notes.[89] Maury County farmer James Houston thought that resurrecting the national bank was the solution to the farmers' problems with state bank notes. "I have some hope of [William Henry] Harrison being elected," he wrote to family members in 1840, "and that a bank will be made that will force the state paper out of circulation or make it sound."[90] Harrison was elected, but the problems persisted, only to reach crisis level again in the 1850s. Robert Cartmell recorded the onset of the Panic of 1857 in Tennessee with a entry in his diary that "banks have generally suspended."[91] James Matthews complained the following year when he received in payment "$8.75 two of which is not at par so I returned them."[92] The editor of the *Southern Agriculturist* understood the predicament many of his Tennessee readers faced. He requested that those in arrears in paying subscription fees "please forward their money by mail, in the best bills they can obtain."[93]

Discounted or worthless bank notes were not the farmers' only concern about money; counterfeiting also caused apprehension. The *Knoxville Gazette* warned readers in the 1790s of bogus notes on the First Bank of the United States and of bogus dollar coins.[94] Some years later, a skillful swindler altered money issued by the Bank of Yeatman, changing one dollar bills into one hundred dollar bills "in a manner calculated to deceive the best judges."[95] At another time, farmers in the Clarksville area had to be on guard for counterfeit ten dollar bills bearing the name of the Bank of Louisville.[96] The problem was common enough by the 1840s that the *Memphis Appeal* ran a weekly column describing bogus bills on banks in the Southeast and Midwest that might be circulating in Tennessee.[97]

Farmers could sometimes avoid the need for paper money by dealing in checks or bank drafts. Herndon Haraldson "recd a return on sale of our cotton with a check on the Bank [of] Philadelphia." Such instruments were readily negotiable if they were drawn on banks with sound reputations, as Haraldson's transactions illustrate. The next day he "indorsed the check to David Hexter merct Browns[ville] for $92."[98] Robertson County farmer George Washington regularly settled his accounts by transferring checks and drafts among banks in New Orleans, New York City, and Philadelphia.[99] The use of checks or drafts, however, was normally an option only for direct sales in distant markets. Farmers selling their produce to local dealers, at local auctions, or through commission merchants rarely received them.

Obtaining credit could present problems. Banks rarely made loans for the purchase of household goods. Local merchants and craftsmen, therefore, usually carried accounts for the supplies and services farmers bought throughout the year.[100] The common practice among farmers was to pay off or pay down those debts on the sale of crops or livestock. But not everyone adhered to the practice, and merchants sometimes had to plead for payment. One desperate Knoxville store owner published a demand for payment to those indebted to him, agreeing to accept cattle in lieu of cash.[101] Another firm took a different tack when it declared Christmas Day 1824 the deadline for settlement of overdue accounts: "Pay Your Debts / All those having accounts with Cozier & Barton, by book account or note, will MAKE PAYMENT by the 25th December."[102] Cozier & Barton left unspecified the fate of debtors failing to meet the deadline. Delinquent accounts forced J. Sommerville of Knoxville to abandon his practice of selling on time; he announced in early 1792 that from then on his was a "Money Store (Where no credit whatever will be given)."[103] Although few merchants could afford to go to this extreme, many became more cautious and more selective as uncollected debts mounted. Still, farmers who preserved a reputation for paying their bills in a timely manner normally had little difficulty securing store credit.

Bank credit for other purposes might also be difficult to obtain. Well-established farmers with ample assets could as a rule secure short- and intermediate-term credit on their own signature. Others required endorsements or were turned down altogether. George Washington sometimes cosigned for bank loans to friends or neighbors, as in the case of "William . . . [who came] here to get my Endorsement to a note for $680 which I gave him."[104] James Matthews "indorsed a note for C. H. Davis in bank."[105] Robert Cartmell found his banker uncooperative when he requested seven hundred dollars to pay for a slave girl he had purchased. "I could only raise $350.00," he fumed. "The Bank wont discount a cent."[106] He applied for the loan as the state was beginning to feel the effects of the Panic of 1857. Had he made the request at a time when the economy was sounder, he might have received a more favorable response.

Farmers developed an informal system under which they extended credit to each other as a supplement to inadequate bank credit. James

Matthews, on one occasion, "supped at A. H. Davis, we adjusted our debts, he gave me due bill for $25.40."[107] These arrangements usually involved delayed payment on the purchase of some asset. The seller of the slave girl Cartmell had bought eventually agreed to accept the $350 the bank would loan him and a note for the balance.[108] Wiley Bagwell consented to a similar arrangement on the sale of a slave woman and her child. Late one spring, a time when farmers were likely to be short of cash, he "sold them . . . on a credit until Christmas for $600."[109] Sometimes, though, the transactions were outright cash loans, as when Washington "let him [Mr. Ogg] have $200/00 & took his note for same."[110] Farmers occasionally extended credit to local merchants by accepting notes in payment for farm commodities. Cartmell sold a load of cotton at the ginhouse in Jackson in February 1856, for which he received "$600.00 down—balance in good notes payable 25th Dec next."[111] Bagwell "let moore & Broaddus have $507.12 for which I took their note to be paid when called."[112] The diary entry is curious because Bagwell ran an account of his own with Moore & Broaddus, a general store in Clarksville. Because the transaction occurred in January, around the time Bagwell normally settled his accounts, the "loan" probably represented a credit against which he drew for purchases later on in the year.

Ad hoc transactions could run into problems. On reconsideration, Cartmell apparently decided that the arrangement with the Jackson ginhouse on the sale of his cotton was overly generous. "The notes ought to have been due now and drawing interest," he protested shortly after agreeing to the conditions.[113] "Dr. Lockert has not paid my note," groused Washington. "I think it likely I shall have some trouble getting the money." "Samuel Watson here yesterday & I paid him a bill I had paid before," he grumbled on another occasion.[114]

Banks almost always refused to extend the long-term credit necessary for the purchase of land. Early settlers in need of credit normally obtained financing from the speculators who sold them their property. Subsequent land transfers often depended on informal arrangements. Parents customarily extended credit to offspring for purchase of the family farm. Cartmell decided to use money from the sale of his cotton to the Jackson ginhouse to reduce a mortgage debt to his father: "The notes which I'll get I will pay over to my Father as I owe him $1500 for the land I live on." Earlier Cartmell had added to the holdings he had bought from his father, and the seller agreed to payments over a period of two years.[115] When Washington considered purchasing land from a neighbor, he had two options: "His price is $14,000 in cash or 15000 on time."[116] Montgomery County farmer John Barker was obviously relieved when he "sent . . . $1014.50 to pay off my note to J. C. Bryan for land."[117] Wiley Bagwell was probably equally relieved to receive final payment on land he had sold on time to a neighbor.[118]

The informal credit system that evolved among farmers, merchants, and craftsmen was in many respects inefficient and certainly fell short of the needs of rural Tennesseans in the antebellum period. But it was a necessary expedient. Scarce specie, undependable bank notes, stringent bank credit, and intermittent economic downturns placed constraints on business transactions. Ad hoc arrangements might not have been entirely satisfactory, but they allowed the agricultural economy to function despite a number of institutional problems.

The commercial network in which Tennessee farmers operated also offered them a broad spectrum of information. Newspapers and agricultural journals published commercial data, analyses of supply and demand, and financial advice. Their purpose was to enable farmers to make informed and timely business decisions. It was a tacit recognition that information was vital to successful participation in a market economy.

The most basic and useful information related to prices. Shortly after the turn of the century, Nashville's *Tennessee Gazette* began printing a list of commodity prices at Natchez.[119] Within a short while, newspapers in all of the state's principal market centers included such information. They normally gave prices offered in their local market and in the major outside markets, such as New Orleans, St. Louis, Cincinnati, and New York City. In time they began including prices of some commodities in the foreign markets. For instance, offerings in Liverpool for cotton or in Amsterdam for tobacco often appeared. The Clarksville newspapers were especially thorough. In addition to publishing tobacco prices at outside centers, they included detailed information on sales at each of the local warehouses during the auction season.[120] Agricultural magazines sometimes provided price information in their monthly or biweekly editions.[121]

Newspapers printed regular columns on the value of state and national bank notes. They gave the discounts and premiums offered on the principal notes available in the local economy. Knoxville's *Argus and Commercial Herald* went beyond most newspapers with the inclusion of quotations on gold and silver and on federal securities.[122] A few newspapers gave similar information on the New Orleans and north-eastern money markets.

Some newspapers offered economic analyses and advice. "TOBACCO, is coming in slowly with but slight demand," read a typical account in the *Clarksville Jeffersonian.* "Late accounts from London and Liverpool represent dull market, but no disposition on part of holders to take lower prices."[123] On another occasion, the newspaper advised "farmers to hold on to their crops, for they are sure of an increased price by doing so." The newspaper was open to dissenting views, as a letter to the editor criticizing this advice indicated: "[The farmer] certainly should not hold too long, if he wishes to do the very best with his crop."[124] The *Memphis Appeal* surveyed the commodities trade and recorded ship arrivals and departures at New Orleans on a weekly basis. The newspaper carried elaborate information on the cotton market. One article, for instance, evaluated anticipated supply and demand among the different grades of cotton. Another reported on the amount and types of agricultural goods received in New Orleans.[125] During the growing season, the *Nashville Gazette* regularly published articles on the condition of crops in Middle Tennessee and on their commercial prospects. It, too, assessed the situation in the New Orleans market, especially as it related to cotton and tobacco.[126] Farm journals, which tended to focus on production rather than marketing questions, occasionally offered commercial advice. The *Southern Cultivator* reported on the surplus wheat crop in 1839, assuring readers that it would stay abreast of the situation: "We will take pleasure in giving in due time everything in our reach that will aid in making a profitable disposition of the present crop, which it seems will be over abundant." It failed to keep its promise.[127]

How much Tennessee farmers availed themselves of this information is uncertain. First of all, it is impossible to know what portion of the state's farmers subscribed to newspapers and journals. References to paying subscription fees indicate that most of those who left diaries received a newspaper and perhaps an agricultural magazine. That they left written records, however, suggests that they were more literate than the rural population in general and therefore more likely to obtain sources of useful information. Likewise, the degree to which those with access to such information used it for making business decisions is impossible to determine. Diary writers were certainly knowledgeable about commercial matters and apparently inclined to employ published accounts as a guide to market activity. But again, they were hardly typical of all farmers. Perhaps the strongest evidence that many farmers tapped published accounts to inform their decisions was the proliferation of commercial information itself. Newspapers and magazines were clearly responding to a growing demand for the kind of data and advice that would enable farmers to operate effectively in the antebellum market system.

The comprehensive commercial network that emerged before the Civil War, though used for other purposes, addressed the needs primarily of Tennessee's farmers. It provided them a number of options for marketing their goods. For those who desired the convenience and assurance of immediate sale, local dealers or auctions provided an outlet. For those who preferred to gamble on a better price in the coastal markets, local commission merchants could arrange for the shipment and sale of their commodities. For those in a position to deal directly with the coastal markets, all of the facilities and services required to complete the transactions were readily available. Although sellers of nonagricultural commodities, such as lumber and lime, employed some of those same services, the overwhelming majority of goods that moved through the marketing system were farm products.

Transportation played a vital role in the commercial network. From the rough roads of the early years through the steamboats and railroads on the eve of the Civil War, Tennessee developed a system that served the agricultural sector well. Some farmers in remote sections of the state, to be sure, had access only to primitive road and flatboat facilities to carry their products to the nearest market center. But even they usually found participation in commercial production worthwhile. Those located closer to more efficient steamboat and railroad services found such participation that much more profitable. Transportation development was not confined to intrastate traffic. Tennessee acquired vital links to outside commercial centers, such as New Orleans and Mobile on the Gulf Coast, Charleston and Philadelphia on the Atlantic coast, and Cincinnati and Pittsburgh on the Ohio River. The transportation system carried other goods, as well as passengers, but its chief purpose was to connect the state's farmers with the most lucrative markets for their products.

Financial institutions were the weakest facet of the commercial network. Banks provided circulating currency, checks and drafts, and credit. But the bank notes were notoriously undependable, the checks and drafts were limited in availability, and the credit was inadequate. Farmers compensated in some cases by creating their own informal arrangements, but these failed to meet all of their needs. A more efficient financial system would doubtlessly have enhanced agricultural expansion and development.

Sources of market information completed the commercial network. Newspapers and agricultural journals offered a variety of information on prices, supply and demand, and market conditions. Farmers could, if they chose, take advantage of these publications to plan and implement their commercial strategies.

6

Acquiring Land

Land played an ambivalent role in the lives of antebellum Tennessee farmers. It was, on the one hand, a basic component of the agricultural system, an essential factor of production. To engage in farming the operator had to obtain access to this factor of production under some form of land tenure. It was, on the other hand, an almost sacred element of rural society, the acquisition of which was one of its core cultural values. Participation in what farmers referred to as a rural way of life rested on the ownership of land. The centrality of land to the lives of antebellum farmers ensured that it would occupy a crucial place in their beliefs, their aspirations, their plans, and their decisions. Rural Tennesseans devoted much of their time and energies to securing the use of land, to acquiring and expanding ownership of land, and to passing land on to the next generation of farmers.

Most farmers preferred ownership to alternative forms of land tenure, but for some it was not feasible or even possible. The principal impediment to ownership was cost. Land, which had been relatively inexpensive and plentiful in the early nineteenth century, increased in value as each region of the state moved from the pioneer to the mature stage of settlement. Land that sold earlier for two dollars or less an acre brought from two to thirty times that amount on the eve of the Civil War. The average value of land for the state in 1860 was about thirteen dollars per acre.[1] However, as map 6.1 illustrates, county averages varied enormously across Tennessee, depending on quality of soil, proportion of improved acreage, and proximity to transportation and cities. For instance, average land value in the central basin county of Davidson, in which Nashville was located, was about fifty-six dollars an acre, and in Shelby County, situated in southwestern Tennessee and containing the city of Memphis, about thirty dollars an acre. By contrast, the corresponding figures for East Tennessee's Morgan, Middle Tennessee's Fentress, and West Tennessee's Benton counties were below five dollars. A small farm of, say, forty acres ranged in value from a few hundred to several thousand dollars. Many aspiring farmers could not afford ownership of land at prices prevailing in the late antebellum period.

Tenancy offered an alternative that gave farmers the use of land without requiring them to purchase it. Speculators, farmers with land in excess of their needs, retired farmers, and widows were usually anxious to rent out land to tenants. Owners advertised their rental property through newspapers, agricultural journals, and neighborhood informational networks, such as churches, general stores, county courthouses, or word of mouth.[2] Families often rented out farms to brothers, sons, sons-in-law, and nephews.

Tenants and owners chose from several different forms of leasing arrangements. One form required renters to make improvements—clearing and breaking land, erecting fences, building structures—in return for the use of the farm. On his tour across Tennessee in the early nineteenth century, François André Michaux discovered that speculators were eager to rent out their land under such arrangements. It was a way, he noted, for them to attract settlers and improve property, which "speedily enhances the value of their possessions."[3] A few years later, the owner of 647 acres, only thirty of which were cleared, was following such a strategy when he advertised for a renter who would "engage to make improvements to a certain extent."[4] This form of tenancy was common during the early stage of settlement when much of the land was unimproved, but declined in importance as the agricultural sector matured. Still, it remained part of the land tenure system throughout the antebellum period.

Other leasing arrangements required the tenant to pay for the use of land in either kind or cash. Under share rent, the owner and the tenant divided the produce of the farm in some predetermined proportion, the owner usually receiving a third or a half. Maury County farmer James Matthews used a share arrangement to rent out some of his excess land. "I rent my bottom field (1/3 of the corn)," he recorded in his diary.[5] In East Tennessee, according to a report in the 1840s, "it is customary for the Proprietor to receive one-third the crop for the Uplands, and some of the River Bottom Lands; but on very superior River Bottom Lands, from one-third to one-half."[6] Another rental form required the tenant to pay a specific amount of cash for each acre. Rates varied with the productive potential of the land and the availability of commercial services. A letter to the editor of the *Agriculturist* indicated that

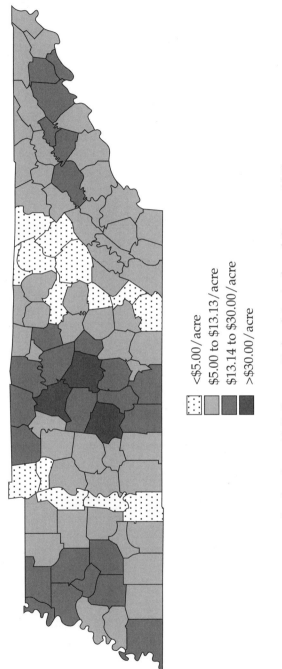

Map 6.1. Average county land values, 1860. Source: Federal Agricultural Census, 1860.

<$5.00/acre
$5.00 to $13.13/acre
$13.14 to $30.00/acre
>$30.00/acre

rental rates averaged about two dollars per acre in the early 1840s.[7] Samuel Alsbrook agreed "to pay George A. Washington on order one dollar and fifty cents per acre on the 25th day of December 1855 for the rent of all the cleared land."[8] Standing rent, used infrequently, called for the tenant to pay a prescribed amount of produce for the use of a piece of land. Herndon Haraldson employed such an arrangement when he "rented Purvis place to Fortune for 6 barrels of corn."[9] The report on East Tennessee agriculture noted that some owners "rent their River Bottom Lands at so many bushels of corn to the acre, without reference to the crop."[10]

It is impossible to know with certainty how many farmers had or chose to rent land in order to engage in agriculture. The pre–Civil War federal censuses failed to record information on tenancy. Frank L. Owsley and his students at Vanderbilt University devised a method, later refined by Allan G. Bogue, for estimating the percentage of landless farmers in the rural population from information on the manuscript censuses.[11] Applying a version of this method to the eight sample counties provides the estimated tenancy rates given in table 6.1.[12]

The figures indicate that tenancy was a common form of land tenure in antebellum Tennessee. The estimated rates for 1850 range from about 4 percent of farmers in Robertson County to 24 percent in Haywood County. Ten years later, they ran from 8 percent in Robertson County to just under 30 percent in Hardin County. For both years the rates for the eight counties combined were about 17 percent.[13] Although a large majority of farmers owned their land, a sizable portion rented land from others. By the 1850s, tenancy allowed about one in six farmers to engage in agricultural production without purchasing land. As early as 1825, tenancy was widely enough practiced to require state regulation to assist landowners in collecting rents. The legislature declared that the debt due for rent "shall be a lien on the crop growing or made on the rented premises, and shall receive precedence over all other debts of every description, till said debt for rent shall be discharged."[14]

If tenancy enabled farmers to obtain use of a necessary factor of agricultural production, it also gave them a vehicle for fulfilling one of rural society's cultural values. Some operators used their years as tenants to accumulate the savings necessary to buy a farm of their own. They were rarely able to accumulate funds to cover the entire purchase price, but they could often eventually set aside enough for the down payment. Tenancy also served as an educational institution through

Table 6.1

Percentage of Tenants by County, 1850 and 1860

County	1850	1860
Dekalb	21.8	15.7
Fayette	14.11	3.0
Franklin	21.5	24.3
Grainger	22.5	16.4
Hardin	15.8	29.2
Haywood	24.0	16.8
Johnson	10.3	13.5
Robertson	3.9	8.2
All counties	16.8	17.3

SOURCE: Eight sample counties (see appendix).

which landlord fathers or fathers-in-law passed on to tenant sons or sons-in-law the knowledge they would need to become independent farmers. Coupled with bequest, tenancy was one stage of a two-stage system for transferring control and ownership of family property from one generation to the next. Tenancy, then, provided a social mechanism through which farmers became landowners and thereby achieved a fundamental goal of rural society.[15]

That tenancy performed such functions is clearly shown in tables 6.2 and 6.3. In the eight sample counties, the average age for tenants was 5.6 years lower than for owners in 1850 and 7.6 years lower in 1860. A higher percentage of tenants than of owners fell into the under-forty age groups, and a higher percentage of owners than of tenants fell into the over-forty age groups. Moreover, the lower the age category, the higher the tenancy rate. In both 1850 and 1860, the rates for the under-forty groups were higher than the overall average. In 1850 the rate for the under-thirty group was nearly double the overall rate; in 1860 it was more than double. Age structures in the individual counties replicated those for the eight counties combined. In each county, tenants were on average younger than owners. Differences in average age between the two groups in 1850 ranged from 2.8 years in Robertson County to 9.3. years in Grainger County. Ten years later, they ranged from 3.7

Table 6.2

Percentage in Each Age Category and Average Ages for Tenants
and Owners, 1850 and 1860

Age Category	1850		1860	
	Tenants	Owners	Tenants	Owners
<30	29.6	14.1	33.3	12.8
30–39	31.3	27.8	30.2	26.5
40–49	19.3	26.5	18.4	26.8
50–59	11.9	18.8	12.8	19.7
60–69	6.0	9.2	3.8	11.0
>69	1.8	3.5	1.5	3.3
Mean age	38.3	43.9	37.2	44.8

Source: Eight sample counties (see appendix).

in Fayette and Johnson counties to 10.1 in Grainger County. Tenancy
rates for the under-forty age categories were uniformly higher than for
the forty-and-over age categories across the eight counties.

A clear pattern emerges from these figures. Agricultural tenancy
occurred across the entire adult age spectrum, but it was obviously
more prevalent among younger farmers. Whether tenancy was a stage
for accumulating a down payment or for transferring family property
between generations, this is precisely the age pattern one would expect. In either case, many farmers passed through the tenant ranks on
their way to landownership.

Tracing the careers of renters over a period of time provides another way to examine the dynamics of agricultural tenancy. This is a
difficult task. Tennessee farmers, like farmers elsewhere in the country, exhibited a high degree of geographical mobility. The majority of
tenants found in the 1850 census had left their counties of residence by
1860, and there is no way to know their fate. It is possible, however, to
learn the fate of those who remained in the same county for at least
ten years. Farmers who persisted during the 1850s—that is, those who
appeared in both the 1850 and 1860 manuscript censuses of a particular county—in four of the eight sample counties have been identified

Table 6.3

Percentage of Tenants by Age Category, 1850 and 1860

Age Category	1850	1860
<30	30.4	37.2
30–39	18.9	20.5
40–49	13.1	13.5
50–59	11.6	12.9
60–69	11.8	7.3
>69	9.7	9.3
All categories	16.8	17.3

Source: Eight sample counties (see appendix).

and their experiences with regard to land acquisition have been recorded. Those who persisted represented 35 percent of all farm operators in 1850, and they ranged from 33 percent in Haywood County to 44 percent in Johnson County.

Of the 1,087 farmers who remained throughout the 1850s, 164 (15 percent) began the decade as tenants. As table 6.4 indicates, the tenants of 1850 fared well, with 121, or almost three-quarters of them, becoming landowners by 1860. The portion of successful tenants varied from about 68 percent in Franklin County to more than 80 percent in Johnson County. A substantial group among the persisting tenants, then, employed the institution as a vehicle for attaining ownership of land.[16]

One may question whether the persisting tenants were representative of all tenants, and whether their degree of success in acquiring land was typical of those who could not be found in the census records ten years later. Persisting tenants were on average about three years younger than tenants who did not persist. Some disparity in age would be expected. Isolating farmers who remained in the same county for a full decade eliminates not only those who moved on but also those who died; that is, the procedure culls out a large segment of the oldest age cohort. Still, it is doubtful that this explanation accounts for the entire age differential between persisting and nonpersisting tenants.

Table 6.4

Transition Matrix for Persisting Farmers by County, 1850 to 1860

	1860 Operators (%)	
	Owners	Tenants
1850 Operators		
Dekalb owners	91.6	8.4
Dekalb tenants	75.6	24.4
Franklin owners	93.5	6.5
Franklin tenants	68.3	31.7
Haywood owners	95.6	4.4
Haywood tenants	77.3	27.7
Johnson owners	94.4	5.6
Johnson tenants	83.3	12.7
All owners	93.8	6.2
All tenants	73.8	26.2

SOURCE: Eight sample counties (based on Dekalb, Franklin, Haywood, and Johnson Counties; see appendix).

The relatively young age of the persisting tenants suggests that they may have been atypical in other respects and that the successful tenants among them may have enjoyed some economic advantage that facilitated their acquisition of land.

Table 6.5 points to possible sources of such an advantage. Farmers who stayed and climbed from tenant to landowner status during the 1850s operated larger farms than the nonpersisting tenants. On average, they cultivated farms about one-third more valuable and with about twenty-five more improved acres. They owned roughly one more slave, although almost three-quarters of them held no slaves in 1850. In short, their farms appear to have been somewhat better able to generate the income necessary to maintain the household and at the same time to set aside savings for a down payment on land of their own.

Understanding the reasons for their apparent advantage must rest

Table 6.5

Age and Farm Values for Persisting Farmers and Nonpersisting Tenants, 1850–60

Farmer Category	Average Age	Improved Acres	Farm Value ($)	Number of Slaves
Owner–Owner	41.0	84.1	1586	5.1
Tenant–Owner	38.1	67.5	948	2.9
Tenant–Tenant	35.3	41.9	614	0.2
Owner–Tenant	32.9	42.6	719	1.6
Nonpersisting Tenants	39.9	42.1	721	1.8

SOURCE: Eight sample counties (based on Dekalb, Franklin, Haywood, and Johnson counties).
NOTE: Age and farm values at first census.

on speculation. Some doubtlessly received financial assistance from family members, which enabled them to operate rental units larger than would have been possible if they had to rely solely on their own resources. Many in such fortunate circumstances, of course, acquired their first farms through gift or inheritance, making it unnecessary for them to save for a down payment and incur debt in order to move into the ownership ranks. For those farmers, as noted, tenancy was a transitional stage in their life cycles rather than a vehicle for acquiring land. Successful tenants from less affluent or less accommodating families had to derive whatever advantage they appear to have had from managerial talent and personal initiative. Their special attributes permitted them to operate units larger than those of less gifted tenants and to accumulate more rapidly the savings necessary to purchase farms. For those farmers, tenancy was truly a vehicle for attaining landownership. What portion of the successful tenants fell into each of those categories is impossible to ascertain. Whatever the breakdown, their apparent economic advantage helps to explain why they achieved upward mobility.

About a quarter of the persisting farmers, as table 6.4 shows, began and ended the 1850s as tenants. Table 6.5 indicates that they were younger, on average, by a little under three years, than the successful tenants, which suggests that at least some in this group had had insufficient time to save the money for a down payment. A study of Iowa farmers in the mid-nineteenth century found that successful tenants, on average, acquired farms in their mid- to late thirties.[17] The age information in table 6.2, which registers a sharp decline in the portion of all tenants between the under-forty and the over-forty categories, reveals that this was probably true of Tennessee tenants as well. If this were the case, some of the unsuccessful tenants were simply still saving for an initial down payment or waiting for a bequest.

At the same time, those who failed to acquire land operated smaller and less valuable farms, and owned fewer slaves than their more successful counterparts. More than 90 percent held no slaves in 1850, compared to about three-quarters of the tenants who eventually entered the ownership ranks. Whether this condition obtained from a lack of family assistance or a paucity of personal talent and ambition, the result was very likely the same: an inability to set aside income sufficient to buy a farm of their own. For many of those farmers, landownership was forever out of reach.

If tenancy served as a stage through which some farmers moved on their way to landownership, it also served as a receivership into which some farmers dropped after losing their land to foreclosure or bankruptcy. Table 6.4 shows that about 6 percent of the 1850 owners who persisted had fallen into tenancy by 1860. They were generally younger than those who began and ended the decade as owners (table 6.5), suggesting that many of them in 1850 had recently acquired land and incurred a large debt. Perhaps the most significant characteristic was that they operated smaller-than-average units, also suggesting that many were relatively new landowners who had had neither the time nor the opportunity to expand their assets. Their improved acreage and land value were about half and their slave numbers about a third of the corresponding figures for those who remained owners throughout the 1850s; and, for that matter, they were substantially less than the figures for the successful tenants. Furthermore, more than three-quarters of them owned no slaves in 1850, compared to about half of those who began and ended the decade as owners.

The evidence, admittedly circumstantial, implies that a sizable portion of these downwardly mobile farmers operated uneconomic units. They were unable to generate the income needed to sustain their households and meet their mortgage payments. As a result, they lost their land to creditors and retreated to tenancy. Those who experienced this reversal of fortune represented a small percentage of the farming population, but they demonstrated that economic mobility operated in two directions.

Aggregate quantitative evidence can mask diversity in behavior and fortune. A few examples illustrate a great variety of experience among farmers. Isaac Bain, twenty-eight years old and a tenant in Dekalb County in 1850, was typical of many farmers. He rented a farm valued at four hundred dollars and containing forty improved acres; he owned no slaves. At the beginning of the following decade, he owned—and was probably paying on—a farm worth two thousand dollars with thirty-five improved acres; he still owned no slaves. In 1850 Johnson County tenant John Stalcup was thirty-four years old and working a farm with sixty improved acres and worth twelve hundred dollars. During the 1850s he acquired a twenty-five hundred dollar farm with 175 improved acres. He owned slaves in neither census year. Haywood County tenant James Shirley, twenty-five years old and working a farm valued at four hundred dollars with fifteen improved acres in 1850, elevated his economic position significantly over the next ten years. By 1860 he owned a farm worth ten times the amount of his rental unit and containing 125 more improved acres. Moreover, he increased his slaveholding from one to five during the same period. Given the sizable growth in his assets, Shirley was very likely one of those receiving family assistance.

Not all tenants, as the aggregate numbers reveal, succeeded in attaining land. In 1850 Amos Richardson, forty-two years old, rented a farm in Franklin County worth $240 and containing forty improved acres. Ten years later, he was renting a unit worth $1,750 but with five fewer improved acres. Fifty-six years old and a tenant in 1850, J. M. Wilkson was still renting a small Dekalb County farm in 1860. Over the decade, the number of improved acres on his rental units dropped from forty-five to twenty, their value from $240 to $100. William Strayhorn, a Haywood County tenant, was renting a unit valued at $1,500 with 125 improved acres in 1850, when he was twenty years old. He was still a tenant in 1860, now renting a farm of only thirty improved acres. His case is curious. He acquired six slaves during the 1850s, suggesting that he continued to rent land by choice, not by necessity. Moreover, because thirty acres could not have occupied the labor of six slaves, he was probably hiring them out.

Another group of farmers moved from owner to tenant status. In 1850 J. P. Keith seemed well established as the thirty-eight-year-old owner of a

Franklin County farm containing eighty-five improved acres and valued at $2,000. But at the end of the decade, he was renting thirty improved acres on a $600 farm. Haywood County farmer John A. Johnson experienced a similar change in circumstances. In 1850 he was forty-seven years old, owned forty-five improved acres on a farm worth $900, and held one slave. Although he increased his slaveholding to three over the next ten years, he had become a tenant on a $2,500 farm with fifty-eight improved acres. Jesse Cole, at age thirty-two in 1850, owned a Johnson County farm containing seventy-five improved acres and worth $1,500. In 1860 he was renting a $6,000 farm with one hundred improved acres. He had acquired one slave during the 1850s.

The recollections of a group of Civil War veterans who came of age during the 1850s reveal, like the quantitative evidence, a mixed picture. Surveys of these veterans conducted by the Tennessee State Library and Archives in 1915 and 1920 included several questions on social and economic conditions in the pre–Civil War decade.[18] One query asked specifically about opportunities for young men of modest means to acquire farms. Two-thirds of a random sample of responses said without qualification that they were favorable; an additional 10 percent agreed but with some reservations. A few veterans maintained that young farmers had little chance to obtain land. Wilburn T. Barnes complained that a "pour man are boy didn't have no opportunity to own a farm." George A. Mills remembered that "young men made their expenses but couldn't save anything." William D. Beard echoed these views, claiming that a "renter had no chance to save anything."[19] Thomas S. Arnold held a much different opinion about conditions in the 1850s: "In this country land was cheap[;] . . . yung men could hav dun varry well at that time." George W. Alexander recalled that "if a young man would work and save his earnings he could soon have a home of his own."[20] William Y. Willey's response was probably closer to the truth than most: "With perseverance he [a young farmer] could eventually own a little home but [it was] a slow and hard process."[21] The accuracy of perceptions remembered after some sixty years is certainly open to question, but it is at least suggestive that they coincided with inferences drawn from the quantitative material.

Tenancy, in addition to providing the use of land to those who did not own farms, clearly worked as a mechanism for acquiring land. Almost three-quarters of the persisting tenants succeeded in acquiring farms during the pre–Civil War decade. Moreover, some of the owners in 1850 had obviously come through the tenant ranks earlier, and some of the nonpersisting tenants undoubtedly became owners elsewhere. The persisting tenants appear to have had an advantage over other tenants, but the nature and the sources of that advantage remain unclear. A combination of personal circumstances and general economic conditions determined the fate of each individual. Those who became landowners probably came from favorable family situations and/or possessed personality traits that enhanced economic mobility. Those who failed to reach the ownership ranks very likely enjoyed neither of these advantages.

As the figures above indicate, the vast majority of farmers—more than 80 percent—owned the land they worked. What the figures fail to reflect is the great disparity in the size of these holdings. Some owned small farms of less than twenty-five improved acres. A few owned huge plantations of more than one thousand improved acres. Most owned medium-sized farms of fifty to one hundred improved acres. Many owners, furthermore, began with relatively small purchases and expanded their holdings over the years, whereas others saw their holdings decline as they sold off, gave away, or lost land.[22]

Table 6.6 shows the decile distribution of improved acreage held by farmers in the eight sample counties. The figures depict a high degree of concentration in landownership. For both 1850 and 1860, individuals in the top decile owned more than 40 percent of the total improved acreage, and those in the top two deciles owned about 60 percent. At the opposite end of the spectrum, those in the bottom two deciles owned less than .5 percent of all improved acreage. Most of the farmers in this fifth of the farm operators, as noted, were tenants. The broad middle range of landowners—the 60 percent who comprised the third through the eighth deciles—held about 40 percent of the total improved acreage.

Farm value provides a more comprehensive measure of agricultural holdings. It included the value of land, both improved and unimproved, and the value of structures and fencing on the land. The distribution of farm value, like the distribution of improved acreage, was highly skewed. The figures ran from farms worth a few hundred dollars to ones worth more than a quarter of a million dollars. Most farmers, with units valued at a few thousand dollars, fell within these extremes. The decile distributions given in table 6.6 reveal this concentration in farm value. The top decile owned a little less than half of the total value in 1850 and a little more than half ten years later. The first

Table 6.6

Agricultural Wealth Distribution, 1850 and 1860

Decile	Percentage of Total Improved Acres		Percentage of Total Farm Value	
	1850	1860	1850	1860
1	41.7	45.1	47.1	51.6
2	17.2	17.5	18.5	17.5
3	12.1	11.2	11.4	10.8
4	9.1	8.6	7.9	7.5
5	7.1	6.6	5.8	5.2
6	5.6	4.9	4.3	3.5
7	4.2	3.7	3.0	2.4
8	2.7	2.2	1.8	1.3
9	0.4	0.2	0.2	0.1
10	0.0	0.0	0.0	0.0

SOURCE: Eight sample counties (see appendix).

and second deciles combined had accumulated about two-thirds of all farm value by the end of the antebellum period. By contrast, the two bottom deciles held a minuscule portion of total value, and the middle group held roughly a third.

The Gini coefficients given in table 6.7, which measure overall concentration, reveal differences among the eight sample counties in improved-acreage and farm-value distributions. The variation seems to have been random. Haywood County, which was a major cotton producer in West Tennessee, registered relatively high coefficients in both years. Considering the association between cotton cultivation and plantation agriculture, such a result might be expected. But Fayette, another cotton county just to the south of Haywood, had coefficients that were below the numbers for the eight counties combined. The East Tennessee counties of Johnson and Grainger registered relatively low concentrations, which were consistent with an agricultural system that emphasized livestock raising and grain farming. But so too did Middle Tennessee's Robertson County, which was heavily involved in commercial tobacco and grain production. Although location and type of

Table 6.7

Wealth Gini Indexes for Individual Counties, 1850 and 1860

County	Improved Acres		Farm Value	
	1850	1860	1850	1860
Dekalb	52.9	50.3	61.4	58.8
Fayette	54.9	57.1	58.7	61.8
Franklin	56.5	58.7	65.7	64.7
Grainger	50.4	52.9	61.0	63.3
Hardin	46.1	62.5	57.3	70.2
Haywood	61.4	61.8	63.4	65.7
Johnson	47.3	43.4	52.8	51.7
Robertson	41.7	48.5	50.2	57.6
All counties	55.5	58.8	61.6	65.2

Source: Eight sample counties (see appendix).

agricultural system may have played a role in the distributions of improved acreage and farm value, other less obvious factors appear to have been operating within the individual counties.

Although the distributions of improved acreage and farm value were similar in most respects, they exhibited one important difference. Farm value was somewhat more concentrated than improved acreage. The top deciles' percentages of total value were six to seven points higher than their corresponding percentages of improved acreage. The Gini coefficients for farm value in the eight counties combined exceeded those for improved acreage by roughly the same degree.

Several possible conditions could explain these differences. If owners of larger units invested proportionately more in structures and fencing than owners of smaller units, farm value would have been more concentrated than improved acreage. The differences would simply have reflected the more lavish improvements on plantations and large farms. Images of the great house and elaborate grounds on antebellum plantations notwithstanding, their dwellings and yards were in most cases fairly modest.[23] Investments in improvements on larger units no doubt exceeded those on smaller units, but they hardly represented a greater proportion of the overall value. Differences in unimproved acreage holdings between large and small owners might also explain differences in distribution of farm value and improved acreage. Higher concentrations of farm value might reflect relatively greater holdings of unimproved acreage on the larger units. This does not appear to have been the case in Tennessee. The evidence fails to show a higher percentage of unimproved acreage on plantations and large farms. In fact, breakdowns for 1860 indicate that, on average, the more valuable the unit, the lower the proportion of unimproved land.

Another possible explanation appears to have been more plausible. Farm value was determined not only by the amount of total acreage and improvement but also by the quality of the soil. A greater concentration of farm value than of improved acreage might, therefore, reflect generally higher quality land on larger units than on smaller units. The evidence from antebellum Tennessee suggests that planters and large farmers possessed a double advantage. Their units were both larger and of better soil quality than those of smaller farmers. Still, the comparison between farm-value and improved-acreage distributions indicates, at most, a relatively small disparity in soil quality.[24]

Changes in distributions during the 1850s point up another characteristic of rural landholding. The changes were small but mainly in the direction of greater concentration. For both improved acreage and farm value, the shares of the first deciles and of the top two deciles combined increased, whereas the shares of every decile from the third through the eighth declined. The tenancy rate of approximately 17 percent meant, as noted, that landless farmers in both years made up most of the bottom two deciles. The combined and individual county Gini coefficients, which for the most part registered small increases between 1850 and 1860, summarize the trend toward a slightly more skewed distribution. The growth rates in farm value given in table 6.8 tell a similar story. All deciles participated in the asset expansion of the 1850s, but in unequal degrees. The higher the decile, the greater the rate of growth. The decade witnessed, in short, a modest increase in the concentration of agricultural wealth.[25]

The record of the persisting owners sheds further light on the dynamics of land distribution during the 1850s. Table 6.9 indicates that the farmers who remained owners throughout the decade more than tripled their real estate values. Part of the growth resulted from further acquisitions of land, part from appreciation in the values of land

Table 6.8

Annual Compounded Growth Rates in Farm Value by Decile Category,
1850–60

Decile	Percentage
1	12.2
1–2	11.7
3–8	10.0
9–10	3.6
All deciles	11.2

SOURCE: Eight sample counties (see appendix).

already held. Increases in household wealth occurred across all farm-value categories. In fact, the small and middling owners increased their real estate worth proportionately more than large owners. Those with less than two hundred dollars in farm value in 1850 enjoyed more than a tenfold increase over the following decade; those with two thousand or more dollars in farm value saw only a threefold increase.

Two reinforcing processes were at work. Landowners, like the successful tenants, obviously took advantage of economic opportunities in the 1850s to expand their real estate assets. In addition, they apparently experienced the accumulation of wealth that often accompanies advancing years. The figures in table 6.9 depict a clear pattern: higher farm values were associated with older age groups. As persisting owners grew older, they increased their agricultural holdings. At the same time, many of them rose in the wealth distribution structure; that is, they moved to higher deciles within the rural population. But not all experienced increases in wealth and improvements in relative holdings. About 15 percent of the persisting owners saw a decline in landholding over the decade. Although some no doubt lost property because of financial distress, this was not uniformly the case. Others willingly passed land on to children or sold off surplus acres. How much of the decline in holdings resulted from misfortune and how much from voluntary transfer is impossible to ascertain.

Specific examples illuminate the diversity of fortunes experienced by owners. Thomas Lacy, on arriving from North Carolina in 1810,

Table 6.9

Farm Values and Ages by 1850 Farm Value Category for Persisting Owners

Farm Value Category ($)	Age	Farm Value	Farm Value	Percentage Change
	1850	1850	1860	1850–60
1– 199	35.5	$110	$1,231	1,019.1
200– 499	37.9	319	1,845	478.4
500– 999	40.4	653	2,689	311.8
1,000–1,499	42.9	1,093	3,760	244.0
1,500–1,999	42.5	1,574	5,316	237.8
>1,999	43.8	4,116	12,360	200.3
All categories	41.0	1,586	5,296	233.9

SOURCE: Eight sample counties (based on Dekalb, Franklin, Haywood, and Johnson counties; see appendix).

purchased 175 acres of raw land in Hickman County. Ten years later he moved to Madison County, where he purchased 1,280 acres between 1821 and 1825. He continued to acquire land, and at the time of his death in 1831, he owned 1,694 acres. He owned seven adult slaves.[26] Matthias Boon's farming career followed a similar course. He moved to Madison County from North Carolina in 1824 and bought 150 acres of land. Over the next eleven years he increased his holdings in Madison County to 614 acres. He apparently purchased land elsewhere as well, for at his death in 1835 he owned 2,862 acres. His holdings also included sixteen slaves.[27]

In 1850 W. B. Laurence of Dekalb County owned a farm with eighty improved acres valued at $1,500. He added to his holdings and by 1860 owned 140 improved acres on farm with a value of $12,000. Laurence doubled his slave holdings from five to ten over the same period. Haywood County planter Willie Mann began the decade with 450 improved acres, a $6,000 plantation, and fifty slaves; he ended the decade with one thousand improved acres, a $32,500 plantation, and seventy-one slaves. On a more modest scale, Reuben Dotson increased his real estate assets in Johnson County from nine to fifty improved acres and from $125 to $600; he held no slaves. Those farmers realized upward economic mobility, though obviously in vastly different degrees.

Another group of farmers moved in the opposite direction. In 1850 W. R. Davis owned a farm in Franklin County with twenty-five improved acres and worth $600; by 1860 his improved acreage had declined by nine and his farm value by $100; he owned slaves in neither year. John Davis's improved land in Dekalb County dropped from seventy to fifty acres; but increasing land values more than compensated, as his real estate value trebled from $500 to $1,500. Davis held no slaves. Nicolas Perkins owned a significantly larger unit in Haywood County, with 524 improved acres and $5,000 in real estate assets in 1850; over the following decade he trimmed back to 382 acres on a farm worth $8,400. At the same time his slave force increased, curiously, from fifty-two to sixty-seven. Green Moore, who was sixty-one in 1850, apparently decided it was time to sell off some of his holdings, for he reduced his improved acreage in Johnson County from 150 to fifty, though his real estate value increased marginally; the single slave he held in 1850 was gone by 1860.

Farmers' diaries record a variety of land transactions. One year Wiley Bagwell received payment for land he had sold earlier; four years later he bought land from one of his neighbors.[28] Robert Cartmell recorded buying and selling land in a simultaneous transaction.[29] On one occasion, Herndon Haraldson sold off a piece of his holdings, "100 acres for 3.75 pr acre."[30] John Barker was particularly active in the land market, as the following entries indicate: "Sold M. G. Gholson my land on C[umberland]. river for $2500"; "I bot Neblett land for $12.50 pr acre"; "Bot Ahab Langstons land for $3448"; "sold to H. M. Dudley my Irwin farm for $1200."[31] As their needs and financial circumstances changed, many farmers regularly acquired and disposed of land.

Despite the modest rise in the concentration of agricultural assets, an overwhelming majority of the persisting farmers acquired or expanded land holdings during the 1850s, a phenomenon concealed by the aggregate wealth distributions. Growth in real estate assets was not confined to the wealthier groups; all levels of the free farm community participated. Only the owners who fell to and the tenants who remained in the tenant ranks ended the decade without land; together they made up less than 10 percent of the persisting group. A small proportion of the owners either lost or disposed of part of their holdings.

Table 6.10

Owner Assets and Age for Persisting Farmers and All Farmers, 1850–60

	1850		1860	
	Persisting	All	Persisting	All
Improved acres	81.6	75.3	134.8	101.1
Farm value ($)	1,532	1,387	5,125	4,061
Slaves	4.5	3.8	6.4	4.0
Age	39.9	42.5	49.9	43.0

Source: Eight sample counties (based on Franklin, Dekalb, Haywood, and Johnson counties; see appendix).

The rest of the persisters—almost 80 percent—enhanced their economic well-being in the years leading up to the Civil War.

It is possible that the persisting owners possessed an economic advantage that aided them in accumulating wealth. If this were the case, their accomplishments would distort the extent of economic success during the 1850s. As table 6.10 points up, they enjoyed a relatively stronger financial position than the typical owner. Compared to all owners in both 1850 and 1860, they held farms containing more improved acreage and registering higher values, and they owned more slaves. As wealth accumulation was partly a function of age, as noted, one might have expected them to have had higher than average holdings in 1860, when they were about seven years older than the overall average. But in 1850, when they were some two and a half years younger than the typical owner, their stronger position must have resulted from some advantage or head start they enjoyed over others in their respective age cohorts. The explanations, like those for the successful tenants, were doubtlessly found in individual circumstances. Some benefited from family assistance, others from managerial talents and an acquisitive personality, still others from all three. The apparent advantages of the persisting owners should not, however, obscure the fact that upward economic mobility was common. The success they enjoyed was widespread among the rural population.

Rural society in antebellum Tennessee comprised a varied and fluid structure. The state contained a small number of wealthy planters who held a disproportionate share of the land and an even larger share of the farm value. Alongside this rural elite existed a large group of small- and medium-sized landowners representing some 60 percent of all farmers. Less than a fifth of the farm operators owned no land. Despite a modest increase in the concentration of land during the 1850s, many tenants acquired property and many smaller landowners added to their holdings. Perhaps the most salient feature of the social structure was that all levels of the free population accumulated agricultural wealth during the decade. Most moved up the social ladder no more than a rung or two, and very few narrowed the gap between themselves and those above them in the wealth hierarchy. At the same time, a large portion of the free population enjoyed improvement in material well-being.[32]

Antebellum Tennessee provided extensive opportunities for rural residents to obtain the use of land as a factor of agricultural production and to acquire ownership of land as an expression of a salient cultural value. Those wishing to engage in commercial agriculture could either purchase or rent land; ample amounts were available for either form of tenure. The grand objective of farmers, though, was not simply to secure the use of land, but to obtain the ownership of land. Some, for a variety of reasons, never realized their aspirations, but most farmers eventually achieved their goal. Their real estate holdings were in most cases relatively modest, particularly as compared to those of the great planters, but they nonetheless placed them among the landowner group. For some, ownership entailed nothing more than accepting a gift or an inheritance from a member of the family. For some, it required long years of hard work, astute management, and careful planning; good luck often played a role as well. Acquiring land brought economic independence. The landowning farmer no longer had to buy the use of someone else's property in order to produce agricultural goods. It also brought personal satisfaction. The farmer, no matter how small his holdings, could enjoy the social and cultural rewards that came with landownership and the comfort of knowing that he had property to pass on to his offspring.

7

Work and Leisure

If one feature characterized Tennessee agriculture in the antebellum period more than any other, it was work—dreary, endless, mundane, exhausting work. Toil may have varied in nature and purpose, but it occupied most of the farmers' waking hours. Except for the very young and the very old, everyone in the typical rural household participated. Each working member contributed in some way to the operation of the farm or the management of the household. Each performed a set of tasks that together sustained the farming enterprise and defined a seasonal routine that changed little from year to year. Work comprised a central component of what farmers referred to—sometimes fondly, sometimes cynically—as their way of life. Toil was not without its rewards, of course. Household members took pride in performing tasks well and in the results of work that fulfilled its objective. At the same time, they cherished their meager amount of leisure time and the simple pleasures it brought. They were grateful for diversions, no matter how modest, from the work of the farm.

Crop cultivation made up a good portion of the work routine. Farmers had to plow and sow the fields, tend and harvest the crops, and prepare them for market or household consumption. For most crops, these activities began early in the year and continued well into the fall or even into the winter.[1] The men and teenage boys of the household normally performed the field work, though at particularly busy times women might have assisted.[2]

Tobacco cultivation was particularly demanding. In late January or early February farmers burned the beds to sterilize the soil and remove vegetation. They next scattered seeds on the prepared beds, covering them with a thin layer of fine dirt and a sheet of cheese cloth. Farmers then plowed and harrowed the fields that would eventually receive the young tobacco plants. Beginning in late April, they transferred the plants, now six to eight inches tall, from the beds to the fields, placing them in rows two to three feet apart. "Setting" the tobacco, as this task was called, involved transplanting approximately seven to eight thousand plants per acre and lasted until late May or early June. Farmers often staggered their setting so that the tobacco would mature at different times, allowing them to spread out the harvesting and curing, which were extremely labor demanding. Inclement weather sometimes killed the fragile transplants, requiring a second setting. In 1845 Montgomery County farmer John Barker had to reset his tobacco plants on two occasions, one time after heavy rains in June and another after high winds in July. That year he finally finished his tobacco planting in mid-July, which was probably too late to secure a decent harvest.[3]

Hoeing commenced as soon as the plots were in and continued, usually through July, until the plants were high enough either to choke out or to contend with the competing weeds. Between hoeing runs, farmers removed, one at a time by hand, the worms that had started to feed on the young plants. Tobacco growers sometimes tried to reduce this phase of the work by turning geese and turkeys into the plots to eat the worms. Solon Robinson, a northern journalist who observed deworming in northwestern Tennessee in the 1840s, noted that "some have trained turkeys to perform part of the work." Poultry were very inefficient, however, and someone had to follow them to complete the job.[4] After the plants reached a height of two to three feet, some farmers cultivated the fields with an animal-drawn plow to remove weeds that had grown up between the rows. By August it was usually time for "topping" and "suckering," that is, cutting off the blossom at the top of the plant and then, periodically, the sprouts that erupted at the base of the leaves to improve their quality and size.

Harvesting started in mid-August and, for late crops, could continue through September. Workers split each stalk from the top to near the bottom, cut the plants off at the ground, and hung them upside down over a tobacco stick about four feet in length. They then hauled the sticks to the barn and suspended them across rows of poles running the length of the building and reaching up four or five tiers high. If the tobacco was an air-cured variety, such as burley, the farmer had a respite of approximately a month before the leaf cured. If it was a dark fire-cured variety, the farmer built a smoldering fire on the floor of the barn, which someone had to tend day and night for a week or more to maintain the desired temperature. After the tobacco was properly cured, the farmer took it down, stripped the leaves from the stalks, and tied them into bunches, or "hands." Farmers usually finished this task in December and were then ready to market their tobacco, almost a year after the tedious and exhausting process of cultivation had begun. Tobacco, with good reason, gained the reputation of being Tennessee's most labor-consuming crop.

If tobacco was the most demanding of labor, cotton came in a strong second. Cotton cultivation began almost as early in the year as tobacco cultivation. The first step in preparing the fields came in February, with cutting and clearing stalks on land that had been in cotton the year before. Farmers next plowed the fields and broke up the larger clumps of earth with hoes or animal-drawn harrows or scrappers. They commenced planting in mid-April and finished by early May. Many farmers preferred to get their crop in as early as possible to allow ample time for the slow maturing cotton to ripen before cold weather set in. But they also had to consider the possibility of frost damage to the early plant growth. Robert Cartmell, who farmed in Madison County, expressed the dilemma in a diary entry for early April: "I have heard of some planting cotton, but I think it rather soon. It is useless to try to *lenthen* the season; I shall plant none before the 17th [even] if ready before."[5] Cartmell was a man of his word. On 17 April he recorded: "Commenced planting cotton this morning."

From the time it sprouted in mid-May until it was well established in August, the crop required weeding. "Chopping" the cotton, the phrase used to describe this back-breaking job, took place two or three times a season. Growers normally used hoes, though some employed animal-drawn plows for the last weeding. Hand picking, probably the most physically demanding task of cotton cultivation, occurred in the fall and could extend into the early winter, with the fields worked two or three times before the plants had been cleaned of fiber. Farmers then hauled the cotton in to be ginned and baled, the final step in preparing it for sale. Large farmers and planters usually owned cotton gins and presses for this purpose, but small farmers paid neighbors or the local gin for the service. Cartmell noted in his diary that he was "ginning Mr. Bond's cotton"; a few days later he "baled 3 bales of Mr. Bonds cotton."[6] With the baling finished, the cotton was ready for market, ten to eleven months after it had been planted. Cotton, like tobacco, cultivation involved a variety of tasks, took up a good share of the year, and required an enormous amount of physical effort.

Grains were less exacting in their labor requirements. The cultivation of corn was very flexible in its demands; farmers could often adjust its care to accommodate other activities. They might prepare the cornfields anytime from late fall to early spring. Planting took place in April; replanting necessitated by poor weather might extend the job into early May. After the young plants appeared, farmers hoed the fields, usually twice during the growing season; some farmers also plowed the fields after the plants had reached sufficient height. Stripping the leaves and topping the stalks for fodder, a procedure followed by some farmers, took place in late August before the ears had matured. The corn fully ripened in early fall. If the farmer had stripped and topped the stalks, he hand-picked the dried ears from the half stalks, threw them into a wagon, and hauled them in. If he had not, he cut and shocked the entire stalks and left them in the field to dry; later he pulled the ears and hauled them in.[7] Corn intended for livestock feed was placed in the crib; corn intended for household consumption was shucked and stored in a dry place. The farmer might later retrieve the discarded stalks from the field and store them for fodder.

Small grains took even less effort. In Tennessee, farmers sowed wheat after the fall plowing and harvested it in late spring. Because small grains were broadcast rather than planted in rows, like cotton or corn, wheat required no cultivation during the growing season. Growers harvested the crop with a hand-held sickle, scythe, or cradle—large farmers might have owned reapers after they became available in the 1830s—and tied the stems into bundles, which were stacked in shocks to dry for a few weeks. In July farmers hauled in the wheat to be threshed. They carried out this task either by spreading the stems on the ground or the floor of the barn to be tread on by horses or by flailing the grain from the stems. Those who owned reapers probably also owned animal-powered threshing machines. Farmers cleaned the wheat by tossing it in the air or fanning it, which separated the kernels from the debris. They then sent the grain directly to market or stored it in barns for household consumption or later sale. Tennessee farmers also grew oats, rye, buckwheat, and millet. The cultivation of these small grains was similar to that of wheat, except that oats and millet were normally planted in the spring and harvested in late summer.

Farmers planted pastures in clover or grasses, usually in the fall. When the vegetation achieved sufficient growth the following year, they turned livestock onto the fields to graze. They used natural grasslands for hay, which they cut, raked, and stacked in early fall for animal feed throughout the winter. Farmers broadcast hemp and flax seeds in the spring and pulled up the mature plants in late summer. They normally left the hemp stems scattered on the ground to break-down the outer layer through a process called "dewrotting." A few farmers used water-rotting, which involved placing the recently harvested stems in pools of water. Water-rotting produced a better fiber, but required more labor than dewrotting. Farmers tied the flax stalks into shocks to dry in the fields, after which they soaked them in water to rot the shell. When the hemp and flax plants had sufficiently decomposed, farmers separated the inner fibers with a break. They either sold the fibers or stored them for household use.

Individual farmers, of course, did not grow all of these field crops; each produced some combination of them. If there was one constant in their production choices, it was corn; virtually every agricultural unit cultivated corn. About half of Tennessee's farms produced either or both of the state's principal commercial crops, tobacco and cotton.[8] Most of the farms that produced neither grew small grains, usually wheat; many of the farms that did produce tobacco or cotton also grew small grains. The labor demands of some crops, such as tobacco and cotton, were heavy and inflexible; the demands of others, such as corn, were moderate and elastic; and the demands of still others, such as wheat, were light and periodic. These variations enabled farmers to arrange seasonal working schedules according to the requirements of their particular combination of crops. Each operator established a seasonal routine with a pattern or rhythm determined by his production choices.

Livestock raising placed intermittent demands on the farmers' time. During much of the year, cattle fed on the open grasslands and swine on the forest mast. "Cattle thrive well on the range," reported Christopher Houston to a family member soon after he settled in Maury County.[9] Solon Robinson observed on his tour of West Tennessee that swine there largely raised themselves: "With little feeding and less care, particularly when 'mast' is plenty, they live . . . independent of their owner."[10] Horses, mules, and sheep grazed without tending on the meadows and pastures, although some farmers stabled them at night. Poultry scavenged for food near the homestead.

Farmers customarily rounded up swine in the late fall to be fattened on corn for a month or two; some farmers in East Tennessee, according to one report, allowed them to feed on mast for the entire year.[11] Gathering animals that had run free for most of the year was an arduous, though fairly brief, task. Herndon Haraldson succinctly recorded such activity in his daily log: "Hunting hogs all day."[12] Farmers either penned swine or turned them onto harvested cornfields to eat the ears that had dropped to the ground. One year Robert Cartmell deliberately left a good deal of corn in the field and "turned hogs in. They will have *one* feast at least."[13] After the swine had been finished on corn, farmers either slaughtered and butchered them for household consumption or sold them. They placed the household meat in the smokehouse or packed it in salt to be cured, and rendered the fat trimmings into lard. They slaughtered and processed cattle and poultry as needed, milked dairy cattle twice a day, and gathered chicken eggs once a day. Sheep shearing customarily occurred once a year, usually in late spring, though a few raisers took wool twice a year. The care of livestock required considerable time and attention, if on an irregular basis.

Crop and livestock production claimed most of the farmers' working time, but not all of it. Farmers filled relatively slack periods in the late fall and winter with construction and maintenance on their farms. One year they might build a shed, barn, or smokehouse. Another year they might construct an addition to the house or a detached kitchen. The house and other buildings on Barton Warren's Blount County farm took three year's of intermittent work to complete.[14] Yet another year farmers might paint or shingle the house, put in a chimney, or lay a new granary floor. During the year after he moved onto his Smith County farm in 1849, William Cheek spent the time when he was not in the fields hand digging and lining a well.[15] Sometime during the summer or fall, someone had to cut down trees, and then saw, split, haul, and stack firewood for the approaching winter. Periodically, a member of the household had to clean the henhouse, stables, and cistern and, perhaps, clear the drainage ditches. Some special chore always seemed to demand attention. One day Jane Margaret Jones's husband was "very busy having the grape vines fixed[;] he is having an entire new frame put up[;] it is an immense deal of work."[16] Fencing was a recurrent task. New fields needed enclosing, and old fields needed repairs. In either case, the farmer had to cut chestnut timber, split rails, and, if a post-type fence, hew the posts. Then he had to erect or replace the fence. Robert Cartmell seems to have been particularly weary one day when, after preparing all of the construction materials, he "worked about an hour on fence[;] a quantity has fallen."[17] Stone fences were more durable than rail or post fences, but they took longer to construct. John Motheral began erecting one on his farm in Williamson County soon after he arrived in 1800; his son, Joseph, completed the job after acquiring the property in 1823.[18] A few farmers put in hedge fences of osage orange, but these were less common than in the Midwest.[19] Farmers also had to set aside time to repair tools, harnesses, wagons, and other equipment.

The male members of the household normally provided all of the labor necessary for cultivation, construction, maintenance, and repair. Sometimes, when they fell behind in their work, they had to bring in outside hands. They usually hired neighboring farmers or their sons. Robert Bayless, who grew up on a Washington County farm, recalled that his "father farmed some at home on rented land. He also worked away from home for the land lord upon whose property we lived and for others also."[20] Alexander Cartwright earned extra income as a young man in Davidson County by working "as a hand at six dollars pr month . . . through the crop season of 1838."[21] One year John Barker "paid O. C. Pitt $25.50 for thrashing grain crop." Wiley Bagwell, who had a number of workers in his household, must have been in a bind when he hired two hands to replace the roof on his house. John Milton remembered from his childhood on a Robertson County farm that his "parents did not keep servents. Accasionally a hand was hired."[22] Apparently some disagreement over wages arose when George Washington "paid Ola Amunson $50.00 on the ditch he dug . . . & he says I owe him 31.95 net."[23] Farmers customarily helped each other by exchanging work, particularly on tasks that required more hands than were available in the typical household. Betty Gleaves noted that her husband received assistance with an especially demanding job: "Austin Smith here cutting wheat." James Matthews helped a neighbor thresh wheat, and Wiley Bagwell "sent hands to help Mrs. Morrow."[24]

Men were not the only household members who toiled. Women contributed in essential ways to the farming enterprise. Some of their duties were exacting in their labor demands, others more flexible. Like the men, they had to adjust their seasonal activities to accommodate those varying exigencies. Whatever arrangements they settled on, work filled most of their daytime hours.

Men plowed the garden plots in the early spring, but on most farms the plots became the women's responsibility from then on. It was a responsibility that demanded careful planning and tedious work. Women began putting in the hardier vegetables, such as white potatoes and onions, in March, and beans the following month. They planted the seeds of more fragile varieties, such as tomatoes, cabbage, and peppers, in containers, which they kept inside until the threat of frost had passed and they could transplant them to the gardens. Meanwhile, they sowed sweet potatoes, peas, carrots, celery, cucumbers, radishes, beets, and, perhaps, a strawberry patch. They normally put in turnips in the fall. The only garden crops not the responsibility of the women were squash, pumpkins, and melons, which the men usually planted between corn rows. Even before the women completed the planting, they commenced hoeing the garden, a tiring job that continued intermittently throughout the season. They harvested the different varieties of vegetables and fruits, from the orchards as well as the gardens, as they ripened, and took them to the house for preparation. A task that began in early spring continued well into fall. On 29 October 1859, Betty Gleaves was still "working in the garden."[25]

Women generally handled all of the food preparation, except for butchering and curing meat. They dried vegetables and fruits, pickled cabbage and cucumbers, and preserved jams and jellies to be eaten when fresh produce was no longer available. After sealable jars became available in the 1840s, they might have canned some of the produce. They cooked meat and vegetables, baked breads and desserts, made butter and cheese, and prepared sweeteners and condiments for the household's daily meals. Usually the fare was pretty mundane; occasionally, probably on Sunday, it was something special, like Jane Margaret Jones's "Black berry cordial."[26]

Growing and preparing food, coupled with the weekly laundering and house cleaning, followed a well-defined schedule. Making clothes allowed for greater flexibility, which meant that women could work it in when they found spare time. Some women performed all of the tasks from the raw fiber to the finished stage. Betty Gleaves spun thread, wove and dyed cloth, and sewed garments. Harrison Farrell remembered that his mother had similar responsibilities on their Coffee County farm: "Mothers work to keep the house in order to cord and spin wool and cotten and warp for her cloth and put it in the loom through harness and sleigh and when done and shrunk and dry them iron out and scissors and cut out pants and make them with her fingers mens coats and 1000 other things. she would make pleted bossom sunday shirts and other fine needle work for to make young folks look well."[27]

Others, like Jane Margaret Jones, purchased the material from which they made their clothes. They produced a variety of articles ranging from socks and aprons to dresses and coats. One day Gleaves "cut out some shirts for Mr. G."; a couple weeks later she "commence[d] with Mr. Gleaves pants."[28] One day Jones was "busy making a bonnet"; the next day she was "making dresses for the children."[29] In addition to clothing, women made articles as simple as corn sacks and as complicated as quilts.

Jane Margaret Jones was among a few fortunate farm women who enjoyed the benefits of new technology, though not without some adjustment. One September she entered in her diary that the "sewing machine has come. . . . I fear it is so complicated I cant understand it." She had learned at least the rudiments of its operation by early the following month and began using it. The contraption was still formidable enough, though, for her to refer to it in upper case: "Vry busy sewing on the Machine making aprons." By mid-December the relationship between woman and machine had advanced to the point where she was "at work on the Machine[;] about to finish many things." Early February of the following year saw a real breakthrough. Not only could she operate the sewing machine for several hours at a time, but she could once again write about it in lower case. "I am busy sewing all day on the machine," she recorded. "I have sewed 18 pair of pants and six shirts." The very next day's entry indicated that Jones had finally come to terms with her new technology: "I am sewing on the machine again. I like it very much. I am making some nice pillow slips."[30]

Women in households owning slaves often carried an additional burden. William G. Taylor remarked that his mother "looked after the spinning, weaving and making of their [slaves'] clothing and that of our family."[31] Gleaves and Jones often made references such as "knitting negros socks" or "cuting out pants for the servants." Patsy Hyde remembered from her days as a slave that the owner's wife knitted stockings for her and the other slave children.[32] Women also supervised some of the work of the female slaves and cared for the sick, injured, and pregnant.[33] "My Mother superintended the Negro women and children," Taylor recalled from his childhood on a Jefferson County farm. James McColgan, who grew up in Jackson County, noted that his mother "looked after seven or eight Negro women."[34]

Women contributed mightily to the maintenance of the household. Some also generated money income. Gleaves raised chickens and sold them and their eggs to a local dealer. On one occasion she "sold 44 hens to the chicken man at 12 1/2 cts," and two days later she "got a hundred chickens" to replace them.[35] She was, no doubt unwittingly, following the advice of a woman's column that appeared regularly in the *Southern Agriculturist*. Published somewhat earlier, the article was entitled "On Rearing of Poultry" and was written by "A Lady."[36] John Barker's wife sold honey and beeswax from the hives she kept on their farm.[37] George Washington hired a farm woman in his neighborhood to make some shirts for him: "Pd Miss Harriet[;] Price shirts—$22.50." Wiley Bagwell "paid Mrs. Adams $3.50 for making overcoat."[38] Women in households with a loom found opportunities to sell cloth off the farm. J. S. Welch recalled that his mother "would weave cloth for other people."[39] A Nashville tailor of ready-made clothes advertised: "Encouragement for the Ladies. I will give cash for all kinds of homespun of a good quality."[40] A report on East Tennessee agriculture mentioned that women were exploiting the silk craze of the 1840s. "One lady, with the assistance of the children and females of her household," it commented, "raised last year one hundred bushels of Cocoons, the selling price of which is three dollars and a half per bushel."[41]

The diaries of farm women reveal that their lives were filled not only with hard, tiresome work but also with boredom and loneliness. Men often worked with others and regularly went into town, whereas women worked alone and rarely left the farmstead. Women frequently alluded to a life of seclusion. "Mr. Gleaves gone all day," was a typical entry in Gleaves's diary. Jones often wrote that her husband was in Clarksville, Bolivar, or Memphis, sometimes for several days at a time. "I am all alone and hard at work," she ruefully recorded one day.[42] An undercurrent of frustration and discontent permeated their narrations. "I am up & at the loom early & by dint of hard work get my cloth out," brooded Gleaves. Jones inscribed plaintively in her log that "I am working away on Mr. Jones shirts[;] it seems as if they never will be done."[43]

Women's contributions to rural households prompted one observer to compare the roles of farm women and farm men in East Tennessee and to conclude that the latter shamelessly shirked. He opined that "the men can scarcely be termed over-industrious." Women's chores occupied them throughout the entire year, he pointed out. Men, by contrast, enjoyed a relatively slack period from July to March—from after the wheat harvest until spring planting—which they used "to ride about, gossip, fish, hunt, and shoot."[44] Although many, including women, would have disagreed with his judgment, he did underscore the crucial place of women in rural society. It was a place that many appreciated, as the recollections of C. W. Post, who grew up on a Monroe County farm, warmly indicated: "Mother and sisters cooked on old pots and skillets, stoves being few and unsatisfactory until after the [Civil] war, spun and wove wool into linsy and jeans for outer clothing for winter and flax for summer pants and duster coats. They cut and make by hand, stitching nearly all the clothes for the family, milked two or three cows, raised chickens, carried water for 100 yards etc."[45] Despite the detailed list of tasks, his concluding "etc." covered a good many unenumerated chores.

Children also participated in the work of the farm. Many jobs were light enough that young boys and girls could easily, if not always happily, manage them. After the wheat had been cut, the boys raked the stems into piles for the men to tie into shocks. Boys helped with deworming tobacco plants and shucking corn. On some farms they "worked the flax," as Tom Bryan recalled from his childhood on a Montgomery County farm. This required pulling up the ripened plants, tying them into bundles, and standing them upright to dry. Later, after the plants had been gathered and soaked, they separated the fibers with a flax break.[46] Boys and girls sometimes received the unwelcome assignment of cleaning the chicken house or livestock barns, and they gathered eggs and worked in the garden. Girls assisted their mothers with household chores, such as cooking, cleaning house, and washing clothes. Children even helped earn money. According to the East Tennessee report, girls as well as women took part in silk production. The annual livestock drives offered the opportunity for young boys to make a little money. "It was a great treat to me," Bryan remembered, "for my mother to hyre me out to parties who was buying hogs, sheep, and turkeys to help drive them to Clarksville."[47] He failed to reveal what happened to his wages, but they most likely went into the family coffer. Parents hired out teenage boys to neighbors for incidental farm work.

In light of the enormous amount and the strenuous nature of work performed by members of farm households, it is small wonder that they looked forward to any kind of relief from their toil. Their leisure-time activities were simple and unpretentious. In large measure, they grew out of the values and habits long established in rural societies. They evolved from ancient folkways that reached back over generations and that had been brought to Tennessee by early settlers. Some activities and practices preserved traditional forms; others reflected

adjustments to the circumstances of a new environment. They emphasized group associations, encouraged community relationships, and in
a curious way fused recreation with other human needs, spiritual,
physical, and intellectual.

Religion provided the context—or perhaps the pretext—for much
leisure-time activity in rural neighborhoods. Rural Tennesseans, on the
whole, were intensely devout and took their religion seriously. But
they saw no conflict in mixing spiritual and secular pleasures, a practice they inherited from their colonial ancestors. Many farmers and their
families attended church regularly, as much, it would seem, to socialize
with neighbors as to engage in worship. They chose from a variety of Protestant denominations, usually including Methodist, Baptist, Presbyterian,
and Cumberland Presbyterian; less often, Congregational, Episcopal, and
Church of Christ.[48] Most households became members of one congregation and returned to the same rural church each Sunday. Some people
remained uncommitted, patronizing several denominations without
joining any. Robert Cartmell fell into this category. From mid-1854 to
mid-1855, he attended four different churches, and he apparently enjoyed the spiritual uplift and social intercourse each offered. One Sunday
he managed to work in two services: "Went to church. Presbyterian in
morning. I went to Episcopal in evening."[49] Doctrinal consistency was
plainly unimportant to Cartmell.

For some, part of the fun of going to church was the opportunity
to critique the minister. Jane Margaret Jones faithfully attended services and took delight in registering her impressions of the sermons in
her diary. She had either excellent ministers or modest standards, for
her assessments were uniformly favorable. Others were less charitable
in their judgments on pulpit performance. The oration of an itinerant
man of the cloth displeased Hardeman County planter John Bills. "The
new Circuit Rider McFerrin preaches. A poor preach it is," he grumbled
after church one Sunday. The return to the pulpit of the regular minister two weeks later won his approval: "Revd Mr. Penland preaches
two good sermons today."[50] Herndon Haraldson was obviously dissatisfied with one minister who "lectures on Baptism & offends the
people."[51] Evaluating the minister, even a weak one, provided a wel-
come break from deworming tobacco plants or sewing shirts.

Even if the sermon fell short of expectations, the Sunday trip to the
church grounds was usually well worth the effort. Groups of people,
some of whom perhaps never entered the church, gathered before and

after the service to socialize. The older folks discussed the weather, crop conditions, prices of farm products, politics, and the latest rumors. The teenagers quietly separated from the main group to explore the rituals of courtship. The children played games, hiked in the woods, and told stories. Some people visited the church cemetery to pay their respects to family members or friends buried there. Many in attendance at the Sunday gatherings ended the day entertaining or being entertained in nearby homes.[52]

The annual camp meetings sponsored by the Methodists and Cumberland Presbyterians afforded another opportunity to socialize with neighbors while fulfilling one's spiritual needs. Those outdoor religious retreats, which traced their roots back to the early nineteenth century, took place in late summer after much of the field work had been completed but before the fall harvest had begun. They attracted from a few hundred to as many as several thousand people.[53] The camp meetings were held on specially prepared camp grounds or, if large enough to accommodate the anticipated crowd, on the grounds of a local church. They normally lasted for a single weekend, though some continued for a full week. Participants slept in tents, on or under wagons, or in cabins; they prepared their meals over campfires. The services began with hymn singing, moved on to a fiery sermon, and climaxed with the call to conversion. Between the religious ceremonies, people picnicked, talked, walked about, and simply enjoyed each other's company.

Participants assessed the success of camp meetings in several ways. As diary entries suggest, the number of people in attendance was a major criterion. A large crowd at one he attended led Wiley Bagwell to pronounce it "a glorious camp meeting."[54] Herndon Haraldson went to a meeting in 1837 that ran for a week and attracted two thousand people on its best day.[55] On sheer size alone, few in antebellum Tennessee could have matched it. The behavior of the crowd provided another measure of success. Those in attendance were normally well behaved, but they sometimes became unruly, particularly when aroused by an especially emotional preacher. Haraldson recorded in his diary, with apparent satisfaction, that the 1845 camp meeting in his neighborhood drew a "great crowd but very orderly. Much zealous excitement."[56] The biggest threat of disruption came from those who saw the camp meetings as an occasion for drinking and merriment. Usually young and always men, they came with no intention of participating in the religious activities. Instead, they milled about, often on the periphery of the campgrounds, making noise and nuisances of themselves. As irritating as they might be, their presence rarely dampened the spirits or spoiled the fellowship and fun of the main group.[57]

Most seemed to agree that the key indicator of success was the number of conversions. Despite everything else that went on, people still believed that bringing the unconverted into the fold was the main purpose of the camp meetings. Bagwell reported on one that ran a full week and managed to produce only sixty to seventy conversions, a disappointing result indeed.[58] Haraldson could feel better about another camp meeting that had a significantly better count and was still in progress: "Camp meeting continues[;] about 100 Negroes & 50 Whites professed." He was cautious, however, knowing full well that exaggerated conversion claims frequently circulated through campgrounds. He attached a disclaimer to his figures: "So said."[59]

Churches held other events that took on social purposes. Members of some congregations gathered every Wednesday evening for a prayer meeting, often preceded by a potluck supper. On a less regular schedule, they met for a round of hymn-singing. Sometimes several churches jointly sponsored day-long shape-note festivals. These brought together singers from across a wide area to produce the peculiar voicings and harmonies of the shape-note system, a tradition that reached back to the colonial period and flourished in the antebellum South. Women also met at the church to sew quilts or crochet tablecloths, which they sold to underwrite the congregation's expenses, and to exchange gossip. A few denominations held yearly foot washings. Jeptha Fuston remembered as a boy in Warren County attending such events after his family was through "layin by" the corn. "We finished in June and they [neighbors] by the first Sunday in July[; we went to] the annual Baptist foot-washing at Old Concord Church."[60] All of these activities combined religious devotion and group fellowship.

If spiritual nourishment supplied the setting for many social functions, so too did physical nourishment. The consumption of food brought people together almost as often as religious activities. Sometimes these occasions involved only two families having a meal at one of their homes, frequently after church. The fare included ample amounts of food, often with a special treat, such as bread made from wheat flour or a dessert made from refined sugar. Those receiving assistance from neighbors with grain harvesting or threshing normally served the workers and their families a feast at noon. At other times, such activities involved a large number of people who had been invited to a neighbor's farm or a local business. Robert Cartmell was especially fond of this type of gathering. "I went to a squirrel stew at Jones Mill to day, good as usual," he inscribed in his diary, plaintively adding: "This winds up stews for the season." On another occasion he "went to a fish fry. . . . I say fish fry though we had no fish; had squirrels, corn, ham, chicken &c."[61] Despite being enticed on false promises, he apparently ate well. Community events on Independence Day or some other noteworthy occasion always provided an excuse for a special meal. Jane Margaret Jones could not conceal her elation at attending a "great Barbecue in town."[62]

Obtaining information and intellectual stimulation provided yet another reason to gather with friends and neighbors during leisure time. Political speeches and public debates were popular attractions. "James K. Polk addressed the people 4 hours. 6[00] or 800 attending," recorded Herndon Haraldson after taking in one such event. "Polk and [Newton] Cannon, candidates for Govr address the people[;] 800 attending," he noted at another time. Campaign rallies could produce frustration as well as entertainment, as Haraldson's reaction to a speech on the 1840 presidential race revealed: "[Former Senator] Ephraim H. Foster addressed the people 4 hours abusing Martin V. Buren the President and extalling [William Henry] Harrison. O fudge, fudge, fudge." On another occasion, Haraldson and two thousand others heard Tennessee Senator Felix Grundy speak in Brownsville.[63] Wiley Bagwell preferred smaller settings for his edification and intellectual challenge; he was a member of a private debating society. One Saturday the group "had a verry animated discussion. The querry was this[:] which deserves the greater praise, Columbus for discovering America or Washington for establishing its freedom." The outcome of what must have been a riveting debate remains a mystery, for Bagwell cryptically recorded that "it was decided in favour of the affirmative."[64] Less formal debates on politics, religion, the economy, and a multitude of other subjects certainly took place whenever people got together for any reason.

Rural Tennesseans often found entertainment in practical activities. Neighbors joining together to build a house for a member of the community provided an occasion to socialize. House-raisings, as these events were called, included feasting, conversation, and fellowship, as well as the construction of a dwelling. Log-rollings, in which men from the community cooperated in retrieving downed timber from the woods, also supplied an excuse for families to gather and to enjoy one another's company. Corn shucking brought neighbors together to lighten the burden of a particularly tedious farm task, but it was also an opportunity for social activities. After they had finished with the job, they customarily sat down to an ample meal, followed by dancing, singing, and storytelling.[65] Tom Bryan fondly remembered from his childhood days on a farm in Montgomery County that after the corn had been "hauled up and banked against the crib the neighbors were invited to a corn shucking."[66]

Some recreational activities claimed no justification beyond the entertainment they provided. When the circuit court was in regular session in the spring or the fall, people streamed into the county seat to participate in a variety of festivities. "I went to town this morning as it is *court times*," read an entry in Robert Cartmell's diary, the implications of which would have been lost on few rural Tennesseans.[67] If the docket included any cases of interest—prurient, gruesome, or sensational—people crowded into the small courtroom to hear them argued and to watch the defendants squirm. Outside on the courthouse lawn they played horseshoes, ran foot races, and engaged in contests of physical strength and dexterity. Racing horses on the road around the courthouse was another favorite activity. As the day wore on the dancing began, at least for those whose religious beliefs permitted it. The dancing was sometimes impromptu to a lone fiddler, sometimes scheduled to a larger group of local musicians.[68] John Bills probably exaggerated the elegance of this type of court-days amusement when he penned: "At night a ball at the CourtHouse. I attend."[69] Still, had it been an event of greater refinement, Bills and the others present would not have enjoyed themselves more. Interspersed among these activities was the consumption of large amounts of food and drink. Of course, if one had any business in town—selling produce, buying supplies, paying taxes, arranging a bank loan—circuit-court session was the ideal time to transact it.

Court days concentrated many amusements within a short period of time. Other activities offered similar diversions from work on a more modest scale. John Barker rarely missed the monthly "Barn Dance at Parhams Spring."[70] Many looked forward to the parties that brought wedding days to a close. John Bills and James Matthews mentioned attending musical events, Bills a minstrel show and Matthews a choir concert at the "Female College."[71] Circuses and fairs provided entertainment that ran from innocent to grotesque. Robert Cartmell saw

"*Dan Rice* the renowed clown with his circus & some animals. . . . He had a remarkably fine horses—& also a *educated mule,* very smart." At the divisional fair he was fascinated by a mimic, who "can beat a mocking bird, nightengale, canary, jay bird or anything else—as for a pig or puppy, he goes precisely like them." He also viewed a "giantress" who was seven and a half feet tall and weighed four hundred pounds, and a "dwarf" who barely exceeded two feet in height.[72] John Barker must have taken in the same bizarre show two years earlier, after which he recorded that he "saw the Big 7ft 4ins and the Little 32 ins high and the Bearded Lady at Clarksville."[73] On one occasion Cartmell, with several friends, visited "a Phronologist[;] got *a chart of my head*[;] *found* myself at last a more *considerable* character than I had ever imagined myself to be."[74] Whether this activity fell into the category of entertainment or therapy is difficult to resolve. Often respite from the day's toil was as simple as relaxing in front of the fireplace. On Samuel Smith's Wilson County farm the women "enjoyed sittin in the 'chimney corner' after the chores were finished for the day smoking their corn cob pipes."[75]

Drinking alcoholic beverages was common among rural Tennessee males, a trait that had probably been handed down from their Anglo-Saxon ancestors. Every community of any size had its tavern, some had several. Before Knoxville was barely a decade old, one of its commercial establishments advertised that it was "well supplied with every thing necessary for the accommodation of Gentlemen."[76] Most rural taverns did not cater to gentlemen, and few found it necessary to advertise. Farmers often stopped off at the local tavern when they were in town; sometimes they came to town exclusively for that purpose. In either case, they found camaraderie as well as libation. Others purchased liquor, which was inexpensive, from the general store to consume in their homes, frequently with friends. James Matthews thought it worth jotting in his diary that he had "bought a half gallon of whiskey" for just such occasions.[77] Robert Austin remembered that after working all day, the men on his family's White County farm sometimes "had a big jug of wiskey too boot."[78]

Many drank without becoming unruly; many did not. In fact, rural Tennesseans gained a reputation for untoward behavior while consuming alcohol. François André Michaux was apprehensive about a group of whiskey drinkers he encountered on the road to Nashville: "Fearing lest I should witness some murdering scene or other, which among the inhabitants of this part of the country is frequently the end of intoxication produced by this kind of spirits, I quickly took leave."[79] Another visitor wrote that "I am afraid my brave Tennesseeans indulge too great a fondness for whiskey."[80] At one court-days celebration, Herndon Haraldson observed a common spectacle: "People drunk & fighting in the evening."[81] Robert Cartmell came across a group of men who had become inebriated at a fish fry, and he could not resist the temptation to pronounce moral judgment: "When will men cease drinking & acting like brutes; it is strange & more especially in an enlightened community & christian age."[82] Condemnation by several Protestant denominations, most notably the Methodists, beginning in the 1830s no doubt discouraged drinking among some groups. Still, men continued to include alcohol consumption, often in excessive amounts, in their leisure-time activities.

Rural Tennesseans toiled long hours at tasks ranging from field work and farm maintenance to clothes making and bee keeping. The work kept most members of the household busy throughout the year, allowing little free time to engage in less-demanding and more-enjoyable activities. They made the most of those infrequent occasions when their schedules permitted a break from the tedious and exhausting routine of farm life. Whenever possible they intermingled recreation and other activities. But much of their entertainment required nothing more than the capacity to provide simple amusement. Their behavior could be rude, insensitive, boorish, or violent. It was more often quiet, innocent, harmless, and inoffensive. Whatever type of behavior they provoked, leisure-time activities joined farm work in defining the character of rural life of antebellum Tennessee.

8

Agricultural Slavery

Rural whites were not the only ones who toiled on farms in antebellum Tennessee; slaves also performed much of the agricultural labor. Slavery came to the territory with the first settlers and figured prominently in the agricultural development of the state over the next three-quarters of a century. Slaves provided a flexible labor supply that farmers could tap when they wished to expand their production. But acquiring slaves involved more than simply augmenting the number of household workers. It demanded careful calculation to determine if the potential increase in production warranted the costs of purchasing and maintaining the additional workers. It required a management scheme designed to extract the optimal amount of labor from the slaves. And it necessitated dealing with a set of problems unique to the institution of slavery.

Few of the households that migrated to the eastern valleys and the central basin in the late eighteenth century brought slaves. The territorial census of 1791, taken two decades after the establishment of the first settlements, recorded 3,417 slaves, just under 10 percent of the entire population.[1] By the time of Tennessee's first federal census in 1800, the slave count had risen to 13,684, almost 13 percent of the total population. The number and the proportion continued to grow until 1860, when Tennessee contained more than 275,000 slaves, about a quarter of its population.

Tennessee slaves were unevenly distributed in three respects. The state's three grand divisions differed in the number of slaves, the percentage of slaveholding households varied among the state's agricultural regions, and the slaveholding households themselves showed considerable diversity in the size of their holdings.

The three geographical divisions contained widely varying proportions of the state's slave population. By 1840, after the last agricultural region had passed through the settlement stage, the disparity had become firmly established. East Tennessee was home to 11 percent of

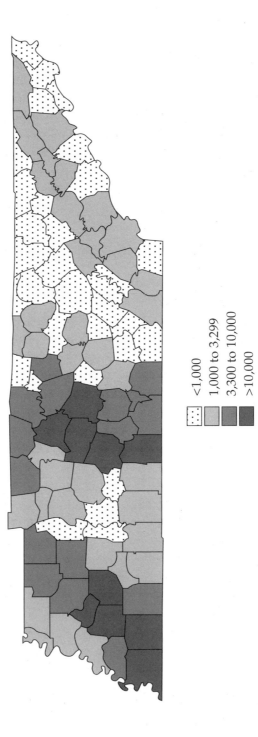

Map 8.1. County slave population, 1860. Source: Federal Population Census, 1860.

the state's slaves, Middle Tennessee to 58 percent, and West Tennessee to 31 percent. Twenty years later, on the eve of the Civil War, the distribution had changed little: East Tennessee had 10 percent; Middle Tennessee, 54 percent; and West Tennessee, 36 percent. As map 8.1 shows, the heaviest concentrations of slaves in 1860 occurred in the central basin of Middle Tennessee and in the western plateau and Mississippi bottom lands of West Tennessee.

The types of commercial agriculture that evolved in each of the divisions explained much of the unevenness in the geographical distribution of slaves. The profitability of slavery depended to a large extent on the capacity of the farming operation to keep workers occupied as much as possible at commercial production. Slavery was better suited to systems that needed labor throughout most of the year than to those that needed labor only intermittently during the growing season.[2] Some agricultural regions in antebellum Tennessee satisfied that requirement; some did not.

The farming regions of East Tennessee concentrated on the commercial production of wheat and livestock, neither of which was particularly labor intensive. Wheat cultivation demanded more workers than the typical farm family could provide only during the spring harvest. Neighbors often tried to stagger their harvests so that they could help one another during this critical period. Farmers also hired hands at times of high labor needs, when cooperative arrangements with neighbors failed to supply the necessary number of workers. During much of the year, most of the livestock fed on range, forest, and pasture lands and required little care. When it came time to bring them in for fattening, butchering, or shearing, the farm family normally supplied the necessary workers, supplemented again if necessary by helpful neighbors. Male members of the household performed the remaining field work in season and the building, repair, and maintenance tasks at relatively slack times. Such a regimen poorly satisfied the profitability requisites for slavery, for it provided little opportunity to keep hands busy at commercial production throughout the year. Small wonder, therefore, that only about one in ten of the state's slaves resided in East Tennessee.

The situation in Middle and West Tennessee was much different. Farmers in these divisions, like those in East Tennessee, produced wheat and livestock for the market. But they also grew sizable quantities of tobacco and cotton, especially in the central basin, western plateau, and

Mississippi bottom lands. Those crops, as noted, demanded considerably more labor. Workers had to prepare the fields, sow the seeds, care for the plants, harvest the crops, and prepare the products for market, tasks that occupied them throughout most of the year. Small farms using exclusively family labor grew both crops, but production on a moderate- or large-scale normally required labor beyond what the male members of the household could provide.

Farmers met those additional labor requirements in two ways. They sometimes employed nonfamily workers by the year; more often they purchased slaves. Fragmentary evidence suggests that a supply of free labor was available for hire. For a few Tennessee counties, the population schedules of the federal manuscript census included "farm laborer" as an occupational designation. Usually, however, all rural occupations were subsumed under the category of "farmer." Some "farmers" on the population schedules owned no land, and some among this group were not included on the agricultural schedules, which listed operators who had recorded production from the year before the census was taken. First-year tenants, of course, comprised an undetermined share of those "farmers without farms," but laborers doubtlessly made up a substantial proportion. Farm diaries provide direct evidence of the use of hired hands. One year tobacco farmer John Barker "employed Wm Murphy to live with me." In 1847 he "employed Dean for next year at $200." Wages apparently increased over the following decade, for he "paid Roach $400 in full for his services for 1857."[3]

The supply of hands willing to work under such arrangements was limited, and the turnover was rapid. Workers normally stayed for only a year or two before moving on to another job or to a farm of their own, usually as a tenant. Slaves were the only labor supply large enough and stable enough to meet the needs of large-scale tobacco and cotton farmers. The production of those labor-intensive crops, in turn, satisfied the crucial requirement for slave profitability, for they kept hands busy over a good share of the year. By the end of the antebellum period, as a result, Middle Tennessee accounted for more than half of the slave population, and West Tennessee for about a third.

The proportion of slaveholding households, as well as the number of slaves, differed among the three regions. In 1850, as table 8.1 indicates, less than 50 percent of the farms in the eight sample counties held slaves; ten years later the portion had declined to less than 40 percent.[4] Slaveholding was concentrated in relatively few households in

Table 8.1

Slave Distribution, 1850 and 1860

Decile	Percentage of Total Slaves	
	1850	1860
1	62.7	66.9
2	21.8	20.4
3	10.5	9.6
4	4.2	3.2
5	0.8	0.0
6	0.0	0.0
7	0.0	0.0
8	0.0	0.0
9	0.0	0.0
10	0.0	0.0

SOURCE: Eight sample counties (see appendix).

each of the three divisions of the state, but in varying degrees. Only about 10 percent of the rural households in East Tennessee owned slaves in 1860. Roughly a third of the operators in Middle Tennessee and just under a half of the operators in West Tennessee fell into this category. The Gini coefficients in table 8.2, which measure overall concentration, clearly show this disparity. The East Tennessee counties of Johnson and Grainger registered relatively high coefficients, reflecting a concentration of slaves in a few hands. The West Tennessee counties of Fayette and Haywood registered relatively low coefficients, reflecting wider slaveholding. With the exception of Hardin, which resembled East Tennessee, the Middle Tennessee counties registered moderate levels of concentration.

The distribution of slaves among slave-owning households was also skewed. In the last two census years before the Civil War, as table 8.1 reveals, the top 10 percent of the farms in the eight sample counties held about two-thirds of all slaves in those counties; the portion for the top two deciles combined approached 90 percent. About half of the slaveholding households owned five or fewer slaves; roughly 70 percent owned ten or fewer; and just under 90 percent owned twenty or fewer.

Table 8.2

Slave Gini Indexes for Individual Counties, 1850 and 1860

County	Slaves	
	1850	1860
Dekalb	86.2	85.9
Fayette	61.2	60.8
Franklin	79.5	79.7
Grainger	86.9	85.8
Hardin	88.1	87.1
Haywood	69.9	73.3
Johnson	89.0	89.5
Robertson	72.7	74.9
All counties	78.3	80.2

SOURCE: Eight sample counties (see appendix).

Approximately 12 percent of the slave owners, representing less than 5 percent of all farmers, held more than twenty slaves. A handful of operators in this group possessed slave forces of enormous size.[5] Fayette and Haywood counties, both major cotton producers, each contained only six planters owning more than one hundred slaves in 1860. John W. Jones, with 182 slaves, was the largest holder in Fayette County; ten years earlier he had owned 235. James Bond, with 221 slaves, and Nathan Adams, with 202, were the only ones in Haywood County holding more than two hundred. The state's largest slaveholder on the eve of the Civil War was Robertson County's George Washington, with 274 slaves.

Although slaveholding became slightly more concentrated between 1850 and 1860, as the table 8.2 Gini coefficients for all counties indicate, the average number of slaves increased across all categories of slaveholders. Table 8.3 records changes in slaveholding for a group of farmers who remained in the same county for at least ten years—that is, those who appeared in both the 1850 and 1860 manuscript censuses of a particular county—in four of the eight sample counties. The persisters, who numbered 1,087, represented 35 percent of all farm operators in the four counties in 1850, and ranged from 33 percent in Haywood County to 44 percent in Johnson County.

Table 8.3

Slaveholdings by 1850 Slave Category for Persisting Farmers, 1850 and 1860

Slave Category	Percentage of Households	Slaves 1850	Slaves 1860	Percentage Change 1850–1860
0	57.8	0.0	0.6	—
1–2	11.4	1.5	3.0	100.0
3–5	8.0	3.9	6.5	66.7
6–10	9.1	7.8	10.7	37.2
11–20	7.8	14.8	19.5	31.8
>20	5.9	36.3	46.2	27.3
All categories		4.5	6.4	42.2

SOURCE: Eight sample counties (based on Dekalb, Franklin, Haywood, and Johnson Counties; see appendix).

The information in table 8.3 depicts a clear pattern. About 17 percent of the farmers holding no slaves in 1850 acquired them over the following decade. Their average holding in 1860 was .6 slaves per household. Those owning one or two slaves in 1850 doubled their slave numbers, and those owning more than twenty increased theirs by more than 27 percent. Overall, the persisting farmers augmented their slaveholdings by more than 40 percent during the 1850s. Not all households participated, of course. About 10 percent of the 1850 slaveholders, for example, had lost or disposed of their slaves by 1860. But most of the persisters either became slaveholders or added to their slave forces during the decade.

The recollections of people who grew up on farms in the antebellum period were consistent with the quantitative portrait of the distribution of slaves. Joseph Crouch recalled from his childhood in northeastern Tennessee that there were "not so many slaves in washington county as further south." John Cooley, whose family's farm was located in the eastern branch of the Tennessee River valley, remembered only "five or six men in our neighborhood [who] owned slaves." By contrast, Robert Dew, who grew up in West Tennessee, observed that "there were few white persons in that territory who did not own negroes." A. B. Webster's comment about his childhood on a plantation in Haywood

County accurately reflected the situation in southwestern Tennessee. "As we had so many slaves," he noted, "it was not necessary for me to work."[6]

Clearly, slave ownership varied widely among Tennessee farmers. A majority, even in areas where large amounts of labor-intensive crops were produced, owned no slaves. Most farmers among the slaveholding group were small operators who owned no more than five slaves. Roughly a third fell into a broad middle group owning between five and twenty slaves. Only about one in twenty Tennessee farmers qualified as large-scale planters, and a very few of those qualified as huge planters.

The household distribution of slaves reflected, for the most part, the overall distribution of agricultural wealth. Farmers with large slave forces nearly always owned large farms or plantations. James Bond's 221 slaves worked on a plantation of seventeen thousand acres, more than four thousand of which were improved, with a value of a third of a million dollars. George Washington, with 274 slaves, owned a plantation that contained thirteen thousand acres, with five thousand improved, and was worth a quarter of a million dollars. Those with few slaves or none at all—the vast majority of operators—generally owned smaller farms or rented farms. Slaves were an expensive asset. Only operators fortunate enough to inherit them or wealthy enough to purchase them joined the slaveholding ranks. And among the farmers in those ranks, the major portion possessed the resources to support only small or moderate-sized farms. Very few commanded the means necessary to acquire slaves and land in quantities large enough to place them among the planter elite.

Tennessee maintained an active slave market during the antebellum period. The legislature prohibited the transport of slaves into the state for the purpose of sale from 1826 to 1855.[7] The law was almost impossible to enforce, however, and the interstate traffic continued virtually unabated. In any case, the restriction did not apply to the intrastate trade. The slave market within the state was convenient, flexible, and reasonably effective.

Slave transactions occurred in several contexts. They often took place between neighbors. On one occasion, tobacco farmer Wiley Bagwell sold a woman and her child to a nearby farmer.[8] Unhappy with a similar transaction, Robert Cartmell went into town "expecting to see Old Mr. Bond concerning a Negro woman Maria I bought of him as sound which Negro is diseased."[9] Plantations held sales to dispose of surplus or estate slaves. John Bills, a planter in Hardeman County, attended several such sales each year, sometimes to purchase slaves, sometimes to keep abreast of current prices.[10] Local communities served as sites for slave sales. "Spend the day in Somerville," Bills noted in his diary. "Many people there, negroes offered in abundance for sale and but few purchasers."[11] Herndon Haraldson took in a "great Negro sale & hireing in town [Boliver]. 1000 people attended."[12] Community sales traditionally occurred on "public day," the first weekday of the year. On 1 January 1856, Cartmell "thought that I would have gone to town to day as there is generally a big crowd there selling hireing &c &c on the first day of the year—but could not conveniently do so."[13] Itinerant dealers occasionally came to the farms. Cartmell recorded that a "Negro trader stoped before the gate this morning with some Negroes." He purchased one.[14] Newspapers in the main commercial centers advertised slaves for sale. Nashville and Memphis held regular auctions.[15] Millie Simpkins remembered that she spent two weeks in the Nashville "slave yard" with many other slaves before her owner purchased her.[16]

Several factors affected slave prices. Gender, age, and skill figured in what slaves brought at sale. The size and location of the market, and the relationship between the number of slaves and the number of buyers played a role. Terms of the sale often affected prices; slaves sold on credit brought more, understandably, than slaves sold for cash. Prices on the agricultural products slaves cultivated were also important factors; when commodity prices were relatively high, so too were slave prices. According to one study, the average price of prime field hands in Tennessee increased from three hundred dollars early in the nineteenth century to $850 on the eve of the Civil War.[17] Average prices for other slaves were correspondingly lower.

Prices fluctuated widely, however. Bills attended an auction in the mid-1840s at which teenage women just entering the working and childbearing ages sold for four hundred dollars. He attributed what he considered unusually low bids to a dearth of buyers, which in turn was probably caused by depressed cotton prices.[18] A decade later, after cotton prices had recovered somewhat, Cartmell paid seven hundred dollars for a woman of roughly the same age.[19] Bills attended a plantation sale in the mid-1850s at which "A-1 slave males went for $1350; A-1 females for $1200."[20] Cartmell thought that prices at the public day sale in 1854 were "enormously high, especially where sold on a credit[;] 1 man sold for $750, 60 years old, 12 months credit[;] 1 woman $1205[;] a woman & 5 children 3415."[21] The *Nashville Gazette* advertised the sale of a slave family in 1852—a male, who was a "number one carpenter," his wife, and two children—for thirty-two hundred dollars.[22] Bills periodically appraised the value of his slaves. In 1845 his estimates ran from $150 for a male child to one thousand dollars for a field hand; fifteen years later the range was from $350 to $1,450.[23] Average prices were, obviously, only rough approximations of the prices slaves brought in a particular market.

For those who were either unable or disinclined to purchase slaves, hiring on an annual, weekly, or daily basis offered an option. In 1816 Maury County farmer Christopher Houston hired out one of his slaves for the year to a physician who owned land nearby: "For his services I am to receive on the 3rd, Feb. next, when year is up, $35. The Dr. pays his tax and clothes him."[24] As Cartmell and Haraldson noted, the community sales usually included slaves for yearly hire. After attending the public day market in 1854, Cartmell recorded that "Women are hiring at about $100 [per year], men from $150 to $180."[25] In one of its editions, the Clarksville newspaper advertised an entire slave force, consisting of fifteen men and boys and several women and children, for hire for the year.[26] Wiley Bagwell sometimes hired his slaves out by the day or the week when he had no work for them on his own farm. John Barker "hired Charles to D. H. Williamson for 1 mo."[27] During his first season in Madison County in 1824, Matthias Boon rented a small farm, which he and several sons worked while he hired out his slaves to neighbors.[28] Frances Batson, who had been born into slavery in Davidson County, recalled her mother telling her that owners routinely rented out their slaves to generate additional income.[29] Buying the use of someone else's slaves was an option worth considering, for the wages and maintenance costs of free laborers exceeded slave rental rates and maintenance costs as much as twofold. The differential doubtlessly reflected the difficulty of attracting and holding relatively scarce free labor for work on the farm. Although slave ownership was far more common in antebellum Tennessee, the hiring of slaves was widely practiced.[30]

The initial costs were, of course, only part of the expense involved in owning slaves; they also had to be maintained. The farm or plantation provided virtually all of the food for the slaves, just as it did for the white family. Slaves normally grew their own vegetables and melons on individual plots. On one occasion, Robert Cartmell "gave the negroes balance of day from about 10 AM to break them up some patches &c." On another day he "gave the negroes part of this evening to plant some watermellons."[31] The owner normally provided slaves with meat, lard, and meal rations regularly, and fruit and molasses on special occasions.[32] Sylvia Watkins recalled from her days as a slave on a farm in Bedford County that their table was always loaded with "good food," but that the slaves grew much of what they ate.[33]

Supplying clothing and shoes was another expense. White women in the household sometimes made slave clothes. Jane Margaret Jones noted one day that "I have not very much to do now except for the servants[;] cuting out the little negros clothing."[34] Robert Dew's mother "would spin and weave and knit and help to make all the clothes for the family, white and black."[35] Diary entries indicate that owners often obtained slave supplies from local merchants. John Barker recorded a typical purchase: "Bot my negroe shoes of Fall."[36] After a visit to the general store, Washington "gave out the Negroes shoes this morning."[37] Each year Wiley Bagwell "bought cloth for negro boys" and paid a neighbor to make it into clothes.[38] Newspapers frequently ran advertisements for "Negro shoes and clothing" or "Negro Goods."[39] In addition to food and clothing, owners provided the slaves with primitive cabins or shacks for living quarters and, on rare occasions, professional health care. Local governments also levied a property tax on each member of the slave force.

Owners confronted a formidable challenge in managing their slaves. They strove for a system that enabled them to exact the maximum amount of work at the least cost. Such a system was not easy to devise or implement. It required a delicate balance among several different, and sometimes competing, elements: supervision, coercion, punishment, cajoling, and incentive. The management techniques varied with differences in type and size of farming operation, ability and personality of the owner, and a host of intangible factors. Few, if any, slave owners achieved the ideal mixture of the basic managerial elements. Most settled on a combination that was compatible with their personalities and that produced an acceptable return on their investments in land, labor, and capital.

Slaves performed a variety of tasks. Their primary duties involved field work: preparing land and planting, cultivating, and harvesting crops. Men broke and plowed the soil. Men and women sowed corn, small grains, and cotton, set out tobacco plants, hoed row crops, dewormed tobacco, picked corn and cotton, and cut tobacco and small grains. On large plantations with the necessary equipment, the men ginned and baled the cotton. Slave men participated in some of the building and maintenance on the farm. They dug wells, cleared drainage ditches, erected and repaired fences, and cut firewood. Owners also sent them to work on the county roads in lieu of paying local taxes.[40] Women cleaned house, washed clothes, prepared food, worked in the garden, and cared for the young white children. "My mother did any work in the house except washing, milking and cooking," recalled Robert Dew. "The negro women did that." Creed Haskin's family had a similar arrangement: "My mother looked after the household duties. She had negro servants who did the cooking etc."[41] Slaves sometimes possessed special skills. Men might perform carpentry, masonry, blacksmithing, or leather work. "Dave . . . [is] making some harnesses," read an entry in Robert Cartmell's diary.[42] Women wove cloth and made clothes. The slave women on James McColgan's childhood farm in Jackson County "manufactured the clothing for the family."[43] Precilla Gray, a slave on a Williamson County farm, carded fiber, spun thread, wove cloth, and made clothes for everyone in her household.[44] On his trip across the state in the 1790s, Francis Bailey encountered a "Mr. Blackamoor . . . [who] possesses several negroes under him, who work upon the plantation; in fact, the whole drudgery (both of house and field) is committed to the slaves."[45] If Bailey's depiction was accurate, Blackamoor delegated more of the work than the typical small slave owner. Still, his observation underscored the point that slaves were employed in a number of capacities.

Slave management on small units was relatively simple. Free members of the household worked in the fields alongside the slaves, which enabled the owners to supervise their labor closely and set the pace of work. They could also keep an eye out for slaves who might be shirking or malingering. On Alexander Cartwright's childhood farm in Davidson County, the white men and two slave men normally handled the field work. "Sometimes at a busy season, like corn-planting and cotton-picking," he recalled, "one or two of the younger negro women and the smaller white boys, were called on for assistance."[46] Robert Austin noted that as a boy on his family's farm in White County, he "plowed and hoed in the field with slaves. We did all kinds of farm work together." Calvin Crook's recollections were similar: "I worked every day both with plow and hoe side by side with slaves and sometimes hired men, both white and negroes." So, too, were Joseph Cardwell's: "I work on farm with neros side by side and row by row."[47] Under this type of arrangement, slaves simply became an extension of the family labor force and worked under a regimen similar to that of the adult

white males. The close supervision ordinarily enabled owners to secure as much effort from their slaves as they did from their sons and
hired hands.

The larger the unit, the more complicated and tenuous slave management became. Owners of moderate-sized units often attempted to
coordinate the supervision of slaves in the fields with the other demands of running a commercial agricultural operation. This at times
necessitated leaving the slaves unattended, which frequently resulted
in a decline in worker output. Robert Cartmell tried this approach,
with predictable consequences, the first year after he acquired his farm.
After being in town on business one day, he "got but *little* cotton when
I came to weigh at night." Another time he had to stay in bed with a
"chill" only to find that the "hands have done almost nothing." He
concluded that "negroes, especially young ones, *will not* work unless
there be some one to see them & make them do."[48] John Bills, who normally left the supervision of his slaves to others, spent a day with some of
his field hands and was unhappy with their effort. "I meet my people at
the break of day at the fields—stay with them all day," he recorded in his
diary; "I have 15 to commence with. 2 are sent home sick at 12. They get
1478 lbs [of cotton]. The highest only 138 lbs."[49] One of the first lessons
a slaveholder learned, no matter how many hands he owned, was that
slaves had little reason or inclination to work up to their full potential
unless motivated by some system of rewards and/or punishment.

One season Cartmell kept meticulous records during the cotton
harvest in an effort to improve the efficiency of his slaves. He constructed an elaborate matrix with the name of each of his twelve field
hands listed down the left-hand column and the calendar days listed
across the top row.[50] Beginning in September 1853 and running through
February 1854, he tallied opposite the names the amount of cotton each
slave picked on each day. At the end of each day, he added up and
recorded the day's total harvest across the bottom row. At the end of
each month, he added up and recorded each slave's monthly harvest
down the right hand column. At a glance he could ascertain the output of his entire slave force or of any single member on a daily or
monthly basis.

Cartmell obviously thought that such elaborate records would reveal workers who consistently performed poorly and enable him to
apply greater leverage in improving labor efficiency. He never com-

mented on whether the effort succeeded, but he seemed pleased with the results when he compared them with those of his father: "I made 46 bales & worked about 9 good hands. My Father with a good over seer, made 53 bales and worked 16 or 17 hands."[51] Nonetheless, a week later he inscribed an especially harsh commentary in his log: "Negroes are an unpleasant animal to have anything to do with, requiring constant watching. They feel intent in nothing—*only punctual* in comeing *regularly* when their meat gives out."[52]

Hiring an overseer, as Cartmell's father had done, offered an alternative to personal supervision on larger units. The overseer had the hapless responsibility of supervising the labor and leisure activities of the slaves, and of answering to the slave owner. Each day he called the slaves to work, coordinated their tasks, and watched over their efforts. He enforced rules of behavior in the slave quarters and elsewhere during free time. A driver, usually an older and trusted male slave, sometimes assisted him in the fields. The overseer reported regularly to the owner on the progress of the work, the condition of the crops, the prospective or actual size of the harvest, and the personal behavior of the slaves. Relieved of the day-to-day responsibilities, the owner could concentrate on the business affairs of the plantation.

The overseer's principal function, of course, was to maximize the field labor of the slaves. On plantations with large slave forces, he typically organized the hands into gangs, each assigned a particular task. He designated one member of each gang as the pacesetter, whose job it was to establish the speed at which the gang worked. He usually chose a person who possessed the physical stamina and the emotional inclination to keep the pace brisk. Pacesetters faced a worrisome dilemma. They had to find a work rate that satisfied the overseer or driver but at the same time was acceptable to the other slaves. Failing to meet the first criterion invited displeasure or worse from their superiors; failing to meet the second invited ostracism from their fellow slaves. It was a delicate balancing act. Overseers on farms with moderate-sized slave forces usually did not employ the gang system. Instead, they personally supervised the field work, much as owners did on smaller units, and attempted through cajoling and intimidation to keep the toil at a suitable pace.

The overseer also watched over the slaves when they were not working. He set bedtimes, maintained quiet after hours, mediated disagreements among slaves, and determined what was acceptable and unacceptable behavior. He decided when and for how long slaves could leave the plantation, and where they could go. He defined and administered punishment for violation of his rules. In short, the overseer supervised virtually all of the slaves' activities outside of the slave quarters.

The overseer's position required a person of special talents and temperament. One advertisement captured some, though certainly not all, of the necessary qualifications: "Overseer wanted; desire sobriety, industry, agricultural skill, and [skill in] management of hands."[53] It might have added to that list patience, discretion, tact, sensitivity, and enormous energy. Many aspects of the job could only be learned, and owners preferred, but could not always find, someone with experience. Cartmell, after an unsatisfactory attempt at managing his own slaves, could find only a novice overseer to hire. "He is young and without experience," he penned in his log, "but I think will do to be with the chaps."[54] In such cases, the slave owner sometimes provided instruction in management. Betty Gleaves noted one day that "Mr. G [is] breaking Frank to work in slaves."[55] Owners often expected the overseer's wife to take on some of the household work. John Bills's agreement with a newly hired overseer stated that "his wife [is] to have cloth made and wove . . . and attend to my interests in sickness and in health." Another of his agreements required the wife to care for the slave children and cook, as well as weave cloth and make clothes.[56]

For all of his responsibilities, the overseer received modest compensation.[57] One of Bills's overseers earned $150, six hundred pounds of pork, and an unspecified amount of meal for the year of 1846. Seven years later, Bills hired another and agreed "to pay him wages $300, find him & his family meat & bread, milk & butter & wheat made on the farm."[58] Cartmell paid his inexperienced overseer $12.50 a month for the 1854 season.[59] An overseer's earnings varied widely, but were on average little better than those of a hired hand.

The limited ability and lack of commitment of many overseers coupled with the unreasonable demands and unrealistic expectations of many owners produced a situation ripe for conflict.[60] Owners' diaries frequently registered dissatisfaction with overseers. Overseers' records, if one had access to any, would doubtlessly have expressed similar dissatisfaction with owners. Bills was particularly incensed at the performance of one Calvin Foltz: "His management is a curse to any one who tries it." Releasing him brought Bills some relief: "That wretched manager Calvin Foltz is off, thank God." It was only temporary relief, however, for a short time later he discovered that Foltz had exaggerated the portion of the cotton harvest for which he was responsible. "Foltz evidently reported false weights upon me," Bills fumed, "to make his own conduct appear better."[61] Foltz's replacement apparently worked out no better. "He is a shabby fellow," Bills grumbled, "and has not cared for my interests since he knew I would not again employ him."[62] The problems were not limited to relations with the overseer. Bills complained one day about a "flare up with my overseer's wife. I find she is a fool and he is [a] good natured, hen pecked husband—They may go." And gone they were, three days later.[63] An overseer hired at the beginning of December won Bills's early approval: "Myrick has . . . done more in 10 days than I would have got done by Christmas under the administration of Cross [the previous overseer]."[64] Bill's daily log did not record whether Myrick remained in favor, however. Cartmell's initial experience with an overseer ended acrimoniously in the first year, causing him to vow that he would never employ another. He later recanted and tried again, but with essentially the same outcome. The second one left him after four months over a disagreement involving slave discipline.[65] Herndon Haraldson succinctly described a problem owners sometimes encountered with their overseers. "Reuben Fuell commences work," read a diary entry. "Fuell gone. Drunk, I suppose," read another two weeks later.[66]

Despite the potential for disagreement between owners and overseers, conflict was not inevitable. George Washington, who employed several overseers at a time to manage his huge slave force, rarely complained, at least in his diary, about their performance. He seemed, on the whole, satisfied with their conduct. Another planter, A. T. Goodloe of Davidson County, obviously had good relationships with his overseers. He advised "treating them with the respect they are entitled to, giving them liberal wages, and retaining them in service as long as possible."[67] Still, satisfied owners seemed to have been the exception.

Supervising the work of slaves joined two quite different management techniques: administering punishment and dispensing rewards. Owners believed that physical coercion was an effective means of exacting work, and they used it freely. Whipping was the preferred—indeed, almost the exclusive—form of physical coercion. Owners, overseers, drivers, and other members of the household delivered the flogging. Cecilia Chappel, a slave in Marshall County, reported that on her plantation the overseer whipped the slaves in the fields and the owner and his wife whipped them in the house.[68] Slaves who failed to work up to expectations invariably felt the whip, the number of lashes depending on the seriousness of the shirking and the ire of the person administering the punishment. When Cartmell discovered that his field hands' cotton harvest was below the amount he anticipated, he "whiped 4." On another occasion, however, he reprimanded an overseer for excessive punishment of a malingering slave.[69] A typical entry in Washington's diary read "had several of the Negroes whipped."[70] Bills resorted to the whip without hesitation if he was dissatisfied with the performance of a slave.[71] Owners and overseers also placed slaves in seclusion, chained them to a post or tree, and subjected them to nonmaiming torture, though such forms of physical punishment were normally used sparingly. Chappel recalled that the owner's wife would sometimes "lock us up in a dark closet en bring our food ter us. I hated bein' locked up."[72]

At the same time, most owners understood that providing positive incentives was an effective supplement to physical coercion. In fact, a judicious mix of punishment and reward held the best chance of producing the optimal labor effort. Slaves customarily received Sundays off from work. A tactic popular among owners and overseers allowed the slaves additional spare time, often with some kind of organized entertainment. Bills prepared pork barbecues at which the slaves ate and engaged in a variety of recreational activities. "My negroes feast & frolic today," he penned in his log.[73] Cartmell apparently felt a touch of guilt when he "gave the negroes the day. I had given them no time for the past 4 weeks."[74] Wiley Bagwell probably took too much credit for a similar concession: "Christmas day[;] gave folks holliday at work." At other times, he appeared a bit more magnanimous in granting "holidays" when there were less obvious reasons to give the slaves the day off.[75] Michel Gaines's owner was more generous to his slaves than most owners. Every other week he brought in Jordan McGowan's string band to play for a barn dance, which began on Friday evening and lasted until midnight Saturday. Particularly enjoyable, at least for Gaines, was the "big barbecue or watermelon feast eve'y time we had a dance."[76]

Owners occasionally permitted slaves to attend outside activities, such as picnics with slaves from other farms and church celebrations. As a slave in West Tennessee, Julia Casey enjoyed the "three days in September" when her owner permitted the slaves to eat their meals on the Baptist Church grounds.[77] Slaves also attended camp meetings, as much for the diversion from work as for the opportunity to save their souls.

Jenny Greer remembered the gatherings from her slave days: "Eve'rbody had a jolly time, preachin', shoutin' en eatin' good things."[78] An important feature of this type of incentive was its flexibility; owners and overseers could promise and then either grant or withhold rewards, depending on the circumstances. Withholding rewards became a form of punishment appropriate for offenses not deemed serious enough to warrant the lash.

Another incentive permitted slaves to earn modest money incomes. They sometimes sold surplus produce from their garden plots. Washington's slaves grew small amounts of their own tobacco, which he sold for them, along with his own tobacco, in New Orleans or Clarksville. He carefully recorded the proceeds from the sale of the "Negroes Tobacco" and reimbursed them when the transaction was completed.[79] Wiley Bagwell used a similar tactic. The day after he settled up in Clarksville for the year's crop, he "paid the negro boys for their tobacco[:] Joe $6.46[,] Anthony $9.16[,] Jacob $1.65[,] Henry $1.48[,] Sam $1.48."[80] Slaves also earned money for working on their days off. Washington paid several of his slaves for working on Christmas one year, and Bagwell "paid Anthony $10.00 for his clearing."[81] The opportunity to earn money was less common than other forms of incentives, but some owners skillfully employed the stratagem in managing their slave forces. The threat to withhold earnings might also provide an effective tactic for generating greater work effort.

Supervising field work and leisure time was only one aspect of slave management; owners and overseers had to deal with other problems. The diaries of slave owners regularly commented on claims by slaves that they were sick or injured and therefore could not work.[82] Sometimes these complaints were justified; sometimes they were feigned. Owners and overseers had to sort out the legitimate from the bogus appeals, not an easy task. If they accepted a false complaint, they lost the labor of a healthy slave. If they rejected a legitimate complaint, they ran the risk of aggravating the slave's condition and losing even more labor later on. They resolved these conundrums with varying degrees of flexibility and uncertainty. Bills reluctantly excused two slaves from picking cotton one day after they complained of illness in the field.[83] "All hands out tho' 3 complaining some," was the way Cartmell handled a similar situation. On another occasion he opted for leniency, but not without underlining his sense of frustration: "Have 2 women in sick[;] *now is the time to pick cotton.*" The frustration carried over to the end of the year: "I should have gotten my cotton out, but . . . I have been hindered more then usual—1 Negro woman (Gracey) has not picked much, on account of Rheumatism. Another pregnant."[84]

Slaves leaving their quarters without permission confronted owners and overseers with another set of management problems. The unauthorized departures were usually brief and fairly harmless. "Mr Hunter here in relation to my Negroes riding his horses," was the way Washington learned of one such offense. At another time, he discovered that several of his slaves had attended a wedding on a neighboring plantation without securing permission.[85] As innocent as these transgressions might seem, owners and overseers believed they had to deal with them firmly if discipline were to be maintained. They almost always resorted to the whip. Ellis Ken Kannon held a vivid recollection of the rules on the plantation where he was a slave. Those who failed to obtain a pass signed by the owner when they visited neighbors always "got a whuppin."[86]

A far more serious situation occurred when slaves left with no intention of returning. Washington and Bills occasionally recorded that slaves had run away. In every case, they recovered them, usually within a few days, and severely punished them with the lash.[87] Frances Batson reported that her younger brother ran away one day, only to be returned and soundly whipped. The punishment failed to deter him, however; he tried again a short while later, this time alluding capture. She never saw him again.[88] Cartmell owned a slave who ran off on several occasions. After one such escapade, Cartmell expressed his frustration:

2 gentlemen . . . brought Dave home to day . . . caught some 8 or 10 miles Nwest of Jackson. I think that it is *very* evident that it was his notion to *try* to get to a free state. . . . I understand from our cook (a good negro) that a free negro woman in Jackson sent Dave's wife word . . . for her not to be uneasy about him. He would go where he would get many *good mouthfull.* . . . I *would like very* much to catch the *wench* or any other free negro about my premises. There is no doubt but that they are an enquiry to our Negroes making them dissatisfied & causing stricter discipline to [be] exercised.

A harsh flogging failed to change the slave's behavior. About four months later, he ran away again. This time Cartmell had to retrieve him from a Kentucky jail: "$95.33—This is what I had to pay to get

Dave out of Blanville jail[;] 'a rascal.'" Cartmell, his patience exhausted, eventually sold the determined slave.[89]

Some offenses were relatively minor, but still invited punishment. Breaking tools, abusing farm animals, making noise after bedtime, or slipping away to engage in romantic activities received, at least when discovered, a temporary loss of privileges, and often something more severe. The misbehavior might have been nothing more than revealing an understandable displeasure or frustration over one's predicament. "Had Big Tom well whipped for insolence and rebellion," wrote Bills. "He is penitent and promises better conduct."[90] Maintenance of slave discipline required punishing even the most innocuous misdeed.

In spite of the myriad of problems associated with slave ownership, the institution was firmly entrenched in antebellum Tennessee. Nonslaveholders desired to become slaveholders and small slaveholders desired to become large slaveholders. Two considerations influenced their thinking. First of all, slave ownership brought social status and recognition. It was a sign of success and position. The larger one's slaveholdings, the greater one's perceived success and the more esteemed one's position. People with slaves commanded more respect, enjoyed greater prestige, and exercised more authority in local affairs than people without slaves. They became the community leaders with influence in civic and religious matters.[91] It was a social advantage slaveholders—particularly large slaveholders—enjoyed and nonslaveholders aspired to.

Slave ownership also brought material rewards. It enabled farmers to produce labor-intensive crops on a larger scale than was possible with family labor alone. It also permitted them to expropriate all worker income that exceeded subsistence costs, something they could not do with wage labor. Some farmers hired free workers to supplement their household labor force, but the supply was limited and unstable. Slaves, readily available in several easily accessible markets, provided a viable alternative, but one that entailed a sizable initial investment and continuous expenses. Farmers needed to ascertain if the increased output possible with more hands warranted the added costs of purchasing and maintaining slaves. For farmers with sufficient land and capital to put the extra workers to productive use, the decision was easy. Acquiring slaves was the surest way to enhance their incomes.[92] Slaveholders faced problems and accepted risks that nonslaveholders avoided. But they also enjoyed a level of income that those without slaves rarely attained.

9

Agricultural Innovations

Methods of farming in Tennessee changed significantly between the time the first white farmers arrived in the late eighteenth century and the outbreak of the Civil War. The transition from a pioneer to a mature stage of settlement naturally accounted for much of the change. As farmers explored the state's agricultural possibilities and sorted out the most viable commodities, they altered their farming methods to accommodate the physical environment. As they shifted from a preponderant concern with subsistence to a broader focus on both household and market goods, they further modified farming practices in an effort to increase the productivity of their land, labor, and capital. But even after those adjustments had occurred, farmers continued to seek better ways to produce food and fiber. Their search brought about the adoption of a diverse array of agricultural innovations. Some innovations involved minor adjustments in farming methods, such as changing crop cultivation or livestock care; others required substantial adjustments, such as using machinery or blooded animals. Farmers responded variously to the availability of new technology. Some embraced it enthusiastically, some approached it cautiously, some rejected it outright. Those who adopted new technology combined to bring about dramatic alterations in Tennessee's agricultural practices during the antebellum period.

Tennessee's early agriculture rested almost exclusively on hand-tool methods.[1] Settlers brought many of the implements from elsewhere. Farmers fashioned others to meet the special conditions and needs they encountered as they spread across the agricultural regions of the state. In time, some of the hand tools gave way to animal-drawn machinery, but many remained in use throughout the pre–Civil War period.

The most widely employed tool was the hoe. A simple device, it consisted of a metal blade attached to a wooden, usually hickory, handle. It was a tool of nearly endless variation. The shape and width of the blade, and the length and configuration of the handle were tailored to its particular purpose and to the type of soil for which it was intended. Farmers used tapered, narrow hoes for planting seeds around tree stumps on newly cleared land. They used square, broad hoes for breaking up clumps on plowed fields or for weeding row crops. Short-handled hoes worked best on dense, heavily rooted soils, long-handled hoes best on thin, loose soils. In the early days, farmers might make their own hoes from materials near at hand; or they might hire the local blacksmith to make them. Later they obtained factory-made hoes from the general store or the agricultural implement dealer, which usually kept several different varieties in stock. Irrespective of who made and sold the tools, the designs continued to change.[2] As late as 1859, one company advertised a newly patented, improved hoe.[3] If one device could be considered crucial to antebellum Tennessee agriculture, it would be the simple hoe. Farmers used it in the cultivation of the state's principal food crop (corn) and its principal commercial crops (cotton and tobacco) as well as in the cultivation of a number of other field and garden crops.

Planting was, in most cases, a hand task. Broadcast crops, such as small grains or hemp, were often sown by casting seeds by hand over broken soil. Some farmers used a makeshift seeder consisting of a long wooden trough with small covered holes in the bottom that could be opened with an attached lever. Filled with seeds and rolled across the ground on a flatbed wheelbarrow, it distributed the seeds as the farmer activated the lever. Another device consisted of a metal cylinder with a rough disc in the bottom that could be rotated with a crank. Farmers filled the cylinder and walked across the field spraying seeds as they cranked the disc. Row crops, such as corn and cotton, were planted by making a hole in the ground with a stick or hoe, dropping in the seed, and covering it with the foot. The chuck-a-luck represented a marginal improvement on that method for planting corn. Usually homemade, it consisted of a cone-shaped wooden container with two handles on top; it was hinged so that when the handles were pressed toward each other, a small hole opened at the point of the cone, delivering seed that had been poured into the container. The farmer made a small hole in the plowed ground with the point of the chuck-a-luck, pressed the handles to "chuck" the seed, and covered the hole with his foot, while he hoped for good "luck" during the crop season. Setting tobacco plants required only a short, stout stick, preferably of hickory, or a hoe to make a hole in the row to receive the plant.

Farmers employed several different hand tools for harvesting. Early in the antebellum period, they used a reaphook or sickle, a curved blade of approximately eighteen to twenty inches mounted on a short wooden handle, to cut small grains. The farmer grasped a handful of stems with one hand, cut them off at the bottom with the reaphook in the other, and laid them out on the ground. Someone followed with a wooden hand rake to gather and tie them into shocks. John Buchanan Murray, an early resident of Williamson County, described the routine: "The first grain I ever saw harvested was with the reaphook, cutting only a handful at a time, throwing it together, later tying into bundles."[4] The scythe was a simple improvement on the reaphook. It had a blade of similar shape, though about twice as long, with a handle of four to five feet. The scythe enabled the farmer to cut a larger swath of stems with a single swing; it also allowed him to stand erect. It therefore speeded up the harvest and took less toll on the user's back. Farmers also harvested hay with a reaphook or scythe and, after allowing it to dry in the field for two or three days, loaded it onto wagons with wooden pitchforks to be hauled in. They then stacked the hay at a convenient location or placed it in the loft of a barn.

The real breakthrough in hand harvesting came with improvements to the cradle, versions of which had been in use since the colonial period. The cradle was essentially a straight scythe attached to a lath platform to catch the cut stems. The advantage of the cradle was that it eliminated the need to rake, as bundles of stems could be combined into shocks directly from the platform. One cradler could harvest up to two acres a day, more than twice the amount possible with a scythe.[5] Besides its greater efficiency, the cradle shook less grain to the ground than the scythe. Tom Bryan remembered from his childhood in Montgomery County in the 1840s that a few farmers still used the reaphook, but most had adopted the cradle. By the 1850s, the slaves on George Washington's Robertson County plantation and on Robert Cartmell's Madison County farm were using cradles to harvest wheat.[6]

Farmers used a tobacco knife for topping, suckering, and harvesting tobacco plants. One version had a short wooden handle attached to a straight, tapered blade of about eighteen inches with a cutting edge on either side. Another was much shorter, perhaps four or five inches, and slightly curved, with the cutting edge on the inside of the arc. Either model enabled the farmer to cut cleanly down the middle of the plant stem and then hack it off at the ground. The longer tool was also ideally suited for stripping and cutting cornstalks for fodder or for clearing fields of cotton plants after the fiber had been picked.

Farmers owned a variety of hand tools for other tasks around the farm. Most had a collection of carpenter tools—handsaws, hammers, chisels, clamps—for building and repair. Some kept a pit saw for cutting logs lengthwise to be used for puncheon walls and floors, benches, and tables. This device was about six feet long and required two operators. One worked from a pit, over which a log had been placed; the second balanced on the log or a plank laid over the pit. As they cut the timber, they moved it periodically to keep the section they were sawing directly over the pit. They used other types of saws, along with different size axes and wedges, to cut and split firewood and fence rails. Farmers needed a large wooden maul for driving fence posts, repairing equipment, and a variety of other purposes. A few had a shingle bench, which was simply a large wooden vice, and a drawknife knife for shaping wooden shingles after they had been riven from a log. Households that wove their own fabric owned wool and cotton cards, a flax brake or heckle, a spinning wheel, and a loom. In the early years, cotton farmers may have owned a small hand-operated gin.

The one farm task that from the beginning of settlement required draft animals was breaking and plowing land. The very earliest plows were made entirely of wood except for a stout iron point. Those plows only broke the ground, but by the end of the eighteenth century, wooden moldboards for turning the soil had been added. Because the early implements were not self-cleaning, plowing was slow and cumbersome. Tom Bryan noted that the plow his father used "had a wood moalboard and the plowman had to carry a paddle to clean the dirt off of it."[7] Plows with cast-iron, wrought-iron, and chilled-steel moldboards and shares appeared later. They did a better job of scouring, but they were more expensive, and many farmers continued to use the old iron-tipped wooden plows.

Plows, like hoes, were designed for specific purposes and conditions. The breaking plows were heavy and bulky, and often had a device attached for cutting through tree roots; they normally needed two operators. Cultivating plows were lighter and more maneuverable, especially those made for use on thin, loose soils.[8] Blacksmiths built plows matched to the special needs of farmers in their neighborhoods. Implement companies later manufactured a number of different plows. The Tennessee Plow Factory in Nashville advertised that its "variety is large, consisting of cast, wrought iron and steel; right and left hand plows, suitable for all conditions and qualities of soil."[9] The design dictated the type of draft animals. The early wooden plows and the breaking plows usually required a pair of oxen, though on loose soil a team of stout horses might suffice. One or two horses or mules, which were faster but not as powerful as oxen, pulled plows used on previously broken land.

Farmers used horses not only as draft animals but also to "tread out" small grain. After the shocks had dried, they spread the stems on a sheet or canvas tarp. Horses walked over the stems to separate the grain, after which workers repeatedly tossed the kernels into the air to blow off impurities.[10] Wiley Bagwell employed this method for threshing his small grain. On one occasion he had "finished tredding wheat"; on another he "tread out floor of oats."[11] Robert Cartmell one day "helped Pa to tramp out his wheat."[12] Another method employed a hand flail, a small stick attached with a leather thong to a longer stick, to beat the grain from the stems. This was more time consuming than treading out, but it recovered more grain and produced fewer impurities.

The development of animal-powered machinery later in the nineteenth century gave farmers a substitute for hand tools for some tasks. The first commercial reaper for harvesting small grains was patented in 1833. It was a large, cumbersome contraption that only cut the grain stems; workers still had to rake them up by hand. Besides, slow-moving oxen had to pull the bulky machine, and the poorly designed cutter bar knocked much of the grain to the ground. The early reapers required frequent repairs and wore out after a few years of operation. Improvements over the following two decades produced a machine that was more efficient and dependable. Reapers became lighter and operated with less draft and friction. They lost less grain, used horses or mules rather than oxen, and gave longer trouble-free service. Moreover, many were self-raking varieties that gathered the cut grain onto a platform, further reducing the amount of labor needed for harvest. Some models easily converted into mowers for cutting hay.[13]

By the 1850s, then, Tennessee grain farmers had an alternative to harvesting small grain by hand. But it was an expensive option. Reapers cost between $150 and $200, a substantial investment for antebellum farmers.[14] John Barker, a tobacco and grain farmer in Montgomery County, bought one in 1856 for $179.[15] George Washington invested in one the same year, but he was apparently not fully satisfied. "Started the Wheat Reaper after a good. . . . lot of trouble," he recorded in his diary; "it cut well, but not so fast as I expected."[16] Some of the more innovative and wealthy farmers adopted the reaper, but the cradle remained the predominant method for harvesting small grain.

Farmers in the 1840s and 1850s had other animal-powered equipment from which to chose. The threshing machine not only separated small grain from the stems faster than treading out or flailing but also produced a cleaner product. At $150 a unit, however, it was also costly. As early as 1846, John Barker was threshing his wheat by machine. James Matthews, a relatively small farmer in Maury County, noted in his log that he had "worked at the wheat Thresher." Robert Cartmell must have put his machine to good use, for he declared one day that the "thrasher is worn out."[17] Mowing and raking machines offered a substitute to scythes and hand rakes for cutting and gathering hay. John Barker's reaper had mowing and raking attachments, but farmers could buy machines that were dedicated to those jobs.[18] Some purchased harrows and scrappers to pull across plowed fields to break up clods, corn and cotton planters, broadcast seeders, cultivators, and straw and stalk cutters, all of which were animal drawn. They also acquired machines to shell corn and fan mills to clean small grain, tasks done by hand in an earlier day.

Cotton farmers had special needs. Their fiber required cleaning, pressing, and baling before it went to market. Larger operators purchased equipment for those purposes. A few, such as Madison County farmer Daniel Hopper, invested in mule-powered cotton gins.[19] Most, such as Hardeman County farmer Herndon Haraldson and Lauderdale County farmer Samuel Oldham, bought steam-powered gins, particularly as the designs of the machines were improved in the 1830s and 1840s.[20] Cotton farmers also needed a cotton press to compress the ginned cotton into bales.[21]

Because much of the new equipment was animal-powered, farmers needed draft stock to operate it. Early plows and reapers, which were heavy and cumbersome, normally required powerful oxen. As the machinery became lighter and more maneuverable, many farmers began switching to horses and mules. Still, oxen retained an important place among the state's draft stock, in large part because they were cheaper to purchase and easier to maintain than the alternatives. As late as 1857 John Barker "bot a yoke of oxen of S. Johnson for $50."[22] A lively debate erupted in the 1830s over the relative merits of different draft animals. The *Tennessee Farmer* took up the fight for mules: "We hope to see the rearing of mules become a more common business in this section of the country, and all absurd prejudices against it utterly eradicted." The editors wished to be fair, however, for about the same time they printed a more dispassionate article comparing oxen and horses.[23] Comparative assessment, individual bias, and, perhaps, simple inertia figured in farmers' preferences for draft stock. Whatever the relative merits of oxen, horses, and mules, their numbers and composition changed in the late antebellum period. Overall, the quantity of animals increased by 20 percent between 1850 and 1860. Oxen represented 20 percent of the total in both years, horses dropped from 63 percent in 1850 to 56 percent in 1860, and mules increased from 17 to 24 percent.[24]

Farmers considered several factors in deciding whether to adopt machine technology. They attempted to determine the amount of labor a piece of equipment would replace, the additional production from the saved labor, and the costs of depreciation and maintenance on the equipment. They next compared the potential revenue from the increased production with the yearly costs of operating the machine. Farmers could readily ascertain some parts of the equation; others they could only estimate. For instance, a worker could harvest ten to fifteen acres a day with a reaper or separate one hundred to two hundred bushels of grain a day with a thresher. The prospective buyer could easily calculate the labor savings over hand-tool methods. The value of the increased production, resting as it did on future prices, was a different matter. So, too, were the operating costs of the machinery, the service records of which were rarely available. Farmers had to approximate those numbers at best, to guess at them at worst. Based on information of uneven precision, they then decided if an investment in a piece of equipment offered an acceptable return.

The critical factor in their decisions was usually the size of the farming unit in relation to its number of workers. If the farm or plantation contained enough acres to utilize fully the labor, either family or slave, that the new technology would replace, the investment was probably justified. If the unit contained so few acres that the new technology would only idle labor, the investment was probably unwise. Many farms contained sufficient amounts of unimproved or underused land to put labor replaced by new technology to work. But shrewd farmers understood the admonition of one agricultural journal: "It is not every farm . . . the product or products of which will justify the expense of erecting machinery to substitute for labor."[25]

Not all farmers, of course, made such systematic analyses. Many based their decisions on the experiences of neighbors or relatives who had purchased machines. Others relied on reports in agricultural journals, which regularly evaluated new equipment and advised farmers on its use, or the claims of manufacturers, who advertised in agricultural journals and newspapers.[26] Still others depended on intuition to guide their actions. Farmers' decisions often reflected personal outlook rather than economic considerations. Some farmers were open to change. Robert Cartmell, for example, "got a new scrapper—it is far superior to the ones I have been using. . . . It is economy to get and use the best kind."[27] Some resisted change, preferring to adhere to traditional methods. The *Agriculturist* was speaking to those farmers when it recommended against purchasing a mechanical corn husker: "Why if such implements were introduced into this country, they would cut off one of the richest sources of pleasure to our stable population. An old fashion corn shucking is worth more to our negroes than all the horse races, chases, theatres and other sports are to the whites. . . . it will never do to deprive them of the autumnal sport of corn huskings."[28] Cartmell employed quite a different criterion in evaluating the advantages of acquiring a corn sheller for his slaves. "The negroes waste a good deal shelling by hand" was the crucial consideration in his decision to purchase one.[29] Clearly, a complicated dynamic was at work among farmers as they pondered the adoption of new technology.

Although it is impossible to ascertain the extent to which Tennessee farmers adopted labor-saving machinery, changes in the value of their farm equipment provides a rough measure. In the years before the Civil War, that value increased faster than the amount of their cultivable land. Between 1850 and 1860, the total value of implements grew by 58 percent, whereas improved acreage grew by 31 percent; the average equipment value per improved acre rose from $1.04 to $1.25. Individual county values varied, however. In 1860, for instance, the value per acre exceeded $1.50 in the West Tennessee counties of Lauderdale and Hardin and barely reached half that amount in the East Tennessee counties of Union and Grainger.[30] The regional disparity apparent in map 9.1 reflected differences in the applicability of machinery to various agricultural products. Small grain farming, for example, was more conducive to mechanization than tobacco and livestock farming, and counties in wheat regions generally recorded above-average equipment values. Topography was another factor, because animal-drawn equipment was less suitable for rough or hilly terrain. Counties in the eastern valleys and the highland rim, where the terrain was uneven, registered relatively low equipment values, whereas counties in the central basin and the western plateau, where the terrain was more level, registered relatively high values. As noted, the capacity to use the labor replaced by machinery was a prime factor in adoption decisions. West Tennessee, where farms were generally larger, tended to have higher equipment values in part because farmers there were better able to absorb labor by expanding the land under cultivation. Farmers across the state took advantage of the new machinery, but obviously with uneven enthusiasm.

Another sign that farmers acquired machinery in significant numbers was the proliferation of companies that manufactured and sold agricultural implements. The Tennessee Plow Factory in Nashville serviced much of Middle Tennessee. The Nashville Agricultural Manufacturing Company employed thirty-five workers and marketed its products throughout the state. The Goodlettesville firm of Reed and Marshall manufactured cotton planters. Union Foundry and Machine Shop in Memphis made equipment for cotton producers in West Tennessee. Urban service centers, such as Knoxville, Nashville, Clarksville, and Memphis, offered farmers a wide variety of equipment for purchase. The Clarksville Agricultural Warehouse claimed to be the place "for everything Farmers want in the way of Farm Tools." Another implement dealer did "not see why Nashville cannot furnish almost every article sought for at this time." A firm in Memphis promised to "keep a constant supply of the various kinds of machinery manufactured at the 'Nashville Agricultural Works.'"[31] Their inventories and those of other dealers in the state supported their claims and indicated clearly that Tennessee farmers provided a flourishing market for farm implements.

Agricultural innovations in antebellum Tennessee encompassed more than the adoption of labor-saving machinery. Farmers also sought to preserve and restore the quality of their soils. The care and conservation of soil had been a matter of little concern during the settlement period, when the state contained seemingly inexhaustible amounts of inexpensive, unoccupied, and fertile land. After the last region had been brought

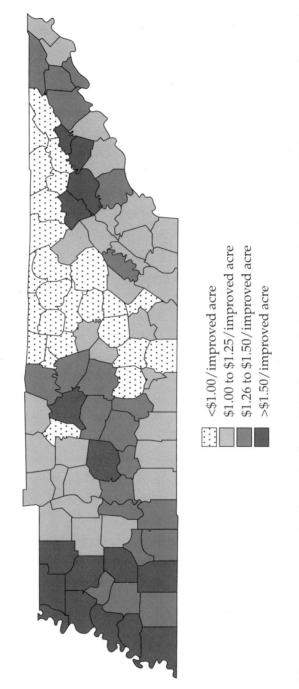

Map 9.1. Average county implement values, 1860. Source: Federal Agricultural Census, 1860.

<$1.00/improved acre

$1.00 to $1.25/improved acre

$1.26 to $1.50/improved acre

>$1.50/improved acre

into production and land values began to rise, more and more farmers became interested in maintaining the productivity of their soils. They adopted a number of different measures, including fertilization, crop rotation, and modification in cultivation.

Perhaps the most widely understood principle among Tennessee farmers was that fertilizers restored nutrients and minerals that crop production withdrew from the soil. Cultivators who chose to apply that principle utilized three basic types of fertilizers: mineral, animal, and vegetable. Farmers believed that calcium, a mineral in the soil that provided a vital plant food, had to be replaced regularly. They normally used limestone from deposits on their own property as a source of calcium. In addition, carbon in the limestone reduced the acidity of soils, thereby providing an additional benefit. Farmers had to break down the chunks to pebble-size by burning the limestone before they applied it to land. Some quasi-experts claimed that burning also removed the unwanted carbonic acid gas naturally contained in limestone.[32] In any case, many farmers built lime kilns for this purpose. John Barker "put up lime kiln" one day, "burnt lime kiln" the next, and "spread lime" a few days later.[33] William M. Crownover dug a huge pit on his Franklin County farm in which to burn limestone for "sweetening croplands."[34] Gypsum, plaster, and marl provided commercial sources of calcium and acid neutralizers, but few farmers appear to have used them.[35]

Animal manure offered another excellent fertilizer. But even for farmers who kept large numbers of livestock, recovering manure was a problem. Because animals typically fed on the open range or in the forest during most of the year, their droppings were lost. Farmers gathered manure from horse stables and from pens after the swine had been brought in for fattening. They also fed animals on cornfields after the harvest and on pastures and meadows, naturally manuring the land. Typical of diary entries were Robert Cartmell's recording that he "took some manure out of the stables" or "put hogs on [corn] field," Wiley Bagwell's that he "hauled out some manure," and John Barker's that he "put hogs in clover."[36] According to one observer, however, too few farmers followed these practices. A report on East Tennessee agriculture complained that "the majority of farmers have been, and even yet, are too indolent to haul out the manure, so that about the old stables it is usual to find it from three to six feet deep."[37]

Farmers also used vegetable manure as a fertilizer. They applied green manure by periodically sowing grasses, such as rye, millet, or timothy, on fields and plowing the crop under when it matured. The decaying vegetable matter returned nutrients to the soil. A writer to the *Tennessee Farmer* recommended such a procedure as a substitute for rotating crops. Green rye, he advised, was a "fine manure for the cotton and corn during the spring. . . . By planting rye upon it, and ploughing it in green for two years running I have been planting the field in cotton every year since with the greatest advantage. I have applied green rye to my corn with the same effect."[38] John Barker obviously recognized value in this practice, for he regularly planted and turned under timothy grass.[39]

Cotton seeds provided another form of vegetable manure. One day Cartmell was "hauling out cotton seed to manure corn with"; another he was "hauling out cotton seed for manuring cotton." His explanation for undertaking the effort was simple: "Crops must be fed as well as animals."[40] One farm journal also recommended wood ashes as a vegetable fertilizer, but apparently few followed the advice.[41]

Farmers sometimes coupled the use of fertilizers with the rotation of crops. They recognized that repeated cultivation of the same soil-depleting crop, such as cotton, tobacco, or grain, gradually drained the soil of certain nutrients and minerals. The more enlightened among them alternated those crops with one another and with grasses and clover to restore these ingredients. The grasses and clover not only built up the soil but also supplied food for livestock. This was apparently Cartmell's thinking when he sowed herd grass on cotton land: "I am determined to have grass both to cut & pasture."[42] Barker followed a fairly rigorous rotation scheme, as the following excepts from his diary indicate: "Sowed rye on corn land"; "planted Tob lot in corn"; "finished sowing tob ground in wheat"; "planted meadow in Tob."[43] Wiley Bagwell was less systematic, but he occasionally noted activity such as "sowing wheat on tobacco land."[44] Another procedure some farmers employed was to plant clover along with small grains, so that after the grain harvest, the clover would take over. Barker "sowed clover on oats" and "commenced sowing clover on rye."[45]

Especially diligent farmers modified their plowing and ground treatment in an effort to protect the soil. Hillside cultivation was particularly destructive. One journal noted that the "deep furrows of the plough, on our hillsides, furnish every facility for the ruinous washings of our soil."[46] Foregoing hillside plowing was the best solution; contour plowing to slow the runoff provided an acceptable alternative that permitted the use of the land. On flat terrain, farmers practiced deep plowing to trap rainwater and to reduce wind erosion. The *Tennessee Farmer* cautioned against shallow plowing, which merely "scratched or furrowed" the surface of the ground: "The first heavy rain after such ploughing carries off a large portion of the loose soil." It recommended two passes, twelve inches deep.[47] Soil conservation provided a supplementary reason for acquiring some types of labor-saving machinery. Harrows, scrappers, and cultivators leveled and rollers packed plowed land, both of which retarded water and wind erosion.[48]

The proportion of farmers who followed soil conservation measures is even more uncertain than the proportion who adopted machine technology. If the attention given to the question by agricultural journals is any indication, it was a matter of intense concern in the farming community. The journals discussed the importance of soil conservation, explained various techniques, and recommended proper methods. Few topics received as much space and enthusiastic attention as the care of land. The *Tennessee Farmer* declared in its first issue that a major objective of the magazine was to inform readers on the "best mode of preserving the fertility of the soil where it already exists" and on "modes of restoring to their original fertility, lands which have been impoverished by injudicious management."[49] Later issues made good on that promise.

Diaries carry evidence that at least some farmers were concerned about soil conservation. Cartmell opened his daily log, and his career as an independent farmer, with a lament on the poor treatment of land in Madison County, where his farm was located, and a call for "a systematic improvement of the soil." Subsequent entries recording his soil conservation practices demonstrated his resolve. Still, a year and a half after putting those views to paper, he confessed that he was failing "to do justice to my ground. But my anxiety to get out of debt prompts me to make the most I can of cotton." Making the most of cotton necessitated delaying or even foregoing certain conservation practices.[50]

Cartmell identified the farmers' fundamental dilemma in adopting soil conservation practices. Some measures cost little, and farmers implemented them extensively. Others cut into short-term profits, and farmers implemented them sparingly. Most made gestures toward preserving the soil; few made full-scale commitments. When they assessed the tradeoff between short-term profits from intensive cultivation and long-term gains from protecting their land, they usually chose the former. Solon Robinson, a northern agricultural journalist who toured the South in 1845, recognized the problem. Tobacco profits, he declared as he observed conditions in northwestern Tennessee, were the "grand desideratum . . . which will be sure to prevent the cultivator from bestowing any care towards the improvement or preservation of his soil."[51] In making choices between commercial production and soil conservation, it is worth noting, Tennessee farmers behaved much as farmers elsewhere in the South and in the Midwest.[52] In general, immediate returns were more compelling than preserving resources.

Farmers tried to improve the quality of their seeds as a way to increase crop yields. They employed the ancient method of seed selection, whereby they preserved seed from the best of a crop to plant the following year. The *Farmer and Mechanic* told farmers what most of them already knew when it advised: "By gathering single heads, remarkable for their size, earliness, etc., and propagating from them, improved varieties may be gradually obtained."[53] The *Tennessee Farmer* suggested an added incentive. "Selecting choice seed" over several successive seasons, the journal told farmers, would result in "a very early and prolific kind of corn, which you can sell to your more careless neighbors for seed, at three or four times the ordinary selling price."[54] Most farmers followed some sort of seed selection routine, but it was probably not as systematic as the farm magazines recommended.

Less often they experimented with new varieties of crops. Tennessee cotton farmers benefited from the introduction of improved strains in the 1830s and 1840s in the lower South. Many of them adopted the cross between Georgia Green and Mexican cotton developed in Mississippi, which was higher yielding, of better quality, and easier to pick than other varieties.[55] Cartmell seemed particularly open to new strains. In 1856 he "planted a few willow cotton seed, blodded." The experiment must have succeeded, for the following year he "planted [only] blooded . . . willow cotton."[56] Several different varieties of grain, including Italian and Siberian spring wheat, appeared about the same time; a few farmers tried them, but with little success.[57] In 1841 the *Agriculturist* reported on experiments with different strains of winter wheat.[58] Cartmell carried out his own experiment with something he identified as a Mediterranean "bearded" wheat, apparently with poor results. "You will *never* catch me sowing a crop of bearded wheat *again*," he vowed. The experience failed to dampen his innovative enthusiasm. The next season he planted "2 small packages of wheat from United States patent office, one of them labelled HARD WHEAT from Algeria, the other RED WHEAT from Turky."[59] Supply dealers often promoted new varieties, a Cuban tobacco at one time, a Canadian corn at another, a Kentucky blue grass at still another.[60]

New varieties of most crops did not significantly improve yields. Impressive claims appeared in various publications citing one hundred bushels of corn per acre, forty bushels of wheat per acre, fifteen hundred pounds of tobacco per acre, or two thousand pounds of cotton per acre.[61] These were at least atypical and probably exaggerated. Yields varied with soil, terrain, and climate, but, with the exception of cotton, the averages probably changed little before the Civil War. The figures reported in 1874 by Joseph B. Killebrew, an agriculturist and educator, very likely approximated those of the antebellum period. They registered twenty-three bushels per acre for corn, fifteen bushels per acre for wheat, about fifteen hundred pounds per acre for cotton, and about 750 pounds per acre for tobacco.[62] Even though the adoption of new crop varieties rarely resulted in significant improvements in yield, it reflected the same innovative bent that underlay the acceptance of other forms of new technology.

No subject caused as much excitement or generated as much debate as the breeding and care of livestock. Other types of new technology were fairly noncontroversial. Farmers agreed that animal-powered machinery could increase profits, conservation measures could preserve and enhance the productivity of soil, and better crop seeds could improve yields. Farmers also agreed on the importance of upgrading livestock, but beyond that the consensus began to breakdown. They differed on the value of blooded animals, on the relative merits of different breeds, and on proper feeding and sheltering practices.

Traditionalist among Tennessee farmers thought that the way to improve livestock, like crops, was through selection. Just as they preserved the best of the crop for the next year's seed, so they used the most productive animals for breeding. Swine that gained weight the fastest, cattle that gave the most and the richest milk, sheep that grew the longest and the strongest fibers, and poultry that laid the most eggs became the breeding stock for the next generation of livestock. The reasoning was simple. By selecting desirable and rejecting undesirable traits, the farmer could improve the quality of his animals over successive generations.

No one denied the wisdom of selective breeding. But many farmers and their spokesmen thought that they could hurry the process along by using blooded animals. Few proposed replacing livestock entirely with purebreds; that would have been far too costly. They recommended instead the introduction of purebred blood lines, either by acquiring a few breeding stock or by purchasing stud services. The *Tennessee Farmer* declared that by "judiciously crossing our present strains, a great and speedy improvement . . . might confidently be expected." The magazine assured farmers that a combination of selective breeding and the introduction of outside lines was the most economically feasible way to upgrade their livestock.[63]

Farmers who followed this advice disagreed over which lines of blooded animals offered the best prospects for improving their herds. Pryor Nance, a livestock dealer in Knox County, obviously sought to satisfy swine farmers of practically any persuasion. He invited "farmers and others interested in improving their breed of HOGS, to call and examine his improved breeds. . . . He has full blooded Irish graziers, Berkshires, Bedfords, and Woburns. He is also crossing these varieties of stock, and can accommodate those who wish to purchase with almost any blood they may chose."[64]

Most farmers considered English lines the best among blooded cattle, but they favored different breeds.[65] Jerseys and Yorkshires were the choices of many farmers, primary for the high quality of their milk. Durham shorthorns and Devons, with reputations as reasonably efficient producers of both milk and meat, also had their advocates.[66] English Saxony and Bakewell sheep competed with Spanish Merino sheep for favor among Tennessee wool producers. Cartmell bought a pair of sheep bred from English South Downs and Cotswolds, a cross he claimed was good for both fiber and meat.[67] Even the Cashmere goat found its promoters as a source of superior fleece. For farmers truly serious about upgrading all of their livestock, Brahma Pootra and white Shanghai chickens came recommended as "good layers."[68] Farmers contemplating the introduction of new blood lines clearly had many from which to choose and about which to debate.

Improving most livestock through the use of blooded animals was something the average farmer could do. The one exception was horse breeding; this was the province of the large, wealthy farmers. From the settlement period on, Tennesseans held a fascination with raising first-class horses. François André Michaux reported in 1802 that "in this state they are not so famed for rearing horses as in Kentucky; yet the greatest care is taken to improve their breed, by rearing them with those of the latter state, whence they send for the finest mare foals that can be procured."[69]

Although some breeders specialized in draft horses, those who drew the most attention raised fine riding and race horses. William Giles Harding of Belle Meade Farm in Davidson County and Lucius J. Polk of Maury County, two of the most successful breeders, became famous throughout the United States and Europe for their excellent lines of horses.[70] Most strains of blooded horses in the state drew on English thoroughbred lines. But even here there was disagreement, with some breeders insisting that Arabians were superior animals.[71] Horse breeding contributed little to the state's broader agricultural economy, but it was an activity with which Tennessee became identified and from which a few gentleman farmers made a good deal of money.

Using blooded animals was a costly innovation, the returns from which were delayed for a number of years. The space devoted to the subject by farm journals implied, however, that many farmers must have at least considered such an innovation. The frequency of journal and newspaper advertisements for the sale of purebred stock and of stud services suggested that some actually invested in improving their livestock. The editors of the *Agriculturist,* who periodically visited farms in Middle Tennessee, noted that most of them had some blooded stock. On one tour they reported that "in the vicinity of Franklin, and indeed in different parts of the county [Williamson], there are many improved cattle, a few hogs, and a great many blooded horses."[72] The profitability of blooded stock, like the profitability of new machinery, depended to a great extent on the size of the farmer's operation. If he could spread the costs over a large enough number of livestock, the investment was probably sound. If he had few animals, the costs almost always exceeded the potential gains.

The care of livestock was another topic that generated controversy among farmers. Since the time of the first white settlers in the Tennessee territory, animals largely shifted for themselves, feeding on range and forest land during much of the year. In the fall, farmers penned the hogs or turned them onto cornfields before butchering. They put cattle out to pasture, supplementing their diet during the winter months with corn fodder or hay and grain. Cattle, and in some areas sheep, remained outside year round, protected only by windbreaks or lean-tos in the winter. Most farmers believed that traditional methods of animal care were adequate, and they continued to follow them throughout the antebellum period.

Agricultural journals urged farmers to modify their practices. The *Tennessee Farmer* recommended feeding swine on clover and rye in the spring, wheat and oat stubble in the summer, and corn in the fall. Not only would the animals gain weight more rapidly than under standard practices, the journal argued, they would also manure the fields.[73] The *Farmer and Mechanic* also advocated a change in swine feed. In addition to the usual forage and corn, its recommendations included vegetables, buckwheat, and rice. The magazine contended that such a varied and fulsome diet would accelerate weight gain, but acknowledged that it would also be expensive.[74] Some journals proposed grinding, cooking, or curing animal feed. The *Agriculturist* claimed that cattle fed on "sour" grain "will fatten quicker and more economically."[75] Sheltering animals during cold months was another suggestion of several journals. The *Southern Cultivator* maintained that this was especially important for livestock improved through the introduction of blooded lines.[76]

Apparently few Tennessee farmers responded to these recommendations. There was little evidence that they altered feeding routines or constructed adequate shelters. The *Southern Cultivator* lamented in 1839 that hardly any farmers housed their cattle during the winter. A writer to the editor of the *Southern Agriculturist* about the same time noted the poor care of livestock in his Henry County neighborhood.[77] Farmers' diaries revealed little to suggest changes in livestock care. Cartmell, under a reflective mood as he began his diary, decried the treatment of livestock in his county: "They are suffered to stand in every rain, to take every storm and subsist in fields without half enough to eat—*after* everything valuable as food has been hauled out."[78] Yet he followed traditional practices in caring for his own animals. A few progressive farmers with large operations implemented some improvements. Sheep raiser Mark R. Cockrill, for instance, fed his animals on "hay, millet, oats in sheaf, corn fodder, and a moderate supply of Southern corn."[79] But the expense and the ambiguous relationship between innovation and results produced in most farmers tepid enthusiasm for changing their livestock routines.

Farmers needed information if they were going to innovate. Farm journals were their principal source. From the early 1830s until the Civil War, Tennessee farmers had access to at least one and often several agricultural magazines published in the state.[80] Newspaper advertisements for journals such as the *New York Agricultural Review, American Farmer, Southern Cultivator,* and *Farmers' Journal* indicated that they subscribed to out-of-state magazines as well.[81] Journal readers were typically moderate- or large-scale farmers, many of whom were already favorably disposed toward innovation. The editor of the *Tennessee Farmer* recognized the type of person who read journals, but he confused the implications of his insight: "Show me a thrifty, practical and experimental farmer, and I will show you a man who reads works on agriculture, or who borrows his hints from a neighbor that takes an agricultural paper."[82] It was not so much that the journals instilled an innovative disposition, as the editor implied. It was an innovative disposition that drew farmers to the journals.

In any event, the agricultural magazines performed an important service. They informed readers through their articles, letters to the editor, and advertisements on the variety of new technology available. They advised them on the best farming methods for their particular area of Tennessee. Occasionally, they would even offer a financial inducement. "As we wish to improve all kinds of hogs," wrote the editor of the *Agriculturist*, "we offer *one hundred dollars* to any gentleman for a pig of any breed, delivered the day it is two months old, which shall weigh over a hundred pounds."[83] The announcement provoked several claims to having achieved that goal with earlier litters, but there is no record of anyone actually claiming the prize after the offer appeared.

Progressive farmers formed county agricultural societies to exchange information and promote the adoption of new technology. The Cumberland Agricultural Society, launched in Nashville in 1819, was the first such organization. "From this society," declared the charter members, "we anticipate much useful improvem't in the ag[riculture] of our state."[84] The organizational movement gained momentum in the 1830s; indeed, by the 1840s many counties in the state had formed societies. They met, usually once a month, to discuss or demonstrate new agricultural techniques. Cartmell "went . . . to a meeting of the Agricultural Society of Madison County. . . . the Society meets once a month at farms of its members—a committee examining and reports [on] state of farm[ing] &c—essays are read &c."[85] The *Agriculturist* saw collateral benefits: "In addition to the pecuniary advantages arising from improvements in husbandry, Agricultural Societies are well calculated to promote social intercourse and friendship among citizens."[86] Whatever social functions they may have assumed, the main purpose of the agricultural societies was to provide useful information.

On two occasions, once in the early 1840s and again in the early 1850s, the legislature incorporated the Tennessee State Agricultural Society in response to petitions from farm leaders. A private organization at the state level, it was created "for the encouragement of Agriculture and the Mechanic Arts, by premiums and such other means as said corporation may deem proper."[87] The founders intended for the society to establish prizes for the development and testing of agricultural innovations and to disseminate practical information among the state's farmers. During its two brief incarnations, however, it functioned primarily as a lobbying agency to promote measures before the legislature.[88]

In 1854 the legislature created the Tennessee State Agricultural Bureau "to investigate all such subjects relating to the improvement of agriculture in the State." This state agency had several responsibilities. The bureau certified county societies for incorporation after they met certain membership and financial conditions. It distributed annual state subsidies—set at fifty dollars in 1854 and raised to two hundred dollars two years later—to approved county societies. It sponsored agricultural fairs in each of the three grand divisions and at the state level, and reported biennially to the state legislature on agricultural conditions and developments in Tennessee.[89]

Existing county societies qualified immediately for incorporation and state aid under the bureau's auspices. The bureau encouraged the formation of agricultural societies in counties without one. "In union there is strength; and in a multitude of counsel there is safety," declared its first report in 1856. "The time has fully come for us as free and sensible men to unite together, and think and act for ourselves." Qualifying for state aid provided an additional incentive for organizing.[90] The *Farmer and Mechanic* underscored this point when it reminded readers of the increase in the subsidy to two hundred dollars in 1856.[91] Whatever the organizational motivation, societies existed in practically all counties by the end of the decade.

The agricultural fairs emerged as the major achievement of the bureau. Fairs enjoyed a long tradition in the state. In 1797, a year after Tennessee entered the union, the legislature authorized fairs in Knox and Greene counties.[92] In the 1840s, several county agricultural societies, including those in Knox, Sumner, Davidson, and Shelby, held annual fairs.[93] As the number of societies increased, so too did the number of county fairs. Beginning in 1855, the divisional and state fairs sponsored annually by the bureau supplemented the county-level events. Knoxville became the permanent site of the East Tennessee Fair and Jackson the permanent site of the West Tennessee Fair. The Middle Tennessee Fair never received an official location, but Nashville became the site of the Tennessee State Fair when the legislature appropriated funds for the purchase of land in the city for a fairgrounds.[94]

The primary purpose of the fairs was to encourage the adoption of improved agricultural methods. Farmers entered samples of their crops and livestock, and manufacturers entered pieces of equipment to be judged on the basis of an established set of criteria. Educators and journal editors entered essays on agricultural practices. The fairs awarded premiums for the best entries in each category. Winning the competition brought recognition to the successful farmers and essay writers and, usually, enhanced profits to the successful manufacturers. Others benefited as well, for they had the opportunity to inspect the best of the farm products from the county, division, or state and the latest in agricultural equipment. They could attend exhibits and demonstrations of new farming practices and techniques. The fairs also offered entertainment and occasion to socialize with people from other farm households. But, like the monthly meetings of the county agricultural societies, they were primarily a venue for exchanging practical information.

Agricultural leaders comprised another source of useful information. In the antebellum period, a number of aggressive innovators farmed in Tennessee. They performed two vital functions. First, they were risk-takers. They had the financial resources to experiment with new crop varieties and cultivation techniques, to import blooded stock from abroad, and to test new farm machinery. They sorted out the suitable from the unsuitable innovations, those that offered advantages from those that held little promise for Tennessee farmers. Secondly, they publicized and promoted changes that other farmers might implement. Farm journals regularly reported on their activities and cited their experiences in articles on agricultural methods. They took the premiums and exhibited the results of experiments with new crop varieties and breeding stock at the fairs. They spoke at county society meetings, fairs, and other gatherings of farmers. Manufacturers published their endorsements in advertisements for farm equipment. Farmers who could not afford to experiment benefited from the agricultural leaders' examples and their advice on what innovations they should and should not adopt.

Mark R. Cockrill was perhaps the most prominent and most successful of the agricultural innovators. He owned a five-thousand-acre farm in Davidson County at a location along the Cumberland River appropriately called Cockrill Bend. He raised choice cattle, swine, and horses, but he was best know as a breeder of sheep. Solon Robinson visited Cockrill's farm in 1846 and remarked that his "quality of wool, weight of fleeces, size and healthiness of sheep, long life and productiveness of lambs, I think cannot be excelled in the United States."[95] Cockrill imported Saxony and Bakewell sheep from the best herds in England and crossed them to produce a superior line of animals. He routinely took the premiums at the Middle Tennessee Fair and the Tennessee State Fair for his sheep and wool. In 1851 he won the prize for the best wool shown at the World's Fair in London. Three years later, the legislature awarded him a gold medal for his contributions to Tennessee agriculture.[96]

Cockrill was a tireless promoter of wool production. He not only advocated the use of blooded animals to improve existing herds, he also urged farmers throughout the South to raise sheep. *De Bow's Review* wrote that "Mark Cockrill, of Nashville, an experienced and practical farmer, expresses the opinion that as fine wool can be grown in the southern states as can be found in the world."[97] To back up his claim that Tennessee was ideal for raising sheep, he proposed a contest pitting his wool against anyone else's. Both participants would put up between fifty and fifteen hundred dollars, the amount to be decided by whomever accepted his challenge, and the one judged to have the better fiber would take the money.[98] Apparently no one responded, but the gambit drew attention and doubtlessly convinced some farmers to take up sheep raising.

Tennessee boasted a number of other progressive farmers. Gideon J. Pillow of Maury County bred Irish grazier swine, Durham shorthorn cattle, and Merino sheep, all recognized for their superior quality. Davidson County swine producer John Shelby imported Ne Plus Ultra, a famous Berkshire boar that implanted his champion blood line in many herds across Tennessee. Simon Bradford, also of Davidson County, specialized in raising Berkshire swine. Sumner County breeder Wood S. Miller was so confident of the quality of his swine that one year he "challenged any comers to wager $500 on best hogs."[99] William Giles Harding and Lucius J. Polk gained prominence as horse breeders. Former President Andrew Jackson also bred race horses, which he ran on a track maintained on his plantation near Nashville. George W. Mabry of Knox County gained a reputation for his riding horses and high quality red wheat. Tolbert Fanning produced prize-winning chickens on his Davidson County farm. Shelby County planter John Pope won recognition when his cotton took first place at the 1851 World's Fair, the same event at which Cockrill took the prize for wool. In addition to these farmers, who were acclaimed throughout Tennessee and beyond for their innovative methods, less well known farmers engaged in progressive agriculture at more modest levels. They influenced the practices of their neighbors much as their more famous counterparts influenced practices over a wider area.

Some leaders, motivated by the belief that training future generations in proven methods offered the best prospects for the advancement of farming in the state, promoted agricultural education. County societies and other farm organizations appealed to the legislature to provide funding, and they lobbied for courses on agriculture in the public schools and colleges.[100] Their efforts enjoyed little success. Union University, which opened in Murfreesboro in 1841, had a department of agriculture with one teacher. Clinton College in Smith County had an arrangement with the owner of a nearby farm for offering practical training to its students. In 1843 Tolbert Fanning, who was the editor of the *Agriculturist* and a minister in the Disciples of Christ Church, set up the Elm Craig School on his Davidson County farm. Fanning's objective was to combine traditional and agricultural education. Students followed a rigorous program that included study in academic courses and work on the farm.[101] In 1846 the school changed its name to Franklin College, expanded its activities, and appealed for state support. By the early 1850s, however, these experiments with agricultural education had largely disappeared.[102] There is no evidence that they contributed anything of significance to the promotion of farming in the state.

Tennessee farmers were not alone in the adoption of innovations and improvements; they were part of a broader agricultural reform movement taking place across the South.[103] Since the 1820s, agriculturists in the Atlantic states of Virginia and Maryland had experimented with ways to restore and preserve soil fertility. Many of the methods they applied, such as fertilization, crop rotation, and deep plowing, became popular among Tennessee's farmers. Wheat farmers in the grain-producing areas of the upper South abandoned the reaphook and scythe for the cradle. More advanced farmers acquired reapers and other animal-drawn equipment. Farmers in the lower South adopted improved varieties of cotton and ginning equipment. Animal breeders in Virginia and Kentucky shared with those in Tennessee an interest in blooded livestock and introduced many of the same strains of cattle, hogs, and sheep found in the state. Agricultural journals, societies, and fairs appeared in other areas to promote the adoption of new technology and methods. Tennessee's farm leaders had their counterparts elsewhere in the region. Edmund Ruffin of Virginia, James H. Hammond of South Carolina, brothers Henry K. and Thomas P. Burgwyn of North Carolina, Henry Clay of Kentucky, and Eli E. Bass of Missouri vigorously promoted agricultural innovation in their states.

Tennessee agriculture on the eve of the Civil War looked very different from the agriculture of the settlement period. A great deal of the change had resulted from the adoption of new technology. The first half of the nineteenth century witnessed the development of a variety of improved agricultural methods and practices. They were designed to use labor more efficiently, to enhance crop yields, and to upgrade the quality of livestock. Many farmers eagerly incorporated the new technology into their agricultural systems. Their motivations varied, but the vast majority were interested in increasing the productivity and profitability of their operations. Some farmers adopted the new technology more sparingly or not at all. The reasons for their reluctance also varied. Many lacked the financial resources to implement improved methods. Others concluded that they had little to gain from changing their practices. Still others did not have the innovative disposition to break with tradition and accept new methods. Those who possessed the resources, situation, and disposition necessary for the adoption of the new technology had access to rich sources of information on the options open to them. The antebellum period saw the rise of an extensive network for testing, publicizing, and promoting new methods, which innovative farmers tapped as they made their decisions. In adopting new technology and new methods, those farmers participated in a broad agricultural reform movement that significantly changed agricultural practices in Tennessee and across the entire South.

10

The End of an Era

By the outbreak of the Civil War in 1861, Tennessee agriculture had reached maturity. Farmers had long since settled and brought into production every region of the state. Virtually all of the land that could be adapted to farming had passed into private hands. Although much of that land remained unimproved, farmers had placed fully a third of it under cultivation and grazed livestock on a good share of the rest. Over the years since the first white settlers arrived in the territory, farmers had sorted out and refined the crop and livestock systems best suited to their state. Thousands of rural households had made personal decisions involving matters such as farm making, commercial orientation, marketing strategy, landownership, labor requirements, and new technology. Those decisions and the actions they initiated had in turn defined the type of agriculture that evolved in the state. On a broader level, those decisions and actions had also determined, in part, the economic relationship between Tennessee and other areas of the United States and Europe, and they had affected the material well-being of people in Tennessee and throughout the rest of the country.

Tennessee developed a diversified agriculture during the antebellum period. In the 1840s, *Niles' Weekly Register* commented on the broad range of crops and livestock produced in the state. "Of all the states in the union," its editor wrote, "that which probably has, and admits of in the future, the most various productions . . . is Tennessee."[1] Foodstuffs comprised a sizable portion of the crop output. At the approach of the Civil War, Tennessee ranked sixth among the states in corn production and tenth in wheat production. Two nonfood commodities were among its principal products. It ranked third in the country in tobacco output and eighth among the fourteen cotton producing states. It ranked fourth in number of swine and tenth in number of sheep. Its farmers also raised meat cattle, diary cattle, and poultry, and bred fine race and riding horses and draft animals. The state's livestock value was the sixth highest in the nation. In addition, its farmers produced several small grains other than wheat, several fibers other than cotton, and a variety of fruits and vegetables. No other state ranked as high in so many different agricultural goods. Tennesseans, as the *Niles' Weekly Register* observed, had created a uniquely diversified farming sector.

Notwithstanding the state's broad diversification, regional specializations, as table 10.1 and maps 10.1 to 10.8 reveal, became fairly well defined in the last two decades of the antebellum period. The eastern valleys concentrated on wheat and, to a lesser extent, swine production. The southern counties of the central basin and the highland rim specialized in cotton, the northern counties in tobacco, and the entire area in wheat and swine. In the western valley of the Tennessee River, the western plateau, and the Mississippi bottom lands, the northern counties specialized in tobacco and the southern counties in cotton production, with substantial wheat and swine production across all three regions. Only the relatively poor hill country and Cumberland plateau followed a mixed farming regimen with no specific commercial focus. A combination of natural endowments, market conditions, and transportation facilities determined those regional specializations. Farmers, by and large, concentrated on the commercial commodities that brought the highest returns among those naturally suited to their particular locations.

Specialization, at the same time, allowed for considerable flexibility. Despite focusing on a single commercial commodity or combination of commercial commodities, farmers normally produced a variety of goods. Their strategy was sometimes dictated by household needs, sometimes by commercial design, sometimes by habit and tradition. Regions identified with a specific set of commercial products, as a result, always embraced a wider range of agricultural activities. Moreover, as circumstances changed or appeared to change, farmers adjusted their farming practices accordingly and, in the process, altered regional specializations. On the eve of the Civil War, agriculture in Tennessee featured several distinct, but gradually shifting, regional specializations superimposed over a broad, diversified farming base.

Changes in cotton cultivation reflected the dynamics of the situation. Middle Tennessee lay on the northern fringe of the country's cotton belt, which meant that the growing season in most years, but not in all years, was long enough to accommodate the fiber. In the late eighteenth and early nineteenth centuries, when the farmers of Middle Tennessee were testing and selecting products appropriate for their lo-

Table 10.1

Commercial Production by Division, 1840–60

East Tennessee

	1840	1850	1860
Cotton	249	10,471	3,208
Tobacco	257	236	612
Wheat	1,342	714	2,378
Swine	732	724	572
Wool	235	371	424
Silk	501	467	19

Middle Tennessee

	1840	1850	1860
Cotton	10,829	18,754	45,891
Tobacco	17,095	13,184	21,296
Wheat	1,910	565	2,187
Swine	1,480	1,664	1,125
Wool	641	774	734
Silk	572	1,451	52

West Tennessee

	1840	1850	1860
Cotton	16,624	48,587	69,487
Tobacco	12,198	6,729	21,539
Wheat	1,318	341	895
Swine	715	717	650
Wool	184	220	246
Silk	145	5	0

SOURCE: Federal Agricultural Censuses, 1840–60.
NOTE: Cotton, tobacco, and wool measured in thousands of pounds, wheat in thousands of bushels, swine in thousands, and silk in pounds of cocoons; crop production from previous year.

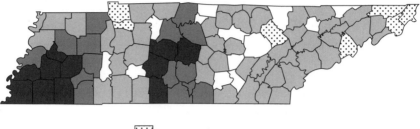

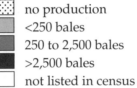

no production
<250 bales
250 to 2,500 bales
>2,500 bales
not listed in census

Map 10.1. County cotton production, 1839. Source: Federal Agricultural Census, 1840.

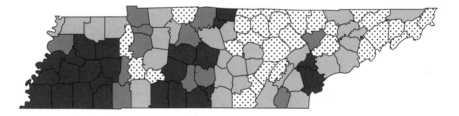

no production
<250 bales
250 to 2,500 bales
>2,500 bales

Map 10.2. County cotton production, 1859. Source: Federal Agricultural Census, 1860.

cation, the area enjoyed relatively short winters that allowed ample time for cotton to mature. After commercial production of the fiber was firmly established in the division, however, late frosts intermittently destroyed the first plantings, delayed germination, and shortened the growing season. As early as 1817, a traveler in the area commented on the change: "About ten years ago cotton was raised in this part of Tennessee in considerable quantities . . . ; but strange as it may seem, it does not succeed here now. It grows as high as ever, but will not open. This defect is said to be owing to the seasons growing colder."[2]

A correspondent to the *Agriculturist* in 1839 echoed this assessment when he wrote that "the culture of Cotton in Middle Tennessee has been precarious since 1812, and by no means a source to be relied on."[3] Mark R. Cockrill, a prominent sheep raiser in the central basin, declared in the 1840s that "the raising of cotton so far north, will not pay interest upon the capital investment."[4] A writer to the *Southern Cultivator* expressed a similar thought more eloquently, if less precisely: "I look upon it as a fixed destiny, that the white coated cotton fields must yield to the green mantled pastures."[5] Even Robert Cartmell, whose Madison County farm was more favorably situated in southwestern Tennessee, had reservations. In April of 1854, he recorded that "I had a good deal of cotton up but I guess this mornings frost killed all. . . . This Country is getting very uncertain. It is the extreme northern part of cotton growing Country."[6]

Some Middle Tennessee farmers adjusted to the weather changes by reducing or abandoning cotton cultivation.[7] Davidson County, at the extreme northern edge of the cotton belt, produced five hundred bales of cotton in 1839 and thirteen hundred bales in 1849, but only four hundred bales in 1859. Williamson County, located immediately south of Davidson County, increased its output from three thousand bales in 1839 to fifty-three hundred bales in 1849, only to see it fall back to twenty-eight hundred bales by 1859. On a visit to Andrew Jackson's Davidson County plantation in 1841, the editor of the *Agriculturist* found that the former president had already adjusted to the precarious nature of cotton cultivation in Middle Tennessee. He reported approvingly that "from the fact that we saw no cotton growing, we infer the General has abandoned this for a more profitable crop. It is just what intelligent farmers will all do, ere long, in the same region."[8] Although Middle Tennessee farmers as a group, as table 10.1 shows, more than doubled production of the fiber in the decade of the 1850s,

☐ no production
☐ <100,000 pounds
☐ 100,000 to 1,000,000 pounds
☐ >1,000,000 pounds
☐ not listed in census

Map 10.3. County tobacco production, 1839. Source: Federal Agricultural Census, 1840.

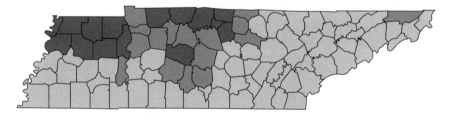

☐ <100,000 pounds
☐ 100,000 to 1,000,000 pounds
☐ >1,000,000 pounds

Map 10.4. County tobacco production, 1859. Source: Federal Agricultural Census, 1860.

many on the edge of the cotton belt followed Jackson's strategy and switched to other commodities.

Wheat became the replacement crop for many Middle Tennessee cotton farmers. Grain prices were relatively stronger than cotton prices during the 1850s. Improvements in transportation, particularly the establishment of railroad links to the Atlantic and Gulf Coasts, widened the market for wheat and enhanced its commercial promise. As cotton production declined in Davidson and Williamson counties between 1849 and 1859, for instance, wheat production quadrupled in the former and more than tripled in the latter. Middle Tennessee as a whole, as shown in table 10.1, saw wheat production rise almost fourfold over the same decade, after declining significantly in the previous decade. Farmers obviously reassessed the potential profits and relative risks of cotton and wheat, and many of them decided to increase their commitment to wheat. In fact, wheat was apparently an attractive commercial crop in southwestern Tennessee as well, even though the climate in the area was less accommodating to small grain than in Middle Tennessee. Between 1849 and 1859, wheat production tripled in Fayette, the state's leading cotton county, and increased 2.5 times in West Tennessee as a whole.

The patterns that characterized Tennessee agriculture at the end of the antebellum period had emerged from a routine that reached back to the settlement period. Each household determined what combination of commodities best suited its needs and aspirations; each household adopted a set of practices tailored to meet its ends. Household decisions rested on two competing models of agriculture, which farmers followed—sometimes explicitly, sometimes implicitly—in deciding what to produce and how to produce it. Because those models narrowed and guided farmers' choices, they imposed regularity on agricultural practices. At the same time, by offering widely divergent conceptions of farming and rural life, they also introduced a measure of variation.

According to one model, farming was a business, an activity subject to the same market forces that affected other economic activities. The editor of the *Tennessee Farmer* obviously had this model in mind when he announced the primary purpose of his journal in its maiden issue: "The first, and the grand objective, then of this paper will be, to promote the interests of Agriculture in all of its branches, by conveying to its readers such information, as will enable them to derive the

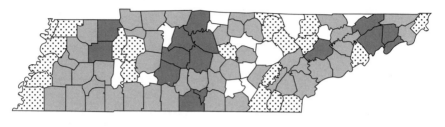

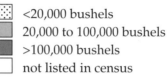

    ⬚ <20,000 bushels
    ■ 20,000 to 100,000 bushels
    ■ >100,000 bushels
    □ not listed in census

Map 10.5. County wheat production, 1839. Source: Federal Agricultural Census, 1840.

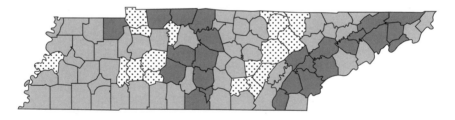

    ⬚ <20,000 bushels
    ■ 20,000 to 100,000 bushels
    ■ >100,000 bushels

Map 10.6. County wheat production, 1859. Source: Federal Agricultural Census, 1860.

greatest permanent profit from their labor and capital."[9] The advice of a Clarksville newspaper drew on a similar set of assumptions. After tobacco prices had remained low for several years, it suggested that farmers consider "some other branch of agriculture, which promised them a better remuneration for their toil."[10] Looking back on his childhood days in Bradley County, M. V. Jones remembered that "farmming was [the] most honorable besness in the country."[11] Under this conception, which emphasized the commercial nature of agricultural life, pecuniary rewards became the principal criteria for making choices among alternative farming practices.

A second model depicted farming as a social organization for perpetuating rural values and leading morally satisfying lives. In this less precise formulation, the critical—if widely divergent—values were independence, family cohesion, community sharing and cooperation, and the virtue of working the land. The editor of the *Tennessee Farmer*, a few years after declaring the promotion of profits as his journal's "grand objective," now stressed the "intrinsic charm" of farming. Although he failed to define the substance of that "intrinsic charm," he strongly recommended a career in agriculture, "the rewards of whose labor is [sic] not made exclusively to consist in prompt returns of dollars and cents."[12] Robert Cartmell seemed to have a similar notion in mind when he complained in his diary that "agriculture has not advanced as fast as it should have. It is now and always has been behind both Law, and Medicine, while it is older than either, and quite as honourable, and affords ample ground for the exercise of the intellectual faculties."[13] Joseph Cardwell agreed, asserting that "farming was an umble but exalted occupahan."[14] Under this conception, which emphasized the moral and cultural content of agricultural life, nonpecuniary rewards became the principal criteria for making choices among alternative farming practices.

As farmers sought pecuniary rewards from agriculture, they naturally adopted practices that promised the greatest financial returns. They produced the most profitable commodities, improved the efficiency of their land and labor, and expanded their productive capacities. Their decisions and actions sustained a number of agricultural developments, such as an increasingly commercial orientation, an expansion of land under cultivation, the spread of slavery, the rise of regional specializations, and the adoption of new technology. As farmers sought nonpecuniary rewards from agriculture, they naturally adopted practices that promoted

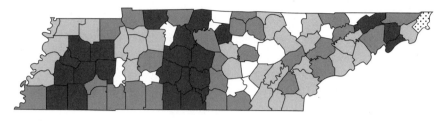

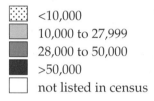

Map 10.7. County swine production, 1840. Source: Federal Agricultural Census, 1840.

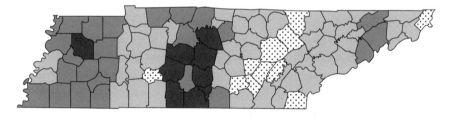

Map 10.8. County swine production, 1860. Source: Federal Agricultural Census, 1860.

the moral and cultural values they embraced. They preserved established farming methods, recognized dignity in tilling the soil, and derived social reinforcement from family and community associations. As a consequence, their decisions and actions tended to perpetuate traditional attitudes and practices and to inhibit certain agricultural developments, such as commercialization and technological innovation.

Despite their conceptual differences, the two models were not necessarily incompatible. Both, for instance, placed great importance on landownership and on production for household consumption. But even in agreement, there was inconsistency. The pecuniary model endorsed landownership because it was normally more profitable than other forms of tenure. The nonpecuniary model endorsed landownership for its intrinsic worth and for the satisfaction of passing property on to one's offspring. Still, whether farmers responded to either model or to both models simultaneously, they vigorously pursued the goal of landownership. The business conception of farming promoted production for household consumption as a way to reduce expenses and keep labor occupied throughout the year. The traditional-values conception of farming encouraged meeting subsistence requirements as a way to reduce household dependence on outside, nonrural sources and to maintain the farm as a self-contained unit. Whatever their orientation, though, farmers endeavored to make the household as self-sufficient as possible.

The vast majority of farmers followed neither of these models to the exclusion of the other. Sometimes their actions were motivated by pecuniary objectives, sometimes by nonpecuniary objectives, sometimes by a combination of the two. But when the two models came into conflict, the business conception of agriculture usually prevailed. Forced to chose, as they often were, between financial considerations and psychic satisfaction, farmers normally gave greater weight to the former in making their decisions. Robert Cartmell explained the dilemma in his diary: "I am *'perfectly' aware* that I *am not* farming. . . on the proper plan to live any thing like [an] easy or comfortable [life]." But, he went on to say, the financial obligations he had incurred in the pursuit of commercial cotton production prevented him from following the "right plan" for realizing his nonpecuniary objectives.[15]

At the same time, the appeal of nonpecuniary rewards could be strong enough to entice farmers even if they conflicted with business objectives. If the financial costs seemed reasonable, farmers might pursue goals that were not strictly economically rational. Most farmers, in fact, followed a strategy that combined pecuniary and nonpecuniary elements. Their objective was not necessarily economically optimal results, but personally satisfying lives that balanced material and psychic rewards. However they weighted their objectives, they could agree on one thing—that agriculture provided the ideal vehicle for realizing their goals. The decisions and actions of farmers in pursuit of those goals in turn shaped the distinctive features that came to typify Tennessee agriculture by the end of the antebellum period.

Much of the output of the agricultural sector found its way beyond the borders of Tennessee. Manufacturers and processors along the East Coast and in Europe purchased virtually all of the cotton and most of the tobacco. According to one study, food production exceeded the needs of Tennessee residents, rural and urban, by a wide margin.[16] Farmers sold the surplus elsewhere. Tennessee wheat, pork, and beef fed people in the staple crop regions of Georgia, Alabama, Mississippi, and Louisiana, in southern ports on the Gulf and Atlantic Coasts, and in the cities of the Northeast and Europe. Farmers, in pursuing their own commercial objectives, produced goods that contributed significantly to the trade between the state and the outside world. Tennessee, in fact, derived the major portion of its money income from the sale of agricultural commodities beyond its borders.

Over the years between settlement and the outbreak of the Civil War, Tennessee farmers and a diverse group of intermediaries improved the productivity of agriculture and of the elaborate commercial network erected to move farm goods through the market system. Settlers cleared, broke, and put into production land that, with the exception of a few tracts worked by Indians before their arrival, had been untamed and unused wilderness. Farmers searched out the most viable crops and livestock for their regions. Many of them adopted technology and managerial techniques designed to increase the productivity of their land and their labor. Merchants and dealers created a flexible and reasonably efficient system for marketing farm goods. Others established transportation facilities to carry products from the farms to their final destinations. Formal institutions and informal arrangements appeared to finance and facilitate commercial transactions. A communication system provided farmers with the information they required to function effectively within the widening exchange economy. Tennessee's entire commercial agricultural complex from production to delivery, in short, became more efficient, more systematic, and more refined during the antebellum period.

People throughout the United States benefited from those improvements. As Tennessee farmers increased their efficiency and expanded their production, they earned higher incomes and raised their standards of living. Commercial agents who handled the farmers' goods participated in the material benefits brought about by changes in the agricultural sector. Commodity merchants, commission agents, and transportation operators generated their own incomes by providing essential services to commercial farmers. So, too, did the bankers and newspaper owners who served the rural community. Manufacturers and dealers who sold the implements, tools, and other supplies used by farmers received a portion of the income originating in the agricultural sector. Nor were the advantages confined to Tennessee. Outside manufacturers and processors who depended on a stable and relatively cheap source of agricultural raw materials benefited from the state's farming developments, as did thousands of households across the eastern section of the United States that consumed foodstuffs produced by Tennessee farmers. Finally, the state's agricultural producers supported a foreign export income that was vital to the economy of the United States in the first half of the nineteenth century. Profits from the sale of Tennessee cotton, tobacco, and grain to other countries contributed significantly to the economic development of the country. Clearly, many people in many places shared in the fruits of Tennessee's agricultural progress.

Changes in Tennessee farming were part of a broader transformation occurring across the United States in the years before the Civil War. The first half of the nineteenth century witnessed enormous increases in farmland and agricultural production throughout the country, coupled with extensive developments in transportation, marketing, and finance. Farmers elsewhere in the nation created highly productive and lucrative sources of cotton in the lower South and of foodstuffs in the Midwest. They altered the agriculture of the Northeast by focusing on perishable goods that had to be produced near markets in large urban centers. Their decisions and their actions reflected, like those of Tennessee farmers, contradictory conceptions of agriculture and rural life. They, too, resolved the ambiguity by selectively drawing on both models, sometimes guided by pecuniary goals, sometimes by nonpecuniary goals. The farming regions to the south and to the north of Tennessee also adopted strong commercial orientations and initiated a variety of agricultural reforms. Much of the change in antebellum Tennessee was unique; much of it grew out of circumstances peculiar to the state. But it is important to recognize that rural Tennesseans also took part in pre–Civil War developments affecting the nation's agriculture and, for that matter, its entire economy.[17]

On 8 June 1861, Tennesseans voted to secede from the Union and join the Confederacy. It was clearly a wrenching decision for the people of the state. Four months earlier they had rejected by a wide margin a proposal of the state legislature to call a secession convention. But events following the inauguration of President Abraham Lincoln in March of 1861 alienated more and more Tennesseans and eventually tipped the balance in favor of secession.[18] With Lincoln's call for troops and decision to blockade southern ports after the firing on Fort Sumter, a special session of the Tennessee legislature decided to submit an ordinance of secession to a public referendum. Almost 70 percent of those participating in the referendum voted to leave the Union and join the Confederacy. Residents of Middle and West Tennessee voted overwhelmingly for secession, those of East Tennessee overwhelmingly against it.[19]

The outcome of the referendum probably mirrored the views of Tennessee farmers. An analysis of the backgrounds of state legislators, which revealed a number of significant social and economic differences, sheds some light on this question.[20] Of the one hundred members of the Tennessee legislature, forty-two were farmers, sixty-six owned slaves, and twelve qualified as planters. Two-thirds of the farmers, two-thirds of the slaveholders, and two-thirds of the planters were secessionists. Roughly the same proportion of the other occupational groups in the legislature and of the voters in the public referendum on secession also favored leaving the Union. Place of residence was the only factor clearly distinguishing secessionists from unionist in the legislature. As in the referendum, the former came largely from Middle and West Tennessee, the latter largely from East Tennessee. Farmers in general very likely conformed to a similar regional division in their positions on secession. Those from Middle and West Tennessee, where slaveholding was relatively widespread and essential to the agricultural economy, identified with the Confederacy and supported secession. Those from East Tennessee, where slaveholding was much more limited and dispensable in the agricultural economy, identified with the Union and opposed secession.

The fateful decision to leave the Union and the Civil War that followed, whatever the attitudes of Tennessee farmers on secession, forever altered agriculture in the state. Tennessee emerged from the conflict with farmland wasted, livestock decimated, agricultural equipment lost or destroyed, and rural structures demolished or in poor repair. Marketing, transportation, and financial systems were in disarray. More than a quarter of a million slaves had gained their freedom. Tennessee would rebuild its farming sector after the Civil War. Some features of the postwar configuration would resemble those of earlier days, but contrast would be far more striking and significant than continuity. The outbreak of the Civil War marked the end of an era in Tennessee agriculture.

Appendix

The Eight Sample Counties

The eight sample counties reflect the range and diversity of Tennessee agriculture in the mid-nineteenth century. The state's three geographical divisions, as map A.1 indicates, are represented. Johnson and Grainger counties, located in East Tennessee, emphasized grain and livestock farming. Robertson, in the northern tier of counties of Middle Tennessee, was one of the state's leading producers of tobacco; it also produced a good deal of wheat. Dekalb and Franklin counties, also in Middle Tennessee, produced a combination of grain, livestock, and cotton. Hardin County, situated on the southern border in the west-central section of the state, supported grain and cotton production. Fayette and Haywood, located in West Tennessee, were two of the state's major cotton counties. Although these counties were not representative of the state in a statistical sense, their agricultural systems delineated the variety of farming across the state. They contained 6,840 farmers in 1850 and 7,462 in 1860.

Much of the agricultural data from these counties were gathered by Blanche Henry Clark Weaver and Harriet C. Owsley from the federal manuscript censuses of 1850 and 1860. Their worksheets, which are available in the Special Collections Division of Vanderbilt University Library, include farm-level information on farm size and value, number of each kind and total value of livestock, value of implements, amounts of various crop productions, and the number of slaves. Clark used the data for her study, *The Tennessee Yeomen, 1840–1860* (Nashville: Vanderbilt Univ. Press, 1942). The age data, which are not included on the worksheets, have been obtained from the microfilm copies of the original manuscript censuses for 1850 and 1860.

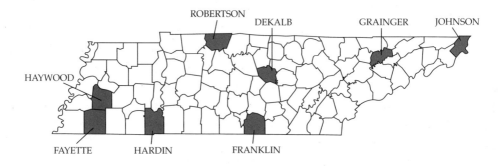

Map A.1. Eight sample counties.

Notes

The abbreviation TSLA denotes location in the Tennessee State Library and Archives.

1. The Setting

1. This account of Tennessee's topography, soil, and climate draws from James M. Safford, *Geology of Tennessee* (Nashville: S. C. Mercer, 1869); Robert Corlew, *Tennessee: A Short History* (Knoxville: Univ. of Tennessee Press, 1981), chap. 1; Stanley John Folmsbee, *Sectionalism and Internal Improvements in Tennessee, 1796–1845* (Knoxville: East Tennessee Historical Society, 1939), chap. 2; and Blanche Henry Clark, *The Tennessee Yeomen, 1840–1860* (Nashville: Vanderbilt Univ. Press, 1942), chap. 2.

2. John Lipscomb, Journal, TSLA, 19 June 1784.

3. Gilbert Imlay, *Topographical Description of the Western Territory of North America* (London: J. Debrett, 1797; rpt. New York: Augustus M. Kelly 1969), 51.

4. Walter B. Posey, ed., "Bishop Asbury Visits Tennessee, 1788–1815: Extracts From His Journal," *Tennessee Historical Quarterly* 15 (1956): 257.

5. François André Michaux, *Travels to the West of the Alleghany Mountains, in the States of Ohio, Kentucky, and Tennessee, and Back to Charleston, by the Upper Carolinas . . . Undertaken, in the Year 1802* (London: D. N. Shury, 1805), 246–47.

6. Lewis Brantz, "Lewis Brantz's Memorandum of a Journey (1785)," in *Early Travels in the Tennessee Country, 1540–1800,* ed. Samuel Cole Williams (Johnson City, Tenn.: Watauga Press, 1928), 286.

7. Michaux, *Travels to the West,* 223.

8. Posey, "Bishop Asbury Visits Tennessee," 261.

9. J. M. Brewer, Journal, TSLA, 6 Mar. 1814.

10. Francis Baily, *Journal of a Tour in Unsettled Parts of North America in 1796 and 1797* (London: Baily Brothers, 1856), 413, 424.

11. Ibid., 412, 417.

12. Michaux, *Travels to the West,* 232–33, 207.

13. Imlay, *Topographical Description,* 521.

14. Ibid., 517.

15. Herbert Anthony Kellar, ed., *Solon Robinson: Pioneer and Agriculturist* (Indianapolis: Indiana Historical Bureau, 1936), vol. 2:447.

16. Quoted in Samuel Cole Williams, *Beginnings of West Tennessee, in the Land of the Chickasaws, 1541–1841* (Johnson City, Tenn.: Watauga Press, 1930), 15, 31.

17. Christian Schultz, *Travels on an Inland Voyage* (New York: Isaac Riley, 1810), vol. 2:110.

18. James M. Safford, *The Economic and Agricultural Geology of the State of Tennessee* (Nashville: State Agriculture Department, 1886), 100–2.

19. Michaux, *Travels to the West*, 147.

20. This account of Indian agriculture draws largely from R. Douglas Hurt, *Indian Agriculture in America: Prehistory to the Present* (Lawrence: Univ. of Kansas Press, 1987), 27–41; Charles Hudson, *The Southeastern Indians* (Knoxville: Univ. of Tennessee Press, 1976), 289–99; and James Gettys McGready Ramsey, *The Annals of Tennessee, to the End of the Eighteenth Century* (Charleston, S.C.: Walker and James, 1853; rpt. Kingsport, Tenn.: Kingsport Press, 1926), 86.

2. Settlement and Farm-Making

1. This account of the resolution of land claims draws from Corlew, *Tennessee*, chaps. 3, 9; Thomas P. Jones, "The Public Lands of Tennessee," *Tennessee Historical Quarterly* 27 (1968); Folmsbee, *Sectionalism and Internal Improvements*, chap. 1.

2. Baily, *Journal of a Tour*, 413.

3. Folmsbee, *Sectionalism and Internal Improvements*, 6; Corlew, *Tennessee*, 50.

4. Thomas P. Abernethy, *From Frontier to Plantation in Tennessee: A Study in Frontier Democracy* (Chapel Hill: Univ. of North Carolina Press, 1932), 8–9.

5. Frank L. Owsley, *Plain Folk of the Old South* (Baton Rouge: Louisiana State Univ. Press, 1949), 56.

6. Corlew, *Tennessee*, 41, 46; Donald Davidson, *The Tennessee: The Old River, Frontier to Secession* (New York: Rinehart, 1946), vol. 1:134.

7. Imlay, *Topographical Description*, 517.

8. *Philadelphia Gazette*, 17 Oct. 1795 (rpt. in Imlay, *Topographical Description*, 526).

9. Joseph White, Hamblen County, Century Farms, Applications (microfilm), TSLA, Reel 2. The application lists the farm in Hamblen County, which was carved out of Jefferson County in 1870.

10. Charles Augustus Starr, Shelby County, Century Farms, Reel 3.

11. John J. Boon, "History of the Boon Family" (private manuscript in possession of V. Jacque Voegeli, Nashville, Tennessee), 3–4.

12. Samuel Henry, Blount County, Century Farms, Reel 1.

13. William Garner, Blount County, Century Farms, Reel 1.

14. Mary Elam Scruggs, Bedford County, Century Farms, Reel 1.

15. William Jeffries, Blount County, Century Farms, Reel 1.

16. Abernethy, *From Frontier to Plantation*, 28; Lewis C. Gray, *History of Agriculture in the Southern United States to 1860* (Gloucester, Mass.: Peter Smith, 1958), vol. 2:867; Malcolm J. Rohrbough, *The Trans-Appalachian Frontier: People, Societies, and Institutions, 1775–1850* (New York: Oxford Univ. Press, 1978), 18.

17. Harriette Simpson Arnow, *Seedtime on the Cumberland* (New York: Macmillan, 1960), 36–39.

18. Imlay, *Topographical Description*, 512–13.

19. *Philadelphia Gazette*, 17 Oct. 1795 (rpt. in Imlay, *Topographical Description*, 526).

20. *Clarksville Jeffersonian*, 25 Dec. 1850.

21. See, for instance, *Knoxville Gazette*, 19 May 1792.

22. *Tennessee Gazette*, 2, 30 July 1811.

23. *Memphis Appeal*, 15 Sept. 1843.

24. Christopher Houston to Placebo Houston, 6 Aug. 1818 (rpt. in Gertrude Dixon Enfield, "Early Settlement in Maury County: The Letters of Christopher Houston," *Tennessee Historical Quarterly* 18 (1959), 61).

25. Baily, *Journal of a Tour*, 415.

26. Michaux, *Travels to the West*, 243–44.

27. Boon, "History of the Boon Family," 3.

28. *Tennessee Gazette*, 1 Mar. 1814.

29. *United States Herald*, 11 Aug. 1810.

30. *Tennessee Gazette*, 30 July 1811.

31. Ibid., 22 Jan. 1814.

32. Ibid., 14 June 1814.

33. Ibid., 2 July 1811.

34. Ibid., 22 Nov. 1814.

35. Ibid., 5 Aug. 1817.

36. Michaux, *Travels to the West*, 244.

37. Quoted in Samuel Cole Williams, *Beginnings of West Tennessee, in the Land of the Chickasaws, 1541–1841* (Johnson City, Tenn.: Watauga Press, 1930), 205.

38. *Tennessee Gazette*, 6 Jan. 1802; 6 May 1812.

39. Albert Steiner, "Report of the Journey of the Brethren Abraham Steiner and Frederick C. De Schweinitz to the Cherokees and the Cumberland Settlements," in *Early Travels in the Tennessee Country, 1540–1800*, ed. Samuel Cole Williams (Johnson City, Tenn.: Watagua Press, 1928), 508.

40.   James A. Crutchfield, "Pioneer Architecture in Tennessee," *Tennessee Historical Quarterly* 35 (1976): 168–74; Corlew, *Tennessee,* 107–8.

41.   Arnow, *Seedtime on the Cumberland,* 222.

42.   *De Bow's Review* (July 1853): 70.

43.   Arnow, *Seedtime on the Cumberland,* 323.

44.   Harriette Simpson Arnow, *Flowering of the Cumberland* (New York: Macmillan, 1963), 260.

45.   Christopher Houston to Samuel Young & Wife, 16 Jan. 1816 (rpt. in Enfield, "Early Settlement in Maury County," 59).

46.   Boon, "History of the Boon Family," 3.

47.   *Acts of Tennessee* (1807), chap. 8, p. 44; J. Crawford King, Jr., "The Closing of the Southern Range: An Exploratory Study," *Journal of Southern History* 48 (1982): 53–54.

48.   Baily, *Journal of a Tour,* 409, 420.

49.   Colleen M. Elliott and Louise A. Moxley, eds., *The Tennessee Civil War Veterans' Questionnaires* (Easley, S.C.: Southern Historical Press, 1985), vol. 4:1532.

50.   Michaux, *Travels to the West,* 206.

51.   Elliott and Moxley, *Tennessee Civil War Veterans' Questionnaires* 4:1509.

52.   Ibid. 4:1592.

53.   Michaux, *Travels to the West,* 205.

54.   William Hunter, Putnam County, Century Farms, Reel 3.

55.   This account of the pace of settlement draws from Corlew, *Tennessee,* chaps. 3–5; Abernethy, *From Frontier to Plantation,* chap. 1; and Folmsbee, *Sectionalism and Internal Improvements,* chap. 1.

56.   Davidson, *Tennessee* 1:134.

57.   Evarts B. Greene and Virginia D. Harrington, *American Populations before the Federal Census* (New York: Columbia Univ. Press, 1932), 194.

58.   Corlew, *Tennessee,* 109.

59.   Imlay, *Topographical Description,* 513, 517.

60.   Brewer, *Journal,* 16 July 1814, 9 May 1814.

61.   Greene and Harrington, *American Populations,* 194.

62.   Michaux, *Travels to the West,* 234.

63.   Quoted in Arnow, *Flowering of the Cumberland,* 234.

64.   Abernethy, *From Frontier to Plantation,* 29.

65.   Davidson, *Tennessee* 1:194–200.

66.   Imlay, *Topographical Description,* 526.

67.   Michaux, *Travels to the West,* 234.

68.   Folmsbee, *Sectionalism and Internal Improvements,* 8.

69.   Imlay, *Topographical Description,* 48.

70. Estwick Evans also reported seeing indigo production when he toured Tennessee in 1818. *A Pedestrious Tour, of Four Thousand Miles, through the Western States and Territories, during the Winter and Spring of 1818* (Concord, N.H.: Joseph C. Spear, 1819), 198.
71. Michaux, *Travels to the West*, 240.
72. Brantz, "Memorandum of a Journey," 285.
73. Corlew, *Tennessee*, 109. Greene and Harrington, *American Populations*, 194, place the population of Nashville at eight hundred families in 1788; this seems much too high.
74. Baily, *Journal of a Tour*, 415, 411.
75. Ibid., 413–18.
76. Brewer, Journal, 6 Mar. 1814.
77. Quoted in Williams, *Beginnings of West Tennessee*, 165.
78. Ibid., 166–67.
79. Ibid., 204; Gray, *History of Agriculture* 2:898.

3. Providing for the Household

1. Michaux, *Travels to the West*, 226.
2. Alexander Cotton Cartwright, Memoir (typescript), TSLA, 99.
3. Albert Holt, "The Economic and Social Beginnings of Tennessee" (Ph.D. diss., Peabody College for Teachers, 1923), 102; Grady McWhiney, *Cracker Culture: Celtic Ways in the Old South* (Tuscaloosa: Univ. of Alabama Press, 1988), 86, 88.
4. John Burtis, Fayette County, Century Farms, Reel 1.
5. John Nick Barker, Diary (microfilm), TSLA, 1 May 1849; Herndon Haraldson, Diary, TSLA, 26 July 1842.
6. Wiley Bagwell, Diary, TSLA, 2 Dec. 1844.
7. John Houston Bills, Diary (microfilm of transcript), TSLA, 31 Jan. 1845.
8. *Weekly Clarksville Chronicle*, 23 Jan. 1857.
9. Robert H. Cartmell, Diary, TSLA, 17 Oct. 1853.
10. Ibid., 2 Jan. 1859.
11. James Washington Matthews, Diary, TSLA, 1 Sept. 1860.
12. Betty A. Gleaves, Diary, TSLA, 4 Apr. 1859.
13. Lipscomb, Journal, 1 July 1784.
14. Haraldson, Diary, 13 July 1842, 10 Jan. 1843, 8 Sept. 1843.
15. Barker, Diary, 28 Dec. 1844.
16. George A. Washington, Diary, TSLA, 21 Apr. 1851.
17. Gleaves, Diary, 14 May 1859.
18. William Hunter, Putnam County, Century Farms, Reel 3.
19. Tom Bryan, Memoir (typescript), TSLA, 3; James Gray Smith, *A Brief*

Historical, Statistical and Descriptive Review of East Tennessee, United States of America; Developing Its Immense Agricultural, Mining, and Manufacturing Advantages (London: J. Heath, 1842), 12–15.

20. Barker, Diary, 12 May 1860; Cartmell, Diary, 16 June 1855; Haraldson, Diary, 27 Apr. 1844.

21. James Harrison, Bedford County, Century Farms, Reel 1.

22. Bagwell, Diary, 6 Jan. 1842, 17 Jan. 1843, 8 Jan. 1844, 14 Jan. 1845.

23. *Knoxville Gazette*, 14, 28 Jan. 1792.

24. Ibid., 3 June 1841, 26 Feb. 1842, 16 Sept. 1844; Barker Diary, 22 Dec. 1848, 19 Apr. 1851.

25. Bryan, Memoir, 2.

26. See Gleaves, Diary; and Jane Margaret Jones, Diary, TSLA.

27. *Southern Agriculturist* 4 (July 1831): 368.

28. Elliott and Moxley, *Tennessee Civil War Veterans' Questionnaires* 4:1478.

29. Gleaves, Diary, 1 Apr. 1859.

30. Barker, Diary, 22 Oct. 1858.

31. Bagwell, Diary, 2 Aug. 1855.

32. John Motheral, Williamson County, Century Farms, Reel 4.

33. *Tennessee Gazette*, 27 Oct. 1812; see also *Tennessee Gazette*, 12 Oct. 1810; *Knoxville Enquirer*, 20 Oct. 1824.

34. Jones, Diary, 30 Jan. 1850.

35. Gleaves, Diary, 26, 28 Apr. 1858.

36. Ibid., 16 Mar. 1858, 15 Mar. 1859.

37. *Tennessee Gazette*, 29 June 1819.

38. Bryan, Memoir, 3.

39. *Tennessee Gazette*, 7 Jan. 1801.

40. Bagwell, Diary, 2 Sept. 1841, 25 Nov. 1842, 8 Feb. 1843, 9 Nov. 1843.

41. Barker, Diary, 25 Aug. 1848.

42. *Knoxville Gazette*, 14 Jan. 1792.

43. Bagwell, Dairy, 21 Dec. 1842, 27 Feb. 1843.

44. Gleaves, Diary, 1 Apr. 1859.

45. Elliott and Moxley, *Tennessee Civil War Veterans' Questionnaires* 4:1323–24.

46. Bagwell, Diary, 23 June 1841.

47. This question is dealt with in greater detail in Donald L. Winters, "Farm Size and Production Choices: Tennessee, 1850–1860," *Tennessee Historical Quarterly* 52 (1993): 212–24.

48. See the appendix for a discussion of the eight-county sample.

49. The manuscript censuses of 1850 and 1860 do not include the amount of improved acreage in various crops. The ratio of the output of a par-

ticular crop—corn, in this case—to total improved acreage, however, provides an index that permits comparison of the relative importance of that crop in the agricultural systems of different size operations. The higher the index, the greater the proportion of improved acreage devoted to the particular crop. The procedure assumes that average crop yields were uniform across all categories of farms. Data on acreage and slaves are from the census years (1850 or 1860); data on production are from the preceding years (1849 or 1859). Information in the tables is identified by census years.

50. The equations regress the corn index (CI) against improved acreage (IA) and the household-acreage ratio (H/A) for individual farms for 1850 and 1860. All coefficients are significant at the 1 percent level; standard errors are in parentheses. The regression equations are:
(1850) CI = 778.80 –1.14IA + 2802.61H/A
　　　　　(.12)　　(71.14)　　　　R^2 = .23
(1860) CI = 724.33 –.70IA + 2288.82H/A
　　　　　(.08)　　(49.93)　　　　R^2 = .25

51. Owsley, *Plain Folk*, 134–36; Morton Rothstein, "The Antebellum South as a Dual Economy: A Tentative Hypothesis," *Agricultural History* 41 (1967): 374–75.

52. I have borrowed the "safety-first" concept from Gavin Wright, who has explored the same question for the antebellum cotton South. See Wright, *The Political Economy of the Cotton South: Households, Markets, and Wealth in the Nineteenth Century* (New York: W. W. Norton, 1978), 62–74.

53. See Winters, "Farm Size and Production Choices," for a discussion of this issue. See also Ralph V. Anderson and Robert E. Gallman, "Slaves as Fixed Capital: Slave Labor and Southern Economic Development," *Journal of American History* 64 (1977): 36.

54. Robert Tracy McKenzie, "From Old South to New South in the Volunteer State: The Economy and Society of Rural Tennessee, 1850–1880" (Ph.D. diss., Vanderbilt Univ., 1988), 32–63.

55. Ibid., 34–43.

56. Edward Anderson, Sullivan County, Century Farms, Reel 4.

57. Barker, Diary, 1 Dec. 1847.

58. Ibid., 26 Sept. 1857.

59. Washington, Diary, 4 Aug. 1856.

60. Matthews, Diary, 4 June 1859.

61. Owsley, *Plain Folk*, 135.

62. ' Cartmell, Diary, 28 Dec. 1853, 24 July 1854, 29 Mar. 1853.

63. Elliott and Moxley, *Tennessee Civil War Veterans' Questionnaires* 4:1623.

64. Cartmell, Diary, 24 Dec. 1853.

65. Haraldson, Diary, 12 Feb. 1838, 14 Mar. 1843.

66. Bagwell, Diary, 1 Nov. 1841, 8 Dec. 1841.

67. Cartwright, Memoir, 99.

4. Producing for the Market

1. Michaux, *Travels to the West*, 222.

2. Baily, *Journal of a Tour*, 416.

3. *Knoxville Gazette*, 17 Dec. 1791.

4. Ibid., 4 May 1793.

5. *Tennessee Gazette*, 15 Apr. 1801, 9 Sept. 1801.

6. *Tennessee Sentinel*, 31 Oct. 1940.

7. *Memphis Appeal*, 13 Oct. 1844.

8. Michaux, *Travels to the West*, 200.

9. *Tennessee Gazette*, 21 Dec. 1810.

10. *Knoxville Enquirer*, 24 Mar. 1825.

11. *Weekly Chronicle*, 18 Apr. 1818.

12. *Tennessee Gazette*, 15 Mar. 1811.

13. *Argus and Commercial Herald*, 14 Sept. 1842; *Tennessee Gazette*, 8 Apr. 1801.

14. David Ragon, Monroe County, Century Farms, Reel 3.

15. *Tennessee Gazette*, 22 Sept. 1802, 2 Nov. 1810.

16. Ibid., 25 Feb. 1800; 11 Mar. 1801.

17. *Knoxville Gazette*, 28 Jan. 1792.

18. *Tennessee Gazette*, 20 Nov. 1821, 10 June 1801.

19. *United States Herald*, 11 Aug. 1810.

20. *Tennessee Gazette*, 13 Jan. 1813.

21. *Knoxville Gazette*, 31 Dec. 1791.

22. Ibid., 17 Mar. 1794.

23. *Tennessee Gazette*, 4 Apr. 1812.

24. Ibid., 3 June 1801, 16 Sept. 1801.

25. *Clarksville Jeffersonian*, 10 Mar. 1858.

26. *Memphis Appeal*, 12 Sept. 1852; see also Smith, *Review of East Tennessee*, 12.

27. Matthews, Diary, 24 Nov. 1859.

28. *Tennessee Gazette*, 19 May 1802.

29. See, for instance, *Tennessee Gazette*, 14 Apr. 1812, 7 July 1812, 7 Oct. 1812.

30. *Knoxville Enquirer*, 28 Oct. 1825.

31. Ibid., 3 Nov. 1825.

32. Ibid., 11 June 1811. Also see Smith, *Review of East Tennessee*, 18.

33. *Knoxville Enquirer*, 25 Apr. 1827.

34. *Tennessee Gazette,* 12 Oct. 1810; see also 22 Mar. 1811.

35. Ibid., 30 Apr. 1813; also see 2 Aug. 1814, 1 Aug. 1820, and *Clarksville Gazette,* 11 Mar. 1820.

36. Ibid., 19 Jan. 1813, 30 Aug. 1814.

37. *Memphis Appeal,* 26 Oct. 1859.

38. *Argus and Commercial Herald,* 11 Oct. 1843.

39. *Nashville Gazette,* 23 Oct. 1858; *Memphis Appeal,* 21 July 1859.

40. *Weekly Clarksville Chronicle,* 16 Jan. 1857.

41. *Tennessee Gazette,* 1 Aug. 1821.

42. Peter Brickey, Blount County, Century Farms, Reel 1.

43. Anne Newport Royall, *Letters from Alabama, 1817–1822,* ed. Lucille Griffith (Tuscaloosa: Univ. of Alabama Press, 1969), 93.

44. *Clarksville Jeffersonian,* 11 Dec. 1849; *Knoxville Gazette,* 18 June 1818.

45. Mary U. Rothrock, ed., *The French Broad-Holston Country: A History of Knox County, Tennessee* (Knoxville: East Tennessee Historical Society, 1946), 75; Edmund Cody Burnett, "Hog Raising and Hog Driving in the Region of the French Broad River," *Agricultural History* 20 (1946): 99–102; Forrest McDonald and Grady McWhiney, "The Antebellum Southern Herdsman: A Reinterpretation," *Journal of Southern History* 41 (1975): 160.

46. *Knoxville Enquirer,* 7 Nov. 1827.

47. Brewer, Journal, 6 May 1814.

48. *Tennessee Gazette,* 29 Dec. 1812.

49. Baily, *Journal of a Tour,* 418.

50. Abernethy, *From Frontier to Plantation,* 29.

51. Arnow, *Flowering of the Cumberland,* 48; Gray, *History of Agriculture* 2:878.

52. Imlay, *Topographical Description,* 48.

53. Michaux, *Travels to the West,* 239–40.

54. Ibid., 201.

55. Robert E. Corlew, "Some Aspects of Slavery in Dickson County," *Tennessee Historical Quarterly* 10 (1951): 238–39; *Tennessee Gazette,* 8 Sept. 1802.

56. Williams, *Beginnings of West Tennessee,* 202

57. Gray, *History of Agriculture* 2:898.

58. Michaux, *Travels to the West,* 221.

59. Rothrock, *French Broad-Holston Country,* 74–75.

60. *Knoxville Enquirer,* 13 Oct. 1825.

61. Ibid., 24 Mar. 1825.

62. *Acts of Tennessee* (1801), chap. 5, 34–39.

63. *Acts of Tennessee* (1811), chap. 42, 50; *Acts of Tennessee* (1837–38), chap. 56, 152.

64. *Acts of Tennessee* (1803), chap. 23, 61–62; the tax was 37 1/2 cents per machine.
65. Michaux, *Travels to the West,* 243.
66. Cartmell, Diary, 15 Dec. 1853.
67. Ibid., remarks on April, 1854.
68. Ibid., 24 Mar. 1859.
69. Bills, Diary, 16 Jan. 1846.
70. Ibid., 31 May 1853.
71. Haraldson, Diary, 13 Jan. 1845.
72. *Niles' Weekly Register,* 69 (13 Sept. 1845): 23.
73. This question is dealt with in greater detail in Winters, "Farm Size and Production Choices."
74. See the appendix for a discussion of the eight-county sample and chapter 3 for an explanation of the production index for cotton.
75. The equations regress the cotton index (CI) against improved acreage (IA) and the proxy for labor per improved acre (L/A) for individual farms for 1850 and 1860. All coefficients are significant at the 1 percent level; standard errors are in parentheses. The regression equations are:

$$(1850)\ CI = 2.67 + .02IA + 11.95L/A$$
$$(.00)\quad(1.06)\qquad\qquad R^2 = .03$$
$$(1860)\ CI = 4.89 + .01IA + 2.32L/A$$
$$(.00)\quad(.81)\qquad\qquad R^2 = .01$$

76. Smith, *Review of East Tennessee,* 2.
77. Gray, *History of Agriculture* 2:754–55.
78. Williams, *Beginnings of West Tennessee,* 209.
79. Gray, *History of Agriculture* 2:758, 886; Joseph Buckner Killebrew, *Introduction to the Resources of Tennessee* (Nashville: State Agriculture Department, 1874), 98–99.
80. Clarksville newspapers contained advertisements for all kinds of services. See especially the *Clarksville Jeffersonian* and the *Clarksville Chronicle.*
81. Gray, *History of Agriculture* 2:754, 774.
82. The practice of inspecting tobacco as a means of regulating trade reached back to seventeenth-century Virginia and Maryland. See Lewis C. Gray, "The Market Surplus Problems of Colonial Tobacco," *Agricultural History* 2 (1928): 30–34.
83. *Acts of Tennessee* (1797), chap. 40, 107–9.
84. *Acts of Tennessee* (1799), chap. 45, 91–95.
85. *Acts of Tennessee* (1811), chap. 42, 50.
86. *Acts of Tennessee* (1817), chap. 105, 108.
87. *Acts of Tennessee* (1845–46), chap. 105, 173; for earlier modifications in the grading procedures, see *Acts of Tennessee* (1819), chap. 17, 47–48,

Acts of Tennessee (1821), chap. 8, 12, and *Acts of Tennessee* (1825), chap. 288, 304.

88. *Clarksville Jeffersonian,* 24 Nov. 1858.

89. *Niles' Weekly Register,* 62 (19 Mar. 1842): 47.

90. Barker, Diary, 8 Feb. 1844, 4 Mar. 1845.

91. See Washington, Diary, July to Dec. 1851.

92. See the appendix for a discussion of the eight-county sample and chapter 3 for an explanation of the production index for tobacco.

93. The equations regress the tobacco index (TI) against improved acreage (IA) and the proxy for labor per improved acre (L/A) for individual farms for 1850 and 1860. Coefficients marked with an asterisk are significant at the 1 percent level; standard errors are in parentheses. The regression equations are:

$$(1850) \text{ TI} = 59.73 + .05\text{IA} + 1783.87\text{L}/\text{A}*$$
$$\qquad\qquad\quad (.24) \qquad (150.14) \qquad\qquad R^2 = .02$$
$$(1860) \text{ TI} = 429.35 - .37\text{IA}* + 390.32\text{L}/\text{A}*$$
$$\qquad\qquad\quad (.15) \qquad (91.38) \qquad\qquad R^2 = .01$$

94. Joseph Edwin Washington, Robertson County, Century Farms, Reel 3.

95. Joyce Appleby, "Commercial Farming and the 'Agrarian Myth' in the Early Republic," *Journal of America History* 68 (1982): 836–41; Diane Lindstrom, "Southern Dependence upon Interregional Grain Supplies: A Review of the Trade Flows, 1840–1860," *Agricultural History* 44 (1970): 101–2.

96. Michaux, *Travels to the West,* 221.

97. Brewer, Journal, 6 May 1814.

98. Gray, *History of Agriculture* 2:883.

99. Folmsbee, *Sectionalism and Internal Improvements,* 13.

100. Ibid., 816–17.

101. Anderson, Sullivan County, Century Farms, Reel 4.

102. Haraldson, Diary, 4 Apr. 1839, 14 May 1839.

103. Cartmell, Diary, 14 Nov. 1854.

104. Barker, Diary, 5, 19 May 1848.

105. Ibid., 26 Sept. 1857.

106. See, for instance, Bagwell, Diary, 12 Aug. 1841, 14 July 1842.

107. See, for instance, Cartmell, Diary, 20, 23 Nov. 1857.

108. Contract dated 7 Nov. 1854 in Washington, Diary.

109. Barker, Diary, 15 Dec. 1846, 30 Nov. 1858, 20 May 1845.

110. Washington, Diary, 4 Aug. 1856, 1 Dec. 1851.

111. David S. Nunn, Crockett County, Century Farms, Reel 1; William Hunter, Putnam County, Century Farms, Reel 3.

112. Gleaves, Diary, 17 Apr. 1858.

113. Matthews, Diary, 10 Dec. 1858.

114. Bryan, Memoir, 5.

115. Burnett, "Hog Raising and Hog Driving," 87–88, 100; Sam Bowers Hilliard, *Hog Meat and Hoecake: Food Supply in the Old South, 1840–1860* (Carbondale: Univ. of Southern Illinois Press, 1972), 193–95; McDonald and McWhiney, "Antebellum Southern Herdsmen," 160.

116. James C. Bonner, *A History of Georgia Agriculture, 1732–1860* (Athens: Univ. of Georgia Press, 1964), 59.

117. Bryan, Memoir, 5.

118. Christopher Houston to Placebo Houston, 15 Oct. 1816 (rpt. in Enfield, "Early Settlement in Maury County," 60).

119. Michaux, *Travels to the West*, 247.

120. *Tennessee Gazette*, 11 Mar. 1801.

121. Barker, Diary, 26 June 1843, 30 Nov. 1859.

122. See, for instance, Haraldson, Diary, 13 May 1837.

123. Bryan, Memoir, 5; Smith, *Review of East Tennessee*, 41; Corlew, *Tennessee*, 229.

124. *Acts of Tennessee* (1801), chap. 5, 25–39.

125. *Acts of Tennessee* (1803), chap. 7, 43.

126. Thomas Ashe, *Travels in America, Performed in 1806* (London: Cramer and Spear, 1808), 267.

127. Ridley Wills, *The History of Belle Meade: Mansion, Plantation, Stud* (Nashville: Vanderbilt Univ. Press, 1991), 55–64.

128. Hubbard Saunders, Sumner County, Century Farms, Reel 4.

129. *Tennessee Gazette*, 11 Mar. 1801, 6 May 1801.

130. Bonner, *History of Georgia Agriculture*, 139.

131. *Acts of Tennessee* (1835–36), chap. 13, 59.

132. Gray, *History of Agriculture* 2:851–52; Arnow, *Flowering of the Cumberland*, 205.

133. John Hebron Moore, *Agriculture in Ante-Bellum Mississippi* (New York: Bookman Associates, 1958), 107; Joseph Lamar, Anderson County, Century Farms, Reel 1; Bonner, *History of Georgia Agriculture*, 137–38.

134. *Agriculturist* 2 (Apr. 1841): 95–96; *Acts of Tennessee* (1835–36), chap. 13, 59.

135. Bagwell, Diary, 26 Apr. 1843; Barker, Diary, 3 Apr. 1845, 6 May 1847, 5 May 1849, 17 Sept. 1846.

136. Cartmell, Diary, 2 Jan. 1859.

137. *Memphis Appeal*, 16 July 1859.

138. *Tennessee Gazette*, 9 Nov. 1810.

139. Smith, *Review of East Tennessee,* 2–3; *Tennessee Gazette,* 12 Oct. 1810, 22 Mar. 1811, 21 Jan. 1814.
140. *Agriculturist* 2 (July 1841): 147.
141. *Acts of Tennessee* (1845–46), resolution II, 339.
142. Clement Eaton, *The Growth of Southern Civilization, 1790–1860* (New York: Harper and Row, 1961), 189.
143. The *Southern Cultivator, Agriculturist,* and *Tennessee Farmer* ran numerous articles on silk production in the late 1830s and the 1840s. See also, Clark, *Tennessee Yeomen,* 135–37.
144. *Southern Cultivator* 2 (28 Mar. 1840): 88
145. Smith, *Review of East Tennessee,* 9–10.
146. Williams, *Beginnings of West Tennessee,* 206.
147. *Tennessee Farmer* 2 (Jan. 1837): 1; *Agriculturist* 2 (July 1841): 146.
148. Receipts of payment dated 1 Apr. 1845, 4 Nov. 1845, Washington, Diary.
149. *Acts of Tennessee* (1841–42), chap. 178, 206; *Acts of Tennessee* (1843–44), chap. 57, 132–33.
150. *Niles' Weekly Register,* 65 (11 Nov. 1843): 170; Paul H. Bergeron, *Paths of the Past: Tennessee, 1770–1970* (Knoxville: Univ. of Tennessee Press, 1979), 46.
151. *Niles' Weekly Register,* 65 (24 Dec. 1843): 272.
152. Bergeron, *Paths of the Past,* 46; Corlew, *Tennessee,* 229.
153. Washington, Diary, 2 May 1851.
154. Barker, Diary, note at end of Apr. 1844; 6 Oct. 1850.
155. Cartmell, Diary, 23 May 1853; 14, 22 June 1853; 6 Sept. 1853.
156. Haraldson, Diary, 31 July 1840; 7 July 1837.
157. Cartmell, Diary, 28 May 1855; Barker, Diary, 27 Aug. 1858.
158. Kellar, *Solon Robinson* 2:446.
159. Barker, Diary, 7 May 1849.
160. *Southern Cultivator* 1 (22 May 1839): 74.
161. Bills, Dairy, 31 May 1853; Cartmell, Diary, 1 June 1854.
162. Barker, Diary, note at end of 1844.
163. Cartmell, Diary, remarks on July 1856.
164. Washington, Diary, 23 June 1854.
165. Barker, Diary, 15 Sept. 1846.
166. Cartmell, Diary, 27 Mar. 1859, 1 June 1859, 1 July 1859, remarks on Aug. 1859.
167. Barker, Dairy, 5 Dec. 1859.
168. *Acts of Tennessee* (1859–60), chap. 45, 45.
169. Haraldson, Diary, 18 Sept. 1844.
170. Cartmell, Diary, 13 Oct. 1853.

171. *Acts of Tennessee* (1791), chap. 52, 110. The legislature later required the publication of a notice in the local newspaper. *Acts of Tennessee* (1807), chap. 80, 132–33.

172. *Acts of Tennessee* (1799), chap. 20, 54.

173. Cartmell, Diary, 5 Feb. 1856, 24 Apr. 1856, remarks on Dec. 1857.

174. Richard Burns, Blount County, Century Farms, Reel 1; John Burtis, Fayette County, Century Farms, Reel 1.

175. Daniel Hopper, Madison County, Century Farms, Reel 1; David Coleman, Carroll County, Century Farms, Reel 1.

176. Cartmell, Diary, 26 Jan. 1854.

177. Baily, *Journal of a Tour*, 420–21.

178. William Carter, Knox County, Century Farms, Reel 2.

179. Elliott and Moxley, *Tennessee Civil War Veterans' Questionnaires* 2:595.

180. Baily, *Journal of a Tour*, 423.

181. Benjamin Prater, Knox County, Century Farms, Reel 2.

182. Isreal Woolsey, Greene County, Century Farms, Reel 1; John B. Bond, Williamson County, Century Farms, Reel 4.

183. Col. Benjamin Elliot, Robertson County, Century Farms, Reel 3; William Kelly, Union County, Century Farms, Reel 4.

184. Elliott and Moxley, *Tennessee Civil War Veterans' Questionnaires* 1:248.

185. Anderson, Sullivan County, Century Farms, Reel 4; *Knoxville Gazette*, 6 Apr. 1793.

186. Michaux, *Travels to the West*, 205.

187. John Stewart, Meigs County, Century Farms, Reel 2; *Weekly Chronicle*, 18 Mar. 1818.

188. Cartwright, Memoir, 113–15.

5. The Commercial Network

1. For a discuss of cotton marketing, see Harold D. Woodman, *King Cotton and His Retainers: Financing and Marketing the Cotton Crop of the South, 1800–1925* (Lexington: Univ. of Kentucky Press, 1968), 15–42.

2. Barker, Diary, 22 Nov. 1845, 15 May 1848, 15 Nov. 1858.

3. Bagwell, Diary, 14 Dec. 1841, 17 Nov. 1842, 12 Nov. 1843.

4. Cartmell, Diary, 5 Feb. 1856.

5. *Weekly Chronicle*, 27 Jan. 1819; *Tennessee Gazette*, 4 Dec. 1821.

6. Barker, Diary, 5 Dec. 1848.

7. *Memphis Appeal*, 7 July 1843.

8. *Clarksville Jeffersonian*, 8 Jan. 1851.

9. Bagwell, Diary, 9 Jan. 1846; see also 14 Apr. 1845.

10. *Tennessee Gazette*, 4 Dec. 1821, 5 Feb. 1822.

11. *Clarksville Jeffersonian*, 9 Oct. 1849, 25 Dec. 1850.

12. Thomas P. Abernethy, "The Early Development of Commerce and Banking in Tennessee," *Mississippi Valley Historical Review* 14 (1928): 317; Lewis E. Atherton, *The Southern Country Store, 1800–1860* (Baton Rouge: Louisiana State Univ. Press, 1949), 26–27.

13. *Clarksville Jeffersonian,* 16 Aug. 1851, 9 Oct. 1849.

14. *Memphis Appeal,* 7 July 1843.

15. *Tennessee Gazette,* 22 Aug. 1820; *Clarksville Jeffersonian,* 19 Dec. 1855, 24 Nov. 1858.

16. *Clarksville Jeffersonian,* 24 Nov. 1858.

17. Ibid., 16 Aug. 1851.

18. Ibid., 28 Mar. 1839.

19. *Memphis Appeal,* 7 July 1843.

20. *Nashville Gazette,* 6 Jan. 1853.

21. *Clarksville Jeffersonian,* 25 Dec. 1850, 10 Mar. 1858, 25 Dec. 1850, 10 June 1857; *Argus and Commercial Herald,* 11 Oct. 1843.

22. H. Phillip Bacon, "Nashville's Trade at the Beginning of the Nineteenth Century," *Tennessee Historical Quarterly* 15 (1956): 15.

23. Washington's diary and account books carefully detail these transactions. Washington, Diary.

24. Cartmell, Diary, 21 Feb. 1854, 6 Mar. 1854.

25. Haraldson, Diary, 13, 14 Jan. 1845.

26. André Michaux, "Travels of André Michaux (1796–1797)," in *Early Travels in the Tennessee Country, 1540–1800,* ed. Samuel Cole Williams (Johnson City, Tenn.: Watauga Press, 1928), 342.

27. Imlay, *Topographical Description,* 516.

28. Michaux, *Travels to the West,* 213.

29. Stanley John Folmsbee, "The Turnpike Phase of Tennessee's Internal Improvements System," *Journal of Southern History* 3 (1937): 453–77.

30. Bergeron, *Paths of the Past,* 51; Corlew, *Tennessee,* 197–201.

31. Smith, *Review of East Tennessee,* 24.

32. *Argus and Commercial Herald,* 11 Oct. 1843; see also Corlew, *Tennessee,* 111.

33. Michaux, *Travels to the West,* 203.

34. Imlay, *Topographical Description,* editorial note, 73.

35. Michaux, *Travels to the West,* 230–31.

36. Ashe, *Travels in America,* 266.

37. Baily, *Journal of a Tour,* 249.

38. Imlay, *Topographical Description,* editorial note, 73.

39. Quoted in Arnow, *Flowering of the Cumberland,* 234.

40. Daniel Smith, *A Short Description of the Tennessee Government of the Territory of the United States South of the River Ohio* (Philadelphia: Mathew Carey, 1793), 12–13.

41. Michaux, *Travels to the West,* 201.

42. Ibid., 221.

43. Davidson, *Tennessee* 1:200–215.

44. *Tennessee Gazette,* 30 Nov. 1810, 30 Aug. 1814, 17 Oct. 1817; Arnow, *Flowering of the Cumberland,* 367–68.

45. Folmsbee, *Sectionalism and Internal Improvements,* 18; Corlew, *Tennessee,* 198–99.

46. Smith, *Review of East Tennessee,* 18.

47. Bryan, Memoir, 5.

48. Quoted in Williams, *Beginnings of West Tennessee,* 165.

49. Kellar, *Solon Robinson* 1:448.

50. Haraldson, Diary, 4 Apr. 1839; Cartmell, Diary, 22 Jan. 1853, 5 Feb. 1856.

51. Davidson, *Tennessee* 1:230–54.

52. Byrd Douglas, *Steamboatin' on the Cumberland* (Nashville: Tennessee Book Company, 1961), 6–8.

53. *Tennessee Gazette,* 14 Dec. 1819, 5 Dec. 1820.

54. *Clarksville Jeffersonian,* 17 July 1849.

55. Ibid., 12 Dec. 1855.

56. *De Bow's Review* 1 (Jan. 1846): 25.

57. Douglas, *Steamboatin' on the Cumberland,* 10–11.

58. Arnow, *Flowering of the Cumberland,* 367.

59. *Southern Cultivator* 1 (27 Mar. 1839): 45.

60. Folmsbee, *Sectionalism and Internal Improvements,* 15.

61. Ibid., 10–12; Corlew, *Tennessee,* 199–200.

62. *Knoxville Register,* 7 Dec. 1831; *Argus and Commercial Herald,* 28 Apr. 1841.

63. *Argus and Commercial Herald,* 12 Nov. 1841.

64. Smith, *Review of East Tennessee,* 24.

65. Williams, *Beginnings of West Tennessee,* 168.

66. See advertisements in the *Memphis Appeal* throughout the 1850s.

67. Kellar, *Solon Robinson* 1:448.

68. Haraldson, Diary, 14 Jan. 1845.

69. Williams, *Beginnings of West Tennessee,* 165–66.

70. James W. Livingood, "Chattanooga: A Rail Junction of the Old South," *Tennessee Historical Quarterly* 6 (1947): 230–46; Corlew, *Tennessee,* 202–6; Bergeron, *Paths of the Past,* 51.

71. Paul M. Fink, "The Railroad Comes to Jonesborough," *Tennessee Historical Quarterly* 36 (1977): 176; see also *De Bow's Review* 27 (1859): 418.

72. *Farmer and Mechanic* 1 (Feb. 1856): 61.

73. Gray, *History of Agriculture* 2:816; Lindstrom, "Southern Dependence upon Interregional Grain Supplies," 108–9.

74. Gray, *History of Agriculture* 2:816, 883, 905.

75. Joseph White, Hamblen County, Century Farms, Reel 2. The application lists the farm in Hamblen County, which was carved out of Jefferson County in 1870.

76. Elliott and Moxley, *Tennessee Civil War Veterans' Questionnaires* 2:677.

77. Cartmell, Diary, 31 Oct. 1854, 14 Nov. 1854, 2 Mar. 1858, 16 Sept. 1857.

78. See, for example, *Nashville Gazette*, 26 Feb. 1858, 4 Mar. 1859; *Memphis Appeal*, 15 July 1859, 23 Sept. 1859.

79. Michaux, *Travels to the West*, 226, 243.

80. *Tennessee Gazette*, 11 June 1811.

81. *Clarksville Gazette*, 25 Nov. 1820.

82. *Acts of Tennessee* (1807–8), chap. 23, 163; *Acts of Tennessee* (1811), chap. 14, 83.

83. Abernethy, "Early Development of Commerce and Banking," 322.

84. Woodman, *King Cotton and His Retainers*, 172

85. *Acts of Tennessee* (1820), chap. 7, 9; *Acts of Tennessee* (1837–38), chap. 34, 153; Bergeron, *Paths of the Past*, 28–29, 51.

86. *Town Gazette*, 5 July 1819.

87. *Weekly Chronicle*, 13 May 1818.

88. Haraldson, Diary, 17, 22 Apr. 1837.

89. *Niles' Weekly Register*, 57 (2 Nov. 1839): 154.

90. James Houston to Placebo and Sarrah Houston, 31 May 1840 (rpt. in Enfield, "Early Settlement in Maury County," 67).

91. Cartmell, Diary, remarks on Oct. 1857.

92. Matthews, Diary, 3 May 1858.

93. *Southern Agriculturist*, n.s., 5 (Dec. 1845): back page.

94. *Knoxville Gazette*, 10 June 1794, 15 May 1797.

95. *Knoxville Enquirer*, 4 Oct. 1826.

96. *Clarksville Jeffersonian*, 2 Oct. 1849.

97. See, for instance, *Memphis Appeal*, 7 July 1843.

98. Haraldson, Diary, 9, 10 Apr. 1845.

99. See Washington, Diary, esp. 1856–60.

100. Atherton, *Southern Country Store*, 52–53.

101. *Knoxville Gazette*, 30 June 1792.

102. *Knoxville Enquirer*, 1 Dec. 1824.

103. *Knoxville Gazette*, 27 Mar. 1792.

104. Washington, Diary, 8 Apr. 1856.

105. Matthews, Diary, 14 June 1858.

106. Cartmell, Diary, 5 Oct. 1857.
107. Matthews, Diary, 28 Feb. 1859.
108. Cartmell, Diary, 24 Dec. 1857.
109. Bagwell, Diary, 24 May 1841.
110. Washington, Diary, 31 Aug. 1856.
111. Cartmell, Diary, 5 Feb. 1856.
112. Bagwell, Diary, 10 Jan. 1842.
113. Cartmell, Diary, 5 Feb. 1856.
114. Washington, Diary, 23 Feb. 1856, 8 Feb. 1857.
115. Cartmell, Diary, 5 Feb. 1856, 28 Dec. 1853.
116. Washington, Diary, 19 Sept. 1851.
117. Barker, Diary, 6 Jan. 1857.
118. Bagwell, Diary, 25 Mar. 1842.
119. *Tennessee Gazette*, 23 Oct. 1802.
120. See, for instance, *Clarksville Jeffersonian*, 10 Mar. 1858; *Weekly Clarksville Chronicle*, 10 Mar. 1858.
121. See, for instance, *Southern Cultivator* 1 (28 Aug. 1839): 136; *Agriculturist* 5 (Dec. 1844): 191.
122. See, for instance, *Argus and Commercial Herald*, 11 Sept. 1844.
123. *Clarksville Jeffersonian*, 8 Jan. 1851.
124. Ibid., 9, 30 Oct. 1849.
125. See, for instance, *Memphis Appeal*, 13 Oct. 1847; 10, 11 Sept. 1851.
126. See, for instance, *Nashville Gazette*, 25 July 1852, 18 Nov. 1852, 24 July 1858.
127. *Southern Cultivator* 1 (3 July 1839): 100.

6. Acquiring Land

1. Average land values are from the Federal Agricultural Census of 1860.
2. See, for instance, *Tennessee Gazette*, 1 Apr. 1801, 25 Dec. 1802; *Knoxville Enquirer*, 20 Oct. 1824; *Argus and Commercial Appeal*, 3 Sept. 1839; *Memphis Appeal*, 6 June 1848; *Agriculturist*, 3 (Feb. 1842): 34.
3. Michaux, *Travels to the West*, 244.
4. *Tennessee Gazette*, 6 May 1812.
5. Matthews, Diary, 17 Mar. 1859.
6. Smith, *Review of East Tennessee*, 42.
7. *Agriculturist*, 2 (July 1841): 162.
8. Washington, Diary, handwritten contract in back of 1860 diary.
9. Haraldson, Diary, 2 Apr. 1842.
10. Smith, *Review of East Tennessee*, 25.
11. Owsley, *Plain Folk*, 152; Frank L. Owsley and Harriet C. Owsley, "The Economic Structure of Rural Tennessee, 1850–1860," *Journal of Southern*

History 8 (1942): 161–82; Clark, *Tennessee Yeomen,* 30–31; Allan G. Bogue, *From Prairie to Cornbelt: Farming on the Illinois and Iowa Prairies in the Nineteenth Century* (Chicago: Univ. of Chicago Press, 1963), 63–65. For a critique of these methods, see Frederick A. Bode and Donald E. Ginter, *Farm Tenancy and the Census in the Antebellum Georgia* (Athens: Univ. of Georgia Press, 1986), 33–44.

12.   See the appendix for a discussion of the sample. The Owsley group classified as "landless" household heads on the population schedules of the manuscript census listed as farmers with no real property. Bogue classified as "tenants" farmers listed on the agricultural schedules and on the population schedules with no real property. Because some of the "farmers" on the population schedules failed to appear on the agricultural schedules, the Owsley group's "landless" category was larger for a given county than Bogue's "tenant" category. The discrepancy results, in part, from the inclusion of farm laborers as "farmers" on the population schedules but not on the agricultural schedules. Bogue's method, which produces a lower bound estimate of tenancy rates, has been used here.

13.   Blanche Henry Clark found county rates ranging from 15 to 47 percent, and overall rates of 35 percent in 1850 and 30 percent in 1860. Because her "landless" category included farm laborers as well as tenants, these rates overstate the corresponding tenancy rates. She noted, however, that tenants generally represented from a quarter to a half of the landless population. Robert Tracy McKenzie found county rates approximating those of this study. See Clark, *Tennessee Yeomen,* 27–31 and McKenzie, "From Old South to New South," 27.

14.   *Acts of Tennessee* (1825), chap. 21, 18–19.

15.   These issues are dealt with in greater detail in Donald L. Winters, "The Agricultural Ladder in Southern Agriculture: Tennessee, 1850–1870," *Agricultural History* 61 (1987): 36–52.

16.   Robert Tracy McKenzie offers an excellent discussion of economic mobility among antebellum Tennessee farmers. His findings are consistent with those of this study, except that his 1850s acquisition rate for tenants in Johnson County, also one of his sample counties, was about thirty percentage points lower. The reason for the discrepancy is not clear. See McKenzie, "From Old South to New South," 112–33.

17.   Donald L. Winters, *Farmers Without Farms: Agricultural Tenancy in Nineteenth-Century Iowa* (Westport Conn.: Greenwood, 1978), 24.

18.   See Elliott and Moxley, *Tennessee Civil War Veterans' Questionnaires.*

19.   Elliott and Moxley, *Tennessee Civil War Veterans' Questionnaires* 1:270, 4:1543, 1:300.

20. Ibid. 1:231, 1:186.

21. Ibid. 5:2187.

22. These issues are dealt with in greater detail in Donald L. Winters, "'Plain Folk' of the Old South Reexamined: Economic Democracy in Tennessee," *Journal of Southern History* 53 (1987): 565–86.

23. Gavin Wright, "'Economic Democracy' and the Concentration of Agricultural Wealth in the Cotton South, 1850–1860," *Agricultural History* 44 (1970): 76–77.

24. Owsley and Owsley, "Economic Structure of Rural Tennessee," 182.

25. Donald Schaefer found similar conditions among tobacco farmers in northern Tennessee and southern Kentucky. Schaefer, "Yeomen Farmers and Economic Democracy: A Study of Wealth and Economic Mobility in the Western Tobacco Region, 1850 to 1860," *Explorations in Economic History* 15 (1978): 421–37.

26. "A Genealogy of Thomas and Kessiah (Griffith) Lacy and Hugh and Margaret (McDonald) Ross, of Anson County, North County" (private manuscript in possession of V. Jacque Voegeli, Nashville, Tennessee).

27. Boon, "History of the Boon Family," 3.

28. Bagwell, Diary, 25 Mar. 1842, 20 Jan. 1846.

29. Cartmell, Diary, 28 Dec. 1853.

30. Haraldson, Diary, 10 Jan. 1837.

31. Barker, Diary, 1, 18, 25 Nov. 1847; 21 Jan. 1853.

32. See Winters, "'Plain Folk' of the Old South Reexamined," for a discussion of the Frank L. Owsley thesis on the yeomanry and its implications for antebellum Tennessee. Donald Schaefer arrived at similar conclusions in his study of farmers in the tobacco region of northern Tennessee and southern Kentucky. See Schaefer, "Yeomen Farmers and Economic Democracy."

7. Work and Leisure

1. The discussion of farm and related work in this chapter is based on the following diaries and memoirs: Wiley Bagwell Diary, John Nick Barker Diary, John Houston Bills Diary, Tom Bryan Memoir, Robert H. Cartmell Diary, Alexander Cotton Cartwright Memoir, Betty A. Gleaves Diary, Herndon Haraldson Diary, Jane Margaret Jones Diary, James Washington Matthews Diary, and George A. Washington Diary. These sources record, often in considerable detail, the day-to-day activities on antebellum Tennessee farms. Citations will be used only in cases of direct reference in the text.

2. On many farms slaves also performed field work, as well as a variety of

other tasks. Their role in Tennessee's agriculture will be taken up in the next chapter.

3. Barker, Diary, 25 June 1845, 11 July 1845.

4. Kellar, *Solon Robinson* 1:446.

5. Cartmell, Diary, 4 Apr. 1854.

6. Ibid., 11, 26 Feb. 1856; *Tennessee Gazette*, 8 Sept. 1802.

7. Haraldson, Diary, 30 Aug. 1842; Cartmell, Diary, 30 Aug. 1853; Matthews, Diary, 3 Sept. 1859; Arnow, *Flowering of the Cumberland*, 239–40.

8. This is based on an analysis of farm-level production in the eight sample counties. In 1849, 48 percent produced at least one of the crops; in 1859, 44 percent produced at least one.

9. Christopher Houston to Placebo Houston, 6 Aug. 1818 (rpt. in Enfield, "Early Settlement in Maury County," 62).

10. Kellar, *Solon Robinson* 1:447.

11. Smith, *Review of East Tennessee*, 7–8.

12. Haraldson, Diary, 18 Nov. 1842.

13. Cartmell, Diary, 3 Jan. 1856.

14. Barton Warren, Blount County, Century Farms, Reel 1.

15. William H. Cheek, Smith County, Century Farms, Reel 3.

16. Jones, Diary, 10 Feb. 1857.

17. Cartmell, Diary, 16 Sept. 1853.

18. John Motheral, Williamson County, Century Farms, Reel 4.

19. Cartmell, Diary, 26 Jan. 1857; *Farmer and Mechanic*, 1 (May 1856): 202–4.

20. Elliott and Moxley, *Tennessee Civil War Veterans' Questionnaires* 1:293.

21. Cartwright, Memoir, 101.

22. Elliott and Moxley, *Tennessee Civil War Veterans' Questionnaires* 4:1496.

23. Barker, Diary, 12 Jan. 1861; Bagwell, Diary, 23 June 1841; Washington, Diary, 23 Oct. 1856.

24. Gleaves, Diary, 16 June 1858; Matthews, Diary, 29 June 1859; Bagwell, Diary, 8 Oct. 1842; see also Owsley, *Plain Folk*, 114–15.

25. Gleaves, Diary, 29 Oct. 1858.

26. Jones, Diary, 3 July 1856.

27. Elliott and Moxley, *Tennessee Civil War Veterans' Questionnaires* 5:1796.

28. Gleaves, Diary, 28 Apr. 1858, 10 May 1858.

29. Jones, Diary, 13, 14 May 1856.

30. Ibid., 9 Sept. 1856; 2 Oct. 1856; 11 Dec. 1856; 2, 3 Feb. 1857.

31. Elliott and Moxley, *Tennessee Civil War Veterans' Questionnaires* 5:2040.

32. George P. Rawick, ed., *The American Slave: A Composite Autobiography*, vol. 16, *Tennessee* (Westport, Conn.: Greenwood, 1972), 33.

33. Gleaves, Diary, 5 Apr. 1859; Jones, Diary, 21 Feb. 1856.

34. Elliott and Moxley, *Tennessee Civil War Veterans' Questionnaires* 5:2040, 4:1425.

35. Gleaves, Diary, 2, 4 Apr. 1859.

36. *Southern Agriculturist* 3 (Feb. 1830): 87–89.

37. Barker, Diary, 1 June 1860.

38. Washington, Diary, 4 Aug. 1851; Bagwell, Diary, 27 Feb. 1843.

39. Elliott and Moxley, *Tennessee Civil War Veterans' Questionnaires* 5:2156.

40. *Tennessee Gazette,* 19 Jan. 1813.

41. Smith, *Review of East Tennessee,* 9–10.

42. Gleaves, Diary, 24 Mar. 1858; Jones, Diary, 14 Aug. 1856.

43. Gleaves, Diary, 1 Apr. 1859; Jones, Diary, 27 Nov. 1850.

44. Smith, *Review of East Tennessee,* 27–28.

45. Elliott and Moxley, *Tennessee Civil War Veterans' Questionnaires* 3:1090; see also Fred Arthur Bailey, *Class and Tennessee's Confederate Generation* (Chapel Hill: Univ. of North Carolina Press, 1987), 35–36.

46. Bryan, Memoir, 2–4.

47. Ibid., 5.

48. Owsley, *Plain Folk,* 96–97.

49. Cartmell, Diary, 30 Apr. 1854.

50. Bills, Diary, 3 Dec. 1843, 27 Dec. 1853.

51. Haraldson, Diary, 10 Aug. 1843.

52. Owsley, *Plain Folk,* 97–98.

53. For a discussion of the Cane Ridge camp meeting in Kentucky in 1801 and of camp meetings in general, see Paul K. Conkin, *Cane Ridge: America's Pentecost* (Madison: Univ. of Wisconsin Press, 1990).

54. Bagwell, Diary, 17 Aug. 1848.

55. Haraldson, Diary, 28 July 1837 to 1 Aug. 1837.

56. Ibid., 27 July 1845.

57. Owsley, *Plain Folk,* 103–4.

58. Bagwell, Diary, 30 July 1842 through 10 Aug. 1842.

59. Haraldson, Diary, 18 Sept. 1842.

60. Elliott and Moxley, *Tennessee Civil War Veterans' Questionnaires* 2:871.

61. Cartmell, Dairy, 13 Oct. 1854, 28 July 1854.

62. Jones, Diary, 25 July 1857.

63. Haraldson, Diary, 17 Oct. 1838, 28 June 1839, 30 Sept. 1840, 10 Oct. 1840.

64. Bagwell, Diary, 30 June 1843. The Franklin Debate Society, organized in Clay County, Missouri, in 1842, debated precisely the same question in the early 1840s. See R. Douglas Hurt, *Agriculture and Slavery in Missouri's Little Dixie* (Columbia: Univ. of Missouri Press, 1992), 205.

65.   Owsley, *Plain Folk,* 108–14.

66.   Bryan, Memoir, 4.

67.   Cartmell, Diary, 24 Sept. 1853.

68.   Owsley, *Plain Folk,* 115–18.

69.   Bills, Diary, 25 Dec. 1845.

70.   Barker, Diary, 4, 5 July 1850.

71.   Bills, Diary, 21 Apr. 1859; Matthews, Diary, 26 Jan. 1860.

72.   Cartmell, Diary, 10 June 1854, 20 Oct. 1859.

73.   Barker, Diary, 17 June 1857.

74.   Cartmell, Diary, 2 Apr. 1858.

75.   Samuel Smith, Wilson County, Century Farms, Reel 4.

76.   *Knoxville Gazette,* 5 May 1792.

77.   Matthews, Diary, 24 May 1860.

78.   Elliott and Moxley, *Tennessee Civil War Veterans' Questionnaires* 1:246.

79.   Michaux, *Travels to the West,* 147.

80.   Royall, *Letters from Alabama,* 93; see also, McWhiney, *Cracker Culture,* 92.

81.   Haraldson, Diary, 24 Oct. 1837.

82.   Cartmell, Diary, 7 June 1854.

8. Agricultural Slavery

1.   The account of the amount and distribution of the slave population draws on the territorial census of 1791 and the federal censuses, 1800–1860.

2.   For a discussion of this concept, see Anderson and Gallman, "Slaves as Fixed Capital," 29–36.

3.   Barker, Diary, 14 Jan. 1846, 13 Dec. 1847, 14 Jan. 1858.

4.   The analysis of slave distribution among rural households rests on data from the eight sample counties for 1850 and 1860. See the appendix for a discussion of the sample.

5.   Owsley and Owsley, "Economic Structure of Rural Tennessee," 179.

6.   Elliott and Moxley, *Tennessee Civil War Veterans' Questionnaires* 2:599, 2:553, 2:678, 5:2151.

7.   *Acts of Tennessee* (1826), chap. 26, 30; *Acts of Tennessee* (1855–56), chap. 22, 23.

8.   Bagwell, Diary, 24 May 1841.

9.   Cartmell, Diary, 24 Jan. 1853.

10.   Bills, Diary, 3 Apr. 1847, 23 Jan. 1848, 29 Feb. 1856.

11.   Ibid., 20 May 1845.

12.   Haraldson, Diary, 3 Jan. 1842.

13.   Cartmell, Diary, 1 Jan. 1856.

14. Ibid., 25 Sept. 1857.
15. See, for instance, *Knoxville Gazette,* 18 June 1818; *Clarksville Jeffersonian,* 12 Dec. 1855; *Nashville Gazette,* 19 Aug. 1852; *Memphis Appeal,* 15 Sept. 1843.
16. Rawick, *American Slave* 16:66.
17. Chase C. Mooney, "Some Institutional and Statistical Aspects of Slavery in Tennessee," *Tennessee Historical Quarterly* 1 (1942): 199; Chase C. Mooney, *Slavery in Tennessee* (Bloomington: Indiana Univ. Press, 1957), 37–38.
18. Bills, Diary, 20 May 1845.
19. Cartmell, Diary, 5 Oct. 1857.
20. Bills, Diary, 29 Feb. 1856.
21. Cartmell, Diary, 2 Jan. 1854.
22. *Nashville Gazette,* 19 Aug. 1852.
23. Bills, Diary, 1 Jan. 1845, 1 Jan. 1860.
24. Christopher Houston to Samuel Young & Wife, 16 Jan. 1816 (rpt. in Enfield, "Early Settlement in Maury County," 59).
25. Cartmell, Diary, 2 Jan. 1854.
26. *Clarksville Jeffersonian,* 18 Dec. 1849; see also *Knoxville Enquirer,* 20 Oct. 1824.
27. Bagwell, Diary, 10 Nov. 1841, 25 Dec. 1841; Barker, Diary, 21 Feb. 1853.
28. Boon, "History of the Boon Family," 3.
29. Rawick, *American Slave* 16:2.
30. Mooney, *Slavery in Tennessee,* 29–34.
31. Cartmell, Diary, 22 May 1854, 17 May 1856.
32. Williams, *Beginnings of West Tennessee,* 211.
33. Rawick, *American Slave* 16:76.
34. Jones, Diary, 24 Nov. 1857.
35. Elliott and Moxley, *Tennessee Civil War Veterans' Questionnaires* 2:678.
36. Barker, Diary, 12 Mar. 1845.
37. Washington, Diary, 7 Dec. 1851.
38. Bagwell, Diary, 6 Feb. 1843.
39. *Memphis Appeal,* 22 Sept. 1843; *Clarksville Jeffersonian,* 24 Nov. 1858.
40. Haraldson, Diary, 24 Feb. 1837; Bagwell, Diary, 28 Oct. 1842, 10 Oct. 1843.
41. Elliott and Moxley, *Tennessee Civil War Veterans' Questionnaires* 2:678, 3:1039.
42. Cartmell, Diary, 26 Feb. 1857.
43. Elliott and Moxley, *Tennessee Civil War Veterans' Questionnaires* 4:1425.
44. Rawick, *American Slave* 16:24.
45. Baily, *Journal of a Tour,* 420.

46. Cartwright, Memoir, 97.
47. Elliott and Moxley, *Tennessee Civil War Veterans' Questionnaires* 1:246, 2:595, 2:446.
48. Cartmell, Diary, 24 Sept. 1853, 10 Nov. 1853.
49. Bills, Diary, 22 Sept. 1845.
50. Cartmell, Diary, cotton chart, Sept. 1853 to Feb. 1854.
51. Ibid., remarks on December, 1853.
52. Ibid., 7 Jan. 1854.
53. *Tennessee Gazette*, 19 July 1814.
54. Cartmell, Diary, 6 Feb. 1854.
55. Gleaves, Diary, 10 Mar. 1858.
56. Bills, Diary, 23 Nov. 1845, 30 July 1853.
57. William Kauffman Scarborough, *The Overseer: Plantation Management in the Old South* (Baton Rouge: Louisiana State Univ. Press, 1966), 23–31.
58. Bills, Diary, 23 Nov. 1845, 30 July 1853.
59. Cartmell, Diary, 6 Feb. 1854.
60. For a discussion of the relationship between owners and overseers see Scarborough, *Overseer*, 102–37.
61. Bills, Diary, 24, 28 Dec. 1845; 14 Jan. 1846.
62. Ibid., 24 Dec. 1846.
63. Ibid., 28, 31 Jan. 1846.
64. Ibid., 10 Dec. 1853.
65. Ibid., 18 Dec. 1854; 12, 26 Apr. 1858.
66. Haraldson, Diary, 14, 26 Apr. 1841.
67. Quoted in Scarborough, *Overseer*, 130.
68. Rawick, *American Slave* 16:6.
69. Cartmell, Diary, 24 Sept. 1853; 12, 26 Apr. 1858.
70. Washington, Diary, 19 June 1854, 8 Mar. 1856, 16 June 1856.
71. Bills, Diary, 30 Mar. 1860.
72. Rawick, *American Slave* 16:6.
73. Ibid., 24 July 1858.
74. Cartmell, Diary, 8 July 1854.
75. Bagwell, Diary, 25, 30 Dec. 43; 8 Apr. 1844.
76. Rawick, *American Slave* 16:17–18.
77. Ibid., 4.
78. Ibid., 27; see also Cartmell, 17 Sept. 1857; Haraldson, Diary, 18 Sept. 1842.
79. Washington, Diary, 28 Aug. 1851, 16 Jan. 1852, account books.
80. Bagwell, Diary, 7 Feb. 1843.
81. Washington, Diary, 15 Feb. 1857; Bagwell, Diary, 11 Jan. 1842.
82. See, for instance, Bills, Diary, 22 Sept. 1845; Cartmell, Diary, 24 Sept. 1853; Washington, Diary, 15 June 1856; Gleaves, Diary, 28 Aug. 1856.

83.   Bills, Diary, 22 Sept. 1845.

84.   Cartmell, Diary, 26, 24 Sept. 1853; remarks on December, 1853.

85.   Washington, Diary, 12 May 1854, 19 June 1854.

86.   Rawick, *American Slave* 16:38.

87.   See, for instance, Washington, Diary, 5, 10 May 1851; Bills, Diary, 10 Dec. 1853.

88.   Rawick, *American Slave* 16:1.

89.   Cartmell, Diary, 24, 26, 28 June 1854; 30 Oct. 1854; 15 Nov. 1854; 16 Dec. 1854.

90.   Bills, Diary, 4 Jan. 1845.

91.   Bailey, *Class and Tennessee's Confederate Generation*, 75–76.

92.   If the average rates of return in Tennessee were comparable to those elsewhere in the South, slave owners in the state earned about 10 percent per year on their investment. See Robert William Fogel and Stanley L. Engerman, *Time on the Cross: The Economics of American Negro Slavery* (Boston: Little, Brown, 1974), 1: 70.

9. Agricultural Innovations

1.   The discussion of farm tools and machinery draws on information obtained from Dorothy Curtis on a tour of the Oscar Farris Agricultural Museum in Nashville, 29 June 1992.

2.   Arnow, *Flowering of the Cumberland*, 237–38.

3.   *Tennessee Gazette*, 2 Mar. 1859.

4.   Quoted in Holt, "Economic and Social Beginnings of Tennessee," 103–4.

5.   Smith, *Review of East Tennessee*, 6.

6.   Bryan, Memoir, 4; Washington, Diary, 20 June 1856; Cartmell, Diary, 19, 24 June 1856.

7.   Bryan, Memoir, 4.

8.   Clark, *Tennessee Yeomen*, 130.

9.   *Tennessee Farmer and Mechanic* 2 (Feb. 1857): back cover.

10.   Holt, "Economic and Social Beginnings of Tennessee," 104.

11.   Bagwell, Diary, 10 July 1841, 22 June 1842.

12.   Cartmell, Diary, 31 July 1854.

13.   Alan L. Olmstead, "The Mechanization of Reaping and Mowing in American Agriculture, 1833–1870," *Journal of Economic History* 35 (1975): 327–52.

14.   *Clarksville Jeffersonian*, 10 June 1857.

15.   Barker, Diary, 27 July 1856.

16.   Washington, Diary, 20 June 1856.

17. Barker, Diary, 18 Aug. 1846; Matthews, Diary, 3 July 1860; Cartmell, Diary, 31 July 1854.

18. Barker, Diary, 27 July 1856.

19. Daniel Hopper, Madison County, Century Farms, Reel 1.

20. Haraldson, Dairy, 13 Jan. 1845; Samuel Oldham, Lauderdale County, Century Farms, Reel 1; see also, Cartmell, Diary, 5 Dec. 1853; *Southern Agriculturist* 8 (Sept. 1835): 473–80; *Southern Agriculturist*, n.s., 5 (Feb. 1845): 78–79.

21. *Memphis Appeal,* 16 July 1859.

22. Barker, Diary, 21 July 1857.

23. *Tennessee Farmer* 3 (Sept. 1838): 324; *Tennessee Farmer* 2 (Nov. 1837): 172.

24. These figures are based on data from the federal agricultural censuses for 1850 and 1860.

25. *Tennessee Farmer* 3 (Nov. 1838): 356.

26. See, for instance, *Southern Cultivator* 3 (Jan. 1830): 54–55; *Southern Cultivator* 4 (Dec. 1831): 662–63; *Southern Agriculturist*, n.s., 5 (Feb. 1845): 78–79; *Tennessee Farmer* 3 (Nov. 1838): 340–57.

27. Cartmell, Diary, 11 May 1859.

28. *Agriculturist* 2 (June 1841): 132.

29. Cartmell, Diary, 2 Mar. 1855.

30. These figures are based on data from the federal agricultural censuses for 1850 and 1860.

31. *Weekly Clarksville Chronicle,* 9 Jan. 1857; *Agriculturist* 5 (Dec. 1844): 188; *Memphis Appeal,* 22 Sept. 1843.

32. *Southern Cultivator* 1 (17 Dec. 1839): 186.

33. Barker, Diary, 31 Oct. 1844; 1, 8 Nov. 1844.

34. William Milton Crownover, Franklin County, Century Farms, Reel 1.

35. *Tennessee Farmer* 1 (Dec. 1834): 3; *Agriculturist* 4 (Nov. 1843): 165.

36. Cartmell, Diary, 20 Jan. 1857, 1 Nov. 1853; Bagwell, Diary, 14, 15 Apr. 1842; Barker, Diary, 29 Apr. 1848.

37. Smith, *Review of East Tennessee,* 5.

38. *Tennessee Farmer* 2 (Jan. 1837): 10–11; see also *Farmer and Mechanic* 1 (July 1856): 308.

39. Barker, Diary, 10, 16 Sept. 1844.

40. Cartmell, Diary, 7 Mar. 1853, 2 Mar. 1854, note at beginning of 1853.

41. *Tennessee Farmer* 3 (May 1838): 271.

42. Cartmell, Diary, 19 Feb. 1857.

43. Barker, Diary, 26 Sept. 1843, 25 Apr. 1844, 29 Sept. 1849, 26 June 1850.

44. Bagwell, Diary, 21 Oct. 1844.

45. Barker, Diary, 9 Mar. 1844, 28 Feb. 1845.

46. *Tennessee Farmer* 3 (Oct. 1838): 340.

47. Ibid. 1 (Dec. 1834): 4.

48. Ibid. 3 (Oct. 1838): 340; 1 (Dec. 1834): 5.

49. Ibid. 1 (Dec. 1834): 1.

50. Cartmell, Diary, statement at beginning of diary dated Jan. 1853; remarks on May, 1854.

51. Kellar, *Solon Robinson* 1:447–48.

52. Eugene D. Genovese, *The Political Economy of Slavery* (New York: Random House, 1961), 97–99; Bogue, *From Prairie to Cornbelt*, 62; Winters, *Farmers Without Farms*, 54–55.

53. *Farmer and Mechanic* 1 (Feb. 1856): 56.

54. *Tennessee Farmer* 2 (Oct. 1837): 145.

55. *Southern Agriculturist* 6 (Feb. 1833): 109; John Hebron Moore, *The Emergence of the Cotton Kingdom in the Old Southwest: Mississippi, 1770–1860* (Baton Rouge: Louisiana State Univ. Press, 1988), 27–30; Moore, *Agriculture in Ante-Bellum Mississippi,* 34.

56. Cartmell, Diary, 3 May 1856, 28 Apr. 1857.

57. *Tennessee Farmer* 3 (Feb. 1838): 211; *Tennessee Farmer* 3 (Nov. 1838): 353–54.

58. *Agriculturist* 2 (Apr. 1841): 94.

59. Cartmell, Diary, 25 Aug. 1857, 12 Dec. 1857.

60. *Weekly Clarksville Chronicle,* 6 Feb. 1857; *Clarksville Jeffersonian,* 10 June 1856; *Farmer and Mechanic* 2 (Feb. 1857): back cover.

61. Smith, *Review of East Tennessee,* 4; *Agriculturist* 5 (Mar. 1844): 43.

62. Killebrew, *Introduction to the Resources of Tennessee,* 95–101.

63. *Tennessee Farmer* 3 (May 1838): 265; *Tennessee Farmer* 3 (June 1838): 276.

64. *Argus and Commercial Herald,* 28 Apr. 1841.

65. *Southern Agriculturist* (May 1830): 262.

66. *Farmer and Mechanic* 1 (May 1856): 210–11; *Agriculturist* 2 (Aug. 1841): 169; *Agriculturist* 2 (Apr. 1841): 73 (advertisement).

67. Smith, *Review of East Tennessee,* 8; *Tennessee Gazette,* 28 July 1812; Cartmell, Dairy, 2 Jan. 1859

68. *Southern Cultivator* 1 (11 Oct. 1839): 153; *Farmer and Mechanic* 1 (May 1856): 212; *Farmer and Mechanic* 1 (June 1856): 285; *Farmer and Mechanic* 1 (May 1856): 197.

69. Michaux, *Travels to the West,* 245.

70. Wills, *History of Belle Meade,* 55–64.; Gray, *History of Agriculture* 2:855.

71. *Southern Cultivator* 1 (15 Jan. 1839): 4–5; *Agriculturist* 4 (Nov. 1843): 257.

72. *Agriculturist* 2 (July 1841): 146.

73. *Tennessee Farmer* 4 (Aug. 1839): 147; see also *Memphis Appeal,* 10 Jan. 1851.

74. *Farmer and Mechanic* 1 (May 1856): 201–2; *Farmer and Mechanic* 1 (Aug. 1856): 335–39.

75. *Agriculturist* 4 (Nov. 1843): 162; see also *Farmer and Mechanic* 1 (May 1856): 201–2; *Tennessee Farmer* 2 (Dec. 1837): 188.

76. *Southern Cultivator* 1 (29 Nov. 1839): 180; see also *Farmer and Mechanic* 1 (May 1856): 201–2.

77. *Southern Cultivator* 1 (29 Nov. 1839): 180; *Southern Agriculturist* 6 (Jan. 1833): 29.

78. Cartmell, Diary, statement at beginning of diary dated Jan. 1853.

79. Kellar, *Solon Robinson* 2:8.

80. Clark, *Tennessee Yeomen*, 95–101

81. *Clarksville Jeffersonian*, 19 Dec. 1855; *Tennessee Gazette*, 28 Sept. 1819; *Knoxville Enquirer*, 20 Oct. 1825.

82. *Tennessee Farmer* 3 (May 1838): 266.

83. *Agriculturist* 2 (Oct. 1841): 218.

84. *Tennessee Gazette*, 29 June 1819.

85. Cartmell, Diary, 5 Jan. 1859.

86. *Agriculturist* 4 (Nov. 1843): 173.

87. *Acts of Tennessee* (1841–42), chap. 109, 112; *Acts of Tennessee* (1851–52), chap. 45, 47–48.

88. Clark, *Tennessee Yeomen*, 79.

89. *Acts of Tennessee* (1853–54), chap. 255, 461–67; *Acts of Tennessee* (1855–57), chap. 95, 105.

90. E. G. Eastman, *Biennial Report of the State Agricultural Bureau, of Tennessee, to the Legislature of 1855–56* (Nashville: G. C. Torbett, 1856), 14–15.

91. *Farmer and Mechanic* 1 (May 1856): 285–86

92. *Acts of Tennessee* (1797), chap. 18, 61; *Acts of Tennessee* (1797), chap. 19, 62.

93. *Argus and Commercial Herald*, 27 June 1839; *Memphis Appeal*, 29 Sept. 1843; *Agriculturist* 2 (Oct. 1841): 225–26, 238–39.

94. Clark, *Tennessee Yeomen*, 89–92.

95. Kellar, *Solon Robinson* 2:7.

96. Ibid., 122–23.

97. *De Bow's Review*, 13 (Aug. 1852): 159.

98. *Naturalist* 1 (June 1850): 135.

99. *Agriculturist* 1 (May 1840): 110.

100. *Southern Cultivator* 1 (11 Oct. 1839): 153; *Agriculturist* 4 (Nov. 1843): 162–64.

101. *Agriculturist* 5 (Feb. 1844): 22–23; Anita Shafer Goodstein, *Nashville, 1780–1860* (Gainesville: Univ. of Florida Press, 1989), 168.

102. Clark, *Tennessee Yeomen*, 103–5.

103. For a discussion of agricultural reform in the upper South, see Eaton, *Growth of Southern Civilization*, 177–95.

10. The End of an Era

1. *Niles' Weekly Register* 60 (8 May 1841): 148.
2. Royall, *Letters from Alabama*, 94–95.
3. *Agriculturist* 3 (Feb. 1839): 40.
4. Quoted in Kellar, *Solon Robinson* 2:10.
5. *Southern Cultivator* 1 (13 Feb. 1839): 20.
6. Cartmell, Diary, remarks on Apr. 1854.
7. The following examples are drawn from the Federal Agricultural Censuses of 1840 through 1860.
8. *Agriculturist* 2 (Oct. 1841): 225.
9. *Tennessee Farmer* 1 (Dec. 1834): 1.
10. *Clarksville Jeffersonian*, 9 Oct. 1849.
11. Elliott and Moxley, *Tennessee Civil War Veterans' Questionnaires* 3:1258.
12. *Tennessee Farmer* 4 (Feb. 1839): 21.
13. Cartmell, Diary, statement at beginning of diary dated Jan. 1853.
14. Elliott and Moxley, *Tennessee Civil War Veterans' Questionnaires* 2:446.
15. Cartmell, Diary, remarks on May 1854.
16. McKenzie, "From Old South to New South," 34–43.
17. Developments in Missouri, for instance, were strikingly similar to those in Tennessee during the antebellum period. See Hurt, *Agriculture and Slavery*, especially chaps. 4–7. See also Jeremey Atack and Fred Bateman, *To Their Own Soil: Agriculture in the Antebellum North* (Ames: Iowa State Univ. Press, 1987) and Bogue, *From Prairie to Cornbelt* for developments in northern agriculture, and Gavin Wright, *Political Economy of the Cotton South* for developments in southern agriculture.
18. Mary E. A. Campbell, "Tennessee and the Union, 1847–1861" (Ph.D. diss., Vanderbilt Univ., 1937), 248–94.
19. Ibid., 283–84.
20. Ralph A. Wooster, *The Secession Conventions of the South* (Princeton, N.J.: Princeton Univ. Press, 1962), 173–89.

Bibliography

Primary Sources: Published

Ashe, Thomas. *Travels in America, Performed in 1806.* London: Cramer and Spear, 1808.

Baily, Francis. *Journal of a Tour in Unsettled Parts of North America in 1796 and 1797.* London: Baily Brothers, 1856.

Brantz, Lewis. "Lewis Brantz's Memorandum of a Journey (1785)." In *Early Travels in the Tennessee Country, 1540–1800,* edited by Samuel Cole Williams, 284–86. Johnson City, Tenn.: Watauga Press, 1928.

Elliott, Colleen M., and Louise A. Moxley, eds. *The Tennessee Civil War Veterans' Questionnaires.* 5 vols. Easley, S.C.: Southern Historical Press, 1985.

Evans, Estwick. *A Pedestrious Tour, of Four Thousand Miles, through the Western States and Territories, during the Winter and Spring of 1818.* Concord, N.H.: Joseph C. Spear, 1819.

Imlay, Gilbert. *Topographical Description of the Western Territory of North America.* London: J. Debrett, 1797. Rpt. New York: Augustus M. Kelly, 1969.

Kellar, Herbert Anthony, ed. *Solon Robinson: Pioneer and Agriculturist.* 2 vols. Indianapolis: Indiana Historical Bureau, 1936.

Killebrew, Joseph Buckner. *Introduction to the Resources of Tennessee.* Nashville: State Agriculture Department, 1874.

Michaux, André. "Travels of André Michaux (1793–1796)." In *Early Travels in the Tennessee Country, 1540–1800,* edited by Samuel Cole Williams, 327–42. Johnson City, Tenn.: Watauga Press, 1928.

Michaux, François André. *Travels to the West of the Alleghany Mountains, in the States of Ohio, Kentucky, and Tennessee, and Back to Charleston, by the Upper Carolinas . . . Undertaken, in the Year 1802.* London: D. N. Shury, 1805.

Ramsey, James Gettys McGready. *The Annals of Tennessee, to the End of the Eighteenth Century.* Charleston, S.C.: Walker and James, 1853. Rpt. Kingsport, Tenn.: Kingsport Press, 1926.

Rawick, George P., ed. *The American Slave: A Composite Autobiography.* Vol. 16, *Tennessee.* Westport, Conn.: Greenwood, 1972.

Royall, Anne Newport. *Letters from Alabama, 1817–1822.* Edited by Lucille Griffith. Tuscaloosa: University of Alabama Press, 1969.

Safford, James M. *The Economic and Agricultural Geology of the State of Tennessee.* Nashville: State Agriculture Department, 1886.

———. *Geology of Tennessee.* Nashville: S. C. Mercer, 1869.

Schultz, Christian. *Travels on an Inland Voyage*. 2 vols. New York: Isaac Riley, 1810.

Smith, Daniel. *A Short Description of the Tennassee Government or the Territory of the United States South of the River Ohio*. Philadelphia: Matthew Carey, 1793.

Smith, James Gray. *A Brief Historical, Statistical and Descriptive Review of East Tennessee, United States of America; Developing Its Immense Agricultural, Mining, and Manufacturing Advantages*. London: J. Leath, 1842.

Steiner, Albert. "Report of the Journey of the Brethren Abraham Steiner and Frederick C. De Schweinitz to the Cherokees and the Cumberland Settlements." In *Early Travels in the Tennessee Country, 1540–1800*, edited by Samuel Cole Williams, 445–525. Johnson City, Tenn.: Watauga Press, 1928.

Diaries, Account Books, Memoirs

TSLA denotes location in the Tennessee State Library and Archives.

"A Genealogy of Thomas and Kessiah (Griffith) Lacy and Hugh and Margaret (McDonald) Ross, of Anson County, North County." Manuscript in possession of V. Jacque Voegeli, Nashville, Tennessee.

Bagwell, Wiley. Diary, 1841–53. TSLA.

Barker, John Nick. Diary, 1843–61. Microfilm copy. TSLA.

Bills, John Houston. Diary, 1843–61. Microfilm of typescript. TSLA.

Boon, John J. "History of the Boon Family." 1909. Manuscript in possession of V. Jacque Voegeli, Nashville, Tennessee.

Brewer, J. M. Journal, 1814. TSLA.

Bryan, Tom. Memoir. Typescript. TSLA.

Cartmell, Robert H. Diary, 1849–61. TSLA.

Cartwright, Alexander Cotton. Memoir. Typescript. TSLA.

Gleaves, Betty A. Diary, 1858–59. TSLA.

Haraldson, Herndon. Diary, 1837–47. TSLA.

Jones, Jane Margaret. Diary, 1850, 1856–67, 1859–60. Microfilm copy. TSLA.

Lipscomb, John. Journal, 1784. TSLA.

Matthews, James Washington. Diary, 1858–61. TSLA.

Washington, George A. Diary, 1850–61. TSLA.

Agricultural Journals

Agriculturist and Journal of the State and County Societies
Niles' Weekly Register
Southern Agriculturist, Horticulturist, and Register of Rural Affairs
Southern Cultivator
Southern Cultivator and Journal of Science and Improvement

Tennessee Farmer
Tennessee Farmer and Mechanic
The Naturalist

Newspapers
Argus and Commercial Herald (Knoxville)
Clarksville Chronicle
Clarksville Gazette
Clarksville Jeffersonian
Knoxville Enquirer
Knoxville Gazette
Knoxville Register
Memphis Appeal
Nashville Gazette and Independent Journal
Tennessee Gazette (Nashville)
Tennessee Sentinel (Jonesborough)
Town Gazette & Farmers Register (Clarksville)
U.S. Herald (Clarksville)
Weekly Chronicle (Clarksville)

Government Documents
Acts of the State of Tennessee, 1796–1860.
Eastman, E. G. *Biennial Report of the State Agricultural Bureau, of Tennessee, to the Legislature of 1855–56.* Nashville: G. C. Torbett, 1856.
———. *Biennial Report of the State Agricultural Bureau, of Tennessee, to the Legislature of 1857–58.* Nashville: G. C. Torbett, 1858.
Federal Agricultural Censuses, 1840–1860.
Manuscript Schedules of the Federal Census, 1850–1860.

Miscellaneous
Century Farms of Tennessee. Applications. Microfilm copy. TSLA.

Secondary Sources: Published
Abernethy, Thomas P. "The Early Development of Commerce and Banking in Tennessee." *Mississippi Valley Historical Review* 14 (1928): 311–25.
———. *From Frontier to Plantation in Tennessee: A Study in Frontier Democracy.* Chapel Hill: University of North Carolina Press, 1932.
Anderson, Ralph V., and Robert E. Gallman. "Slaves as Fixed Capital: Slave Labor and Southern Economic Development." *Journal of American History* 64 (1977): 29–36.

Appleby, Joyce. "Commercial Farming and the 'Agrarian Myth' in the Early Republic." *Journal of American History* 68 (1982): 833–49.

Arnow, Harriette Simpson. *Flowering of the Cumberland.* New York: Macmillan, 1963.

———. *Seedtime on the Cumberland.* New York: Macmillan, 1960.

Atack, Jeremy, and Fred Bateman. *To Their Own Soil: Agriculture in the Antebellum North.* Ames: Iowa State University Press, 1987.

Atherton, Lewis E. *The Southern Country Store, 1800–1860.* Baton Rouge: Louisiana State University Press, 1949.

Bacon, H. Phillip. "Nashville's Trade at the Beginning of the Nineteenth Century." *Tennessee Historical Quarterly* 15 (1956): 30–36.

Bailey, Fred Arthur. *Class and Tennessee's Confederate Generation.* Chapel Hill: University of North Carolina Press, 1987.

Bergeron, Paul H. *Paths of the Past: Tennessee, 1770–1970.* Knoxville: University of Tennessee Press, 1979.

Bode, Frederick A., and Donald E. Ginter. *Farm Tenancy and the Census in Antebellum Georgia.* Athens: University of Georgia Press, 1986.

Bogue, Allan G. *From Prairie to Cornbelt: Farming on the Illinois and Iowa Prairies in the Nineteenth Century.* Chicago: University of Chicago Press, 1963.

Bonner, James C. *A History of Georgia Agriculture, 1732–1860.* Athens: University of Georgia Press, 1964.

Burnett, Edmund Cody. "Hog Raising and Hog Driving in the Region of the French Broad River." *Agricultural History* 20 (1946): 87–103.

Clark, Blanche Henry. *The Tennessee Yeomen, 1840–1860.* Nashville: Vanderbilt University Press, 1942.

Conkin, Paul K. *Cane Ridge: America's Pentecost.* Madison: University of Wisconsin Press, 1990.

Corlew, Robert E. "Some Aspects of Slavery in Dickson County." *Tennessee Historical Quarterly* 10 (1951): 238–49.

———. *Tennessee: A Short History.* Knoxville: University of Tennessee Press, 1981.

Crutchfield, James A. "Pioneer Architecture in Tennessee." *Tennessee Historical Quarterly* 35 (1976): 162–74.

Davidson, Donald. *The Tennessee: The Old River, Frontier to Secession.* 2 vols. New York: Rinehart, 1946.

Douglas, Bryd. *Steamboatin' on the Cumberland.* Nashville: Tennessee Book Company, 1961.

Eaton, Clement. *The Growth of Southern Civilization, 1790–1860.* New York: Harper and Row, 1961.

Enfield, Gertrude Dixon. "Early Settlement in Maury County: The Letters of Christopher Houston." *Tennessee Historical Quarterly* 18 (1959): 54–68.

Fink, Paul M. "The Railroad Comes to Jonesborough." *Tennessee Historical Quarterly* 36 (1977): 161–79.

Fogel, Robert William, and Stanley L. Engerman. *Time on the Cross: The Economics of American Negro Slavery.* 2 vols. Boston: Little, Brown, 1974.

Folmsbee, Stanley John. *Sectionalism and Internal Improvements in Tennessee, 1796–1845.* Knoxville: East Tennessee Historical Society, 1939.

———. "The Turnpike Phase of Tennessee's Internal Improvements System." *Journal of Southern History* 3 (1937): 453–77.

Genovese, Eugene D. *The Political Economy of Slavery.* New York: Random House, 1961.

Goodstein, Anita Shafer. *Nashville, 1780–1860.* Gainesville: University of Florida Press, 1989.

Gray, Lewis C. *History of Agriculture in the Southern United States to 1860.* 2 vols. Gloucester, Mass.: Peter Smith, 1958.

———. "The Market Surplus Problems of Colonial Tobacco." *Agricultural History* 2 (1928): 1–34.

Greene, Evarts B., and Virginia D. Harrington. *American Populations before the Federal Census of 1790.* New York: Columbia University Press, 1932.

Hilliard, Sam Bowers. *Hog Meat and Hoecake: Food Supply in the Old South, 1840–1860.* Carbondale: Southern Illinois University Press, 1972.

Hudson, Charles. *The Southeastern Indians.* Knoxville: University of Tennessee Press, 1976.

Hurt, R. Douglas. *Agriculture and Slavery in Missouri's Little Dixie.* Columbia: University of Missouri Press, 1992.

———. *Indian Agriculture in America: Prehistory to the Present.* Lawrence: University of Kansas Press, 1987.

Jones, Thomas B. "The Public Lands of Tennessee." *Tennessee Historical Quarterly* 27 (1968): 13–36.

King, J. Crawford, Jr. "The Closing of the Southern Range: An Exploratory Study." *Journal of Southern History* 48 (1982): 53–70.

Lindstrom, Diane. "Southern Dependence upon Interregional Grain Supplies: A Review of the Trade Flows, 1840–1860." *Agricultural History* 44 (1970): 101–13.

Livingood, James W. "Chattanooga: A Rail Junction of the Old South." *Tennessee Historical Quarterly* 6 (1947): 230–50.

McDonald, Forrest, and Grady McWhiney. "The Antebellum Southern Herdsman: A Reinterpretation." *Journal of Southern History* 41 (1975): 147–76.

McWhinney, Grady. *Cracker Culture: Celtic Ways in the Old South.* Tuscaloosa: University of Alabama Press, 1988.

Mooney, Chase C. *Slavery in Tennessee.* Bloomington: Indiana University Press, 1957.

———. "Some Institutional and Statistical Aspects of Slavery in Tennessee." *Tennessee Historical Quarterly* 1 (1942): 195–228.

Moore, John Hebron. *Agriculture in Ante-Bellum Mississippi.* New York: Bookman Associates, 1958.

———. *The Emergence of the Cotton Kingdom in the Old Southwest: Mississippi, 1770–1860.* Baton Rouge: Louisiana State University Press, 1988.

Olmstead, Alan L. "The Mechanization of Reaping and Mowing in American Agriculture, 1833–1870." *Journal of Economic History* 35 (1975): 327–52.

Owsley, Frank L. *Plain Folk of the Old South.* Baton Rouge: Louisiana State University Press, 1949.

———, and Harriet C. Owsley. "The Economic Structure of Rural Tennessee, 1850–1860." *Journal of Southern History* 8 (1942): 161–82.

Posey, Walter B., ed. "Bishop Asbury Visits Tennessee, 1788–1815: Extracts From His Journal." *Tennessee Historical Quarterly* 15 (1956): 253–68.

Rohrbough, Malcolm J. *The Trans-Appalachian Frontier: People, Societies, and Institutions, 1775–1850.* New York: Oxford University Press, 1978.

Rothrock, Mary U., ed. *The French Broad-Holston Country: A History of Knox County, Tennessee.* Knoxville: East Tennessee Historical Society, 1946.

Rothstein, Morton. "The Antebellum South as a Dual Economy: A Tentative Hypothesis." *Agricultural History* 41 (1967): 373–82.

Scarborough, William Kauffman. *The Overseer: Plantation Management in the Old South.* Baton Rouge: Louisiana State University Press, 1966.

Schaefer, Donald. "Yeomen Farmers and Economic Democracy: A Study of Wealth and Economic Mobility in the Western Tobacco Region, 1850 to 1860." *Explorations in Economic History* 15 (1978): 421–37.

Williams, Samuel Cole. *Beginnings of West Tennessee, in the Land of the Chickasaws, 1541–1841.* Johnson City, Tenn.: Watauga Press, 1930.

Wills, Ridley, *The History of Belle Meade: Mansion, Plantation, and Stud.* Nashville: Vanderbilt University Press, 1991.

Winters, Donald L. "The Agricultural Ladder in Southern Agriculture: Tennessee, 1850–1870." *Agricultural History* 61 (1987): 36–82.

———. "Farm Size and Production Choices: Tennessee, 1850–1860." *Tennessee Historical Quarterly* 52 (1993): 212–24.

———. *Farmers Without Farms: Agricultural Tenancy in Nineteenth-Century Iowa.* Westport, Conn.: Greenwood, 1978.

———. "'Plain Folk' of the Old South Reexamined: Economic Democracy in Tennessee." *Journal of Southern History* 53 (1987): 565–86.

Woodman, Harold D. *King Cotton and His Retainers: Financing and Marketing the Cotton Crop of the South, 1800–1925*. Lexington: University of Kentucky Press, 1968.

Wooster, Ralph A. *The Secession Conventions of the South*. Princeton, N.J.: Princeton University Press, 1962.

Wright, Gavin. "'Economic Democracy' and the Concentration of Agricultural Wealth in the Cotton South, 1850–1860." *Agricultural History* 44 (1970): 63–93.

———. *Old South, New South: Revolutions in the Southern Economy Since the Civil War*. New York: Basic Books, 1986.

———. *The Political Economy of the Cotton South: Households, Markets, and Wealth in the Nineteenth Century*. New York: W. W. Norton, 1978.

Secondary Sources: Unpublished

Campbell, Mary E. A. "Tennessee and the Union, 1847–1861." Ph.D. diss., Vanderbilt University, 1937.

Holt, Albert. "The Economic and Social Beginnings of Tennessee." Ph.D. diss., Peabody College for Teachers, 1923.

McKenzie, Robert Tracy. "From Old South to New South in the Volunteer State: The Economy and Society of Rural Tennessee, 1850–1880." Ph.D. diss., Vanderbilt University, 1988.

Index